MAKING WAR ON THE WORLD

COLUMBIA STUDIES IN INTERNATIONAL
ORDER AND POLITICS

COLUMBIA STUDIES IN INTERNATIONAL
ORDER AND POLITICS

Stacie E. Goddard, Daniel H. Nexon, and Joseph M. Parent, series editors

The Columbia Studies in International Order and Politics series builds on the Press's long tradition in classic international relations publishing while highlighting important new work. The series is founded on three commitments: to serve as an outlet for innovative theoretical work, especially that work which stretches beyond "mainstream" international relations and cuts across disciplinary boundaries; to highlight original qualitative and historical work in international relations theory, international security, and international political economy; and to focus on creating a selective, prominent list dedicated to international relations.

MAKING WAR ON THE WORLD

HOW TRANSNATIONAL VIOLENCE RESHAPES GLOBAL ORDER

MARK SHIRK

Columbia University Press
New York

Columbia University Press
Publishers Since 1893
New York   Chichester, West Sussex
cup.columbia.edu
Copyright © 2022 Columbia University Press
All rights reserved

Library of Congress Cataloging-in-Publication Data
Names: Shirk, Mark, author.
Title: Making war on the world : how transnational violence reshapes global order / Mark Shirk.
Description: New York : Columbia University Press, 2022. | Series: Columbia studies in international order and politics | Includes bibliographical references and index.
Identifiers: LCCN 2021047076 (print) | LCCN 2021047077 (ebook) | ISBN 9780231201865 (hardback) | ISBN 9780231201872 (trade paperback) | ISBN 9780231554305 (ebook)
Subjects: LCSH: Political violence—History. | Non-state actors (International relations)—History. | Transnationalism. | Piracy. | Anarchism. | Qaida (Organization) | War on Terrorism, 2001–2009. | National security. | Security, International.
Classification: LCC JC328.6 .S54 2022 (print) | LCC JC328.6 (ebook) | DDC 303.6—dc23/eng/20211102
LC record available at https://lccn.loc.gov/2021047076
LC ebook record available at https://lccn.loc.gov/2021047077

Columbia University Press books are printed on permanent and durable acid-free paper.
Printed in the United States of America

Cover design: Milenda Nan Ok Lee
Cover image: Edward "Blackbeard" Teach, English pirate.
Science History Images / Alamy Stock Photo

CONTENTS

Acknowledgments vii

INTRODUCTION

1

1. CHANGE AND CONTINUITY IN POLITICAL ORDER

15

2. THE GOLDEN AGE OF PIRACY AND THE CREATION OF AN ATLANTIC WORLD

35

3. "PROPAGANDA OF THE DEED," SURVEILLANCE, AND THE LABOR MOVEMENT

69

4. AL-QAEDA, THE WAR ON TERROR, AND THE
BOUNDARIES OF THE TWENTY-FIRST CENTURY

102

CONCLUSION

133

Notes 151
Bibliography 207
Index 237

ACKNOWLEDGMENTS

They tell you in graduate school that no piece of scholarship is produced solely by its author. It is not until one actually creates something like a book that one understands how true this is. There are so many people to list here and many more whose names will unfortunately not be listed, for which I deeply apologize. This work is the culmination of a lot of discussions and work put in not just by me but by countless others.

I begin with my wonderful wife, Fiona. She has been with me from the start of grad school, supporting me as a grad student, adjunct, and postdoc and providing emotional support as I worked on this project and navigated the academic job market, while displaying a talent for reading eighteenth-century handwriting that I just do not possess. She has been there for me to bounce ideas off of and has endured living in separate cities and moving to another country in pursuit of my career and this project. She is the most important person in the world to me and to me writing this book. I also want to thank my children, Ciaran and Naomi, who, while they will not remember this process, have provided a wonderful distraction and a sense of perspective in its finishing stages. My parents, Alex and Bev Shirk, have been understanding and supportive of their son who has always done well in school but also seems determined to take a quixotic trip through academia and not make any real money. The same goes for my in-laws, John and Elisabeth Burns. Finally, my dog

Cleo. Since 2013 she has had a knack for knowing when I have been stressed out, coming and lying/sitting next to me. If she hadn't licked my face as often as she did, I may not have finished.

I received a grant from the Horowitz Foundation for Social Policy while in graduate school and won their Harold Lasswell Award for best application in international relations. This grant funded my archival research in the UK and France, paid for a translator for the French materials, and allowed me to adjunct fewer classes as I finished up my dissertation. I am very grateful, as who knows what would have happened without this grant!

Professionally there are so many to thank that it is overwhelming. I will start with Ken Conca. It was discussions with him and his willingness to listen to some rather weird ideas early in my grad school career that launched this project. After he left Maryland, I worked most closely with Virginia Haufler. She was the one who really pushed me to get into the archives and to do interviews, without which I have no idea if this project would ever have taken off. I would also like to thank Paul Huth, my first graduate supervisor; David Cunningham; and Meyer Kestnbaum, who all served on my dissertation committee. The latter introduced me to historical sociology. Other professors at Maryland who allowed me to find my own way through this project include George Quester and Karol Soltan. I also want to acknowledge the help that fellow graduate students gave me even as I spouted on about very abstract theories of the international system that, frankly, made little sense. These include, but are not limited to, Jacqui Ignatova, Mary Kate Schneider, Jonathan Hensley, Quddus Snyder, Jen Wallace, Jacob Aronson, Rodrigo Pinto, Jeff Taylor, Brian Gervais, and Maeryn Goldman. Jacqui, in particular, was a big help during this time.

Finally, I found myself in a position where my research interests did not fit my graduate department very well. This meant that I have relied heavily on the help of many others. First to mention here is Patrick Jackson, who has been my mentor and has been the intellectual heavyweight behind this project. I only hope it reflects at least some of his sage advice. I really cannot thank him enough. But I will try, with whiskey. Dan Green has also been instrumental in developing my work. Our twice-yearly lunch or coffees to discuss research have been more helpful than he probably understands. Dan Nexon was gracious enough to meet with me during graduate school and has been an invaluable editor at multiple points. That includes as series editor for this book, which is so much better because of his interventions. Here I should mention the other editors for this books series, Stacie Goddard and Joseph Parent. And of course none of this would have happened without my acquisitions editor Caelyn Cobb, the people at Columbia University Press—Monique Briones, Kathryn Jorge, Adriana Cloud, and I am sure many others I have not interacted with—and the anonymous reviewers of my manuscript.

Anna Ohanyan was department chair at my first real academic job and has been very supportive. Jason Sharman gave me an opportunity at Cambridge and has been willing to look at multiple drafts of chapters and return them with lots of supportive and useful comments. The POLIS department at Cambridge, where I held a three-year lectureship while polishing and revising this book, has been a very fertile one for work such as mine, with supportive and helpful colleagues such as Giovanni Mantilla, Duncan Bell, Ayse Zarakol, and Dan Larsen. Yale Ferguson, a Clare College fellow and attendee of department events, provided valuable feedback at the later stages of this project. Here I should also thank the fellowship at Sidney Sussex College. Sidney was literally my family's home for three years and my favorite part of Cambridge. Jeppe Mulich has read multiple drafts over the years and been invaluable in giving me some window into a historian's view of my work. Mauro Carracioli has helped to organize panels that have led to publications and further developed my work and been a good friend for a while now. Richard Bach Jensen, Kirk Shaffer, Uri Gorden, and Barak Mendelsohn all gave me notes on my work at different stages when they did not have to. Halvard Leira, Benjamin de Carvalho, and Jorg Kustermans have been very helpful as well.

There are also way too many people to name who have been parts of panels and workshops where I have presented. I know I am forgetting people at this point, and I am sorry. Many of these people I met at ISA Northeast, which has a very supportive intellectual community that has stretched my understandings of international politics beyond what I could do myself. There are also scholars cited in this book whose work has been really influential but I find myself criticizing. I just hope they understand.

Finally, I want to thank Annie Rehill. She did translations of archival documents that have led not only to this book but to a journal article as well. Looking at the difference between my translations and hers (best not to mention specifics) shows how important her help has been.

INTRODUCTION

"The most momentous development of our era," writes Rana Dasgupta, "is the waning of the nation state: its inability to withstand countervailing 21st-century forces, and its calamitous loss of influence over human circumstance."[1] Stephen Kobrin agrees: "The modern era [of the nation-state] may be a window that is about to slam shut."[2]

Commentators point to numerous culprits. Grateful Dead lyricist John Barlow proclaimed that cyberspace turns states into "weary giants of flesh and steel."[3] Dasgupta argues in the same article that "20th-century political structures are drowning in a 21st-century ocean of deregulated finance, autonomous technology, religious militancy and great-power rivalry." Martti Koskenniemi highlights the state's "failure to deal with global threats such as climate change, criminality, and terrorism"[4] Susan Strange states that "where states were once the masters of markets, now it is the markets which ... are the masters over governments of states."[5] Max Manwaring describes the "gang non-state actor" as "a triple threat to the authority and sovereignty" of states.[6] Willem Schinkel argues that "the monopoly of legitimate violence is then helpless against globalized forms of terrorist violence."[7] Jan Klabbers observes that "non-state entities have started to compete with states for the scarce resources of politico-legal authority."[8]

Transboundary processes not only threaten the state, but supposedly make sovereignty obsolete. Cynthia Ayers argues that to "malicious cyber actors, the Westphalian form of sovereignty can be considered completely irrelevant."[9] Emily Crawford and Rosemary Rayfuse state that "climate change presents a unique threat . . . to the very concept of statehood itself."[10] Preventing catastrophic damage "perhaps is asking more than the international system is capable of delivering."[11] According to Jost Delbrück, increasing flows of migrants mean that "the traditional understanding of what constitutes the 'nation' . . . is no longer tenable."[12]

The result is that, as James Rosenau argues, "the lessons of history may no longer be helpful."[13] Philip Cerny forecasts that democracy is in peril with a return to "quasi fiefdoms reminiscent of the Middle Ages."[14] Seemingly fulfilling this prophecy, Molly Roberts announced in 2019 that "Facebook has declared sovereignty."[15] Kobrin opines that sovereignty was a "detour rather than an evolutionary step."[16] And Flora Lewis declared "the end of sovereignty."[17]

Not everyone is ready to consign the sovereign, territorial state to the dustbin of history.[18] Many believe that the state has already, or will soon, reassert itself. Syrian migration has been linked to the rise of nationalism in the European Union.[19] The recent global pandemic has caused a rollback of multilateralism[20] and more investment in border restrictions.[21] Henry Farrell and Abraham Newman argue that, far from eroding the state, financial and information networks are becoming tools for great power competition.[22]

Is the state withering away or striking back? The answer to this question is as difficult as it is important. It has also long been a topic of concern. The death of the state and the rise of private authority were a major topic of scholarship in the 1990s and early 2000s.[23] In 1971, the journal *International Organization* devoted a special issue to the rise of transnational politics.[24] In the 1930s, Eugene Staley observed that economics and technology were in conflict with the state.[25] As early as 1903, H. G. Wells argued that scientific and economic progress made a world state both desirable and inevitable.[26]

We could look at this history as a reason to dismiss the question. This would be a mistake. As I argue in this book, transboundary processes have challenged and transformed states and state authority for centuries. They have produced a number of crucial mutations in the territorial, conceptual, and practical boundaries that demarcate states and societies. The proper questions are not "if" and "whether," but "how" and "when."

How do transboundary processes drive political transformation? Instead of looking for erosion or reimposition, we should look for transformation. Not more or less, but different. For example, some have argued that global governance agencies relegate the state to merely one part of larger governing assemblages.[27] This implies erosion. However, these agencies were developed to solve problems that states have interest in, ranging from capital mobility to infectious diseases. They are not really competing with the state if the state is okay with their presence. Further, the state has never been the only global actor. There have always been empires, corporations, organized religions, company-states, etc., existing alongside it. Instead, the development of global governance agencies is an example of transformation, of governance being different—not more or less—than before.

Something similar can be said about the "responsibility to protect" (R2P)—the idea that international intervention is necessary in certain cases when human rights are violated. Many have argued that R2P is an erosion of the norm of sovereignty. But is it? In the very short term, the state experiencing intervention loses sovereignty, and the practice entrenches global North-South power relations. But the entrenching of these power relations is evidence that it is not an erosion. In many cases, sovereignty has never existed for states in the global South. What we think of as traditional sovereignty has long had an exception for international war.[28] Is it erosion when those without sovereignty are denied it? Is it erosion if powerful states decide to create an exception to a weaker state's sovereignty? For both global governance agencies and R2P, who gains from these transformations and how and what they mean for politics going forward are much more interesting questions than whether or not we are seeing state erosion. We almost certainly are not. Yet we are still seeing something important: transformation.

When do transboundary processes drive political transformation? I argue that they do so under specific conditions: when they are *illegible* to governments and their agents. Illegibility is the inverse of, or at least the step right before, James Scott's concept of "legibility": making sense of some thing or process so as to rule it.[29] Legible processes are those that state agents can sort, file, or make sense of in reference to preexisting categories or repertoires of policy instruments. In other words, legible processes can be categorized and acted upon. They can be taxed, controlled, relocated, bounded, etc. Some transboundary processes are either legible or easily made so. These processes are less likely to cause transformation. Illegible processes force state agents to come up with new solutions to deal with resultant problems. The result of these new solutions is political transformation.

As detailed in chapter 4 of this book, the attacks of September 11, 2001, were part of an illegible process—the global jihadist violence of al-Qaeda and its larger network. When September 11 happened, many evoked Pearl Harbor as a similar event in U.S. history. Both attacks were unexpected. Similar numbers of people died in each. Both shocked observers. But Pearl Harbor was an attack that was easily made legible. It was undertaken by a powerful nation-state, Japan, engaged in a war fast engulfing the entire world. The United States and Japan had been rivals in the Pacific for almost a century by December 7, 1941. The Japanese attacked Pearl Harbor as a preventative measure to stop the United States from siding with Allied forces in the Pacific. The next day, President Franklin Delano Roosevelt gave a speech to a joint session of Congress in which he asked Congress to declare war on Japan. They did so later that day. Pearl Harbor was about something very legible: interstate competition and war.

Compare December 7, 1941, to September 11, 2001. As a college sophomore that day, what I remember is not just shock at the event but utter confusion. This is reflected in the accounts of national security officials. It was not clear what kind of problem this was. Some knew it was al-Qaeda but others thought about Iran or Iraq. It was not clear what part of the national security state should deal with the problem. Was it defense? Intelligence? Law enforcement? There was some consensus that the attacks would usher in a "new era," but Secretary of State Colin Powell, National Security Advisor Condoleezza Rice, and Vice President Dick Cheney all had very different ideas of what that meant.[30] There was widespread fear that further attacks were imminent.[31] It took nine days for the term "war on terror" to develop as a response, much longer than the response to Pearl Harbor despite much faster travel and communications technology. Many in the counterterrorism community testify that al-Qaeda was not taken seriously as a threat and many national security officials were only dimly aware of its existence. They were not the only ones who had trouble making sense of the attacks. Observers and analysts still debate what al-Qaeda hoped to gain from the attacks, whether their goals were a caliphate, to get the United States out of the Middle East, to end democracy and freedom, or notoriety; whether they were strategic or irrational, pre- or post-modern.[32] While people were shocked by Pearl Harbor, they knew the Japanese did it, they knew who the Japanese were, and there was little doubt what it meant. Pearl Harbor could be made legible by state agents; September 11 could not. September 11 was narrated as part of a transboundary processes that threatened the state.[33] The result was transformation.

Two mechanisms—shattering and reinscribing—play a crucial role in transformation.[34] Shattering is when transboundary processes render existing practices of governance unworkable. This happens through a combination of material damage to gain the attention of state agents, challenges to legitimacy, the illegibility of the threat, and the failure of contemporaneous tools to solve challenges. Reinscribing is when, in response to shattering, creative solutions to the ensuing crisis are developed. These solutions lead to new practices that remake the state by drawing new boundaries. The remade state can now make sense of and alleviate the threat. The result is not necessarily erosion or reimposition but transformation.

I demonstrate this process of transformation in three focused cases: the golden age of piracy in the early eighteenth-century Caribbean, anarchist "propaganda of the deed" at the turn of the twentieth century, and al-Qaeda in the early twenty-first century. Pirates in the early eighteenth-century Caribbean exploited "the line," which separated "Europe/state" from "Atlantic/empire." There was *no peace beyond the line*. The line, when combined with the rise of trade in the region, aided pirates due to a surfeit of ungoverned land and open markets. They took advantage by wrecking trade and creating a crisis. Existing counter-piracy measures conditioned by the line, such as pardons and the direct protection of trading lanes, proved ineffective, and pirate rhetoric rendered their actions illegible to eighteenth-century state agents. The reactions were to extend the state's judicial systems into the colonies, taking greater control of colonial policy, and enacting a propaganda campaign that labeled pirates "enemies of humanity." The line was functionally erased, and the colonies were brought closer to the metropole. The sea became an open space. This paved the way for the mercantile colonialism of the eighteenth century and the near-constant warfare this system engendered.

Anarchist assassins practicing propaganda of the deed assassinated heads of state and other government officials and conducted lethal attacks in public cafés and landmarks. They utilized the tension between the unregulated movement of people, goods, and information and continued efforts to silence political radicals. Public trials and torture only managed to bring more recruits to the anarchist cause. Unmonitored movement of people and goods allowed anarchists to evade capture and spread violence outside Europe. Anarchism as a political philosophy was illegible to state agents, who claimed that propagandists were against "everything: ideas and property and social relations."[35] New surveillance techniques such as fingerprint databases and universal passports allowed states to track and control anarchist movements, while the legitimation of anarchist ideas and newly relaxed labor laws drove anarchist sentiment into activism and syndicalism. Borders were closed while the domestic sphere was opened. Thus, the campaign against propaganda of the deed played a role in the end of internationalism and the "second wave" of globalization at the turn of the twentieth century, the modern surveillance state, and the labor movement.

Al-Qaeda circa 2001 articulated a vision that disconnected politics from territory while taking advantage of communication technology to transgress borders. Their actions and rhetoric were illegible to state agents, who saw politics through the lens of territory and used borders to exclude threats. Early attempts to defeat al-Qaeda, such as closing down borders and invading other states, did little to alleviate the threat, fully "shattering" the boundaries of the late twentieth century. Two counter-terror innovations have degraded al-Qaeda: targeted killing—often using unmanned aerial vehicles, or drones—and new systems of surveillance facilitated by bulk data collection. These innovations have transformed borders from sites of exclusion designed to keep out undesirables to sites of collection where they can be tracked and controlled. Crossing a border means entering a surveillance system; cyberspace can be bounded, creating space for the nationalization of the internet. Instead of keeping threats located in geographical space, they can now be tracked and dealt with anywhere in the world.

There are important differences between these cases that demonstrate the robustness of shattering and reinscribing. Each case comes from a very different time period, showing that transboundary processes are as old as boundaries themselves. The pirate case deals directly with formal empires; the anarchist case makes use of empire; the al-Qaeda case comes after the supposed end of colonialism. Furthermore, the empires of the pirate and anarchist cases are quite different. Each case takes place in different geographical locations. The anarchist case even takes place in the order's core European cities! The technology prevalent in each case differs widely. The main form of mass communication in the pirate case was locally printed pamphlets. In the anarchist case, widely distributed newspapers are a new phenomenon. In the al-Qaeda case, cable news and the internet are prevalent. Pirates and anarchists had similar antiauthority ideologies; al-Qaeda based its belief system on a major world religion. The anarchist and al-Qaeda cases are conventionally categorized as terrorism, and the pirate case as crime.

Yet, there are also important similarities that justify my case selection. They all challenge the supposed monopoly of legitimate violence that we traditionally associate with the state. They are all instances of transformation that are overlooked and undertheorized. They all take place in, or originate from, the margins of political order: the colonial Atlantic, the working-class neighborhoods of European cities, Central Asia. They allow me the opportunity for granular study to develop and demonstrate the mechanisms of shattering and reinscribing. Most importantly, all three cases are examples of transnational violence that was illegible to state agents, resulting in political transformation. They are what I have elsewhere called "revisionist violence."[36] They produce an ontological threat[37] because they are illegible to contemporaneous state agents and denaturalize current practices. Their illegibility threatens state legitimacy.[38] The next test would be how they travel to other transboundary processes, a topic I return to in the conclusion.

TRANSNATIONAL VIOLENCE AND STATE TRANSFORMATION

This books helps us to understand specific debates about globalization and about how and when transboundary processes drive political transformation. It also has broader implications for state transformation.[39]

There is a large literature on state transformation but very little of it recognizes my cases as drivers of transformation. Nor do scholars recognize the resulting transformations as instances of such. The reason is that *scholars are looking in the wrong places*.

The literature tends to set the bar for change too high. As a result, it infers stability where there is dynamism and misses many causes of state transformation. There is a tendency toward teleology and the post-hoc-ergo-propter-hoc fallacy. Scholars' stories tend to be about the founding of the state in early modern Europe,[40] nineteenth-century developments,[41] or diffusion of the state following decolonization.[42] There is often an end point such as "nation-state," "democracy," or "welfare state."

Often the focus is on events like the Thirty Years' War,[43] the French and American revolutions,[44] and the world wars.[45] While these events were certainly important, what happened before and after them drove state transformation as much as the events themselves. What might look like a major juncture is often just the moment scholars realize change took place. Even those scholars highlighting processes such as capitalism,[46] the Reformation,[47] democratization,[48] and decolonization[49] have similar problems. They too set the bar so high that most transformations go unrecognized. It is hard to say that capitalism has had no impact on the state, but the ways in which it has are dependent on local actors solving problems. This is especially a problem in the international relations (IR) literature on transformation that spotlights system-level norms of sovereignty.[50] There are scholars who have looked at transnational violence, often with a focus on international society.[51] But again, they are too focused on big historical junctures. For similar reasons, other scholars have attempted to apply transnational violence to state transformation only to find a negative.[52]

One consequence of the campaign against piracy in the early eighteenth century was the newly found importance of territory in the colonial Atlantic. Colonial governance was standardized, pirates had to be given nowhere to go, and peace treaties shifted focus from trading rights to territorial concessions sometime in the eighteenth century. Rodney Bruce Hall claims that a change in collective identity from dynastic to territorial sovereignty triggered by the Peace of Westphalia explains the development of a territorial colonial system.[53] The state—or in Hall's case, norms of sovereignty—was stable and changed after a major war from type A to type B. This has causation backward. Westphalia did not condition what happened in the colonial Atlantic in any obvious way. Practices developed to solve concrete problems such as piracy determined the texture of the region's politics in the eighteenth century. The Peace of Westphalia at most[54] conditioned the possible range of actions for state agents, the categories they could use to interpret what happened around them. So you have an event (the Thirty Years' War or the Peace of Westphalia) that was actually a process and a larger process (developing norms of territorial sovereignty) conditioned by actors solving local problems. Neither the event itself nor macro-process are close to sufficient for understanding state transformation in this context.

Partly because the literature is too focused on big historical transformations and processes, scholars have tended to emphasize single-issue drivers. Many debates have been between bellocentric,[55] econocentric,[56] and ideationalist[57] explanations.[58] There is no reason to take a side in this debate. Many of the factors that these scholars point to could be all three. Military technology is a popular driver of change in bellocentric accounts. But military technology, like all technology, is reliant on ideas. Often more powerful national economics have been at the forefront. It is often developed by private corporations. So which is more important here? War, economics, or ideas?

Structuring debate in this way makes it harder to see my cases as instances of state transformation. What is piracy? There is an obvious economic component. But it is also violence; sea raiding has been an important component of navies across time and, during the golden age, the navy was deployed to defeat it. Pirates had proto-anarchist ideas illegible to state agents. Same goes for al-Qaeda. Clearly violence is at play, but is it military violence that al-Qaeda is wielding? Financing is an important part of its organization, and its members attacked the World Trade Center because it was a symbol of U.S. economic might. Al-Qaeda has very different ideas about how to order politics than the state they attacked, and its attacks are often symbolic. Are these cases about war, economics, or ideas? The answer is all and none of them.

Focusing on war, economics, and ideas causes scholars to miss not only my cases but a lot of other important stuff. U.S. logistical capability made D-Day possible and helped to end the Second World War.[59] Obviously, this had a major impact on the postwar order. But are logistics military, economic, or ideational? Who knows? And frankly, does it matter?

There is a tendency to equate warfare with war between states, but it is actually about organized violence. A great example is policing. Early in the common narratives of state transformation, the distinction between police and military is basically nonexistent.[60] On its own terms, the state transformation literature sees the boundary between policing and war making as a fundamental marker. Yet, once this distinction is drawn, policing is often ignored because it is no longer about war.[61] Policing is often privatized, and its funding is intertwined with larger economic processes. Changes in policing practices often depend on the norms and rules accepted by state agents. Is the recent militarization of American policing not a process that transforms the state? Not only are debates about war, economics, and ideas largely unnecessary but they make it harder for scholars to appreciate all of the ways state transformation can happen.

In addition to a specific claims about the state, I draw on a broader framework to meet this challenge: practice theories of the state. The state is a series of practices. Practices are *habitual, patterned actions that both constitute the social world and its inhabitants and structure possible future action.*[62] State transformation, then, is the development of new practices. This approach allows scholars to look at transformation more granularly and in a historical context. It also helps us build to the macro, to understand how major processes are the conglomeration of smaller ones. Practice theories of the state move us beyond war, economics, and ideas into how actors solve problems. There are other implications as well. Practice theories of state transformation emphasize the continuous nature of transformation. Since any practice can change and evolve at any time, the state is always a work in progress. It also takes us beyond a focus on elites and formal government bodies to state agents or those able to act in the name of the state. A state agent can only be defined as such in context and could include presidents, kings, and bureaucrats, but also merchants, Pinkertons, and software engineers. I go into more depth on this in the next chapter.

The practices that construct the state are those that draw boundaries around political authority. These boundaries constitute the state as an entity amidst global and transboundary flows. Transboundary processes, as the name would suggest, are those that flow through and across boundaries. They are threats, or not, by the way in which they are illegible within contemporary boundary-producing practices. So boundaries must be redrawn if threats are to be ameliorated. Boundaries—both conceptual and territorial—are relational,[63] constructing the entities on either side. The relational properties of boundary-drawing practices allow us to scale up and down from the state. Therefore, this framework allows us to talk about political transformation more broadly.

TRANSFORMING GLOBAL ORDER

State-state and state-other distinctions are an important part of global politics. As these distinctions change as a result of new boundary-drawing practices, so does global order. Global order has become a frequent topic of interest in recent IR scholarship. It is another way to talk about what earlier works called the international system. While "system" invokes a mechanical nature, order ropes in a wider range of scholars and viewpoints. Realist scholars describing a system can be in discussion with constructivist and foreign policy scholars who want to consider something broader and/or more granular.

There are generally two different types of scholarship on global order that, while not really in conflict, highlight different things. The first concerns the nature of any order. What are the actors involved? How do they act? Are they similar or dissimilar? This is where we may put studies on anarchy,[64] hierarchy,[65] the nature of the state and/or sovereignty,[66] international society,[67] and attempts to broaden beyond traditional conception of what matters in IR.[68] The second type of scholarship focuses on the content of order. What are the major institutions, practices, and goals of those able to shape order? Recently, this scholarship has been dominated by concerns over the nature and future of the so-called liberal international order.[69] However, scholarship on historical and/or non-Western orders is also common.[70]

This project sits between these two groups. Boundary-drawing practices determine both the actors and characteristics of an order by connecting them. This builds on a new group of scholars characterizing order, hegemony, and power politics in terms of relations, practices, and networks.[71] Traditionally, scholars view global order as either the result of purposeful construction or the natural outcome of an anarchic world (or a combination of both). Practice turn scholars argue that political orders of any type take work to maintain[72] and are nothing more or less than a set of patterned relations. The focus here is on states and state relations, because while states are by no means the only relevant global actors, nor are they constant,[73] they have remained the dominant actors for centuries. This is a heuristic, one with blind spots but also powerful explanatory potential. In fact, state boundaries often determine the character of other actors like empires, social movements, and corporations.

As new boundaries are drawn, the practices of sovereignty and statehood change. Since new practices of sovereignty necessitate new relations, this means a change in global order. For instance, when European states took greater control over their Atlantic colonies (chapter 2) or when passports became universalized (chapter 3), both states and the manner in which they interacted with each other changed. This constitutes a shift in global order. It also highlights collusion as a possible vehicle for transformation. Orders constrain and discipline actors, even hegemons[74] and rising powers,[75] making it more important to conceive of a bottom-up vision of order. Conceptualizing global order in this way opens up new possibilities for change.

The implication for the present is that the current liberal international order is in trouble, because there is a disconnect or mismatch between the order's formal institutions/rules and the actors and patterns of relations they are governing. This differs from, but is complementary to, common claims about the rise of China, illiberal actors, and the decline of the United States. I will discuss the changes in global order resulting from each of my cases and then readdress this point in the conclusion.

PLAN OF THE BOOK

The argument of this book is that transboundary processes drive state transformation when they are illegible. They are illegible when the boundary-drawing practices that construct the state do not help state agents make sense of what is happening. When these practices no longer "work" in the world, a crisis ensues. In the midst of the crisis, state actors develop creative responses that draw new practices and new boundaries. I demonstrate this dynamic in three cases—Caribbean piracy in the eighteenth century, anarchist propaganda of the deed at the turn of the twentieth century, and al-Qaeda in the twenty-first century. The United States that experienced 9/11 was not the same United States that degraded the core of al-Qaeda over the next fifteen years as a result of the War on Terror. Understanding this process helps us to understand the transformation of the state and global order in a globalized world. Chapter 1 further developments the theoretical framework of this book. I argue that the transformation I am highlighting marks both change (the state is different) and continuity (the state perseveres). The change is the cause of the continuity. To demonstrate this, I go into more depth on how boundary-drawing practices construct the state. Then I cover the implications of this position for state transformation. Finally, I discuss the two mechanisms of state transformation—shattering and reinscribing.

The next three chapters apply this theoretical framework to my cases. Chapter 2 draws on colonial correspondence and pirate trials accessed at the National Archives in London, the Calendar of State Papers—Colonial Series, and New York Colonial Documents, in addition to other published collections, to outline how pirates forced state agents to draw North American and Caribbean colonies closer to the state. Utilizing contemporary newspapers, police reports, and international correspondence available at the National Archives in London, the Archive de Prefecture de Police in Paris, and other published sources, chapter 3 details how anarchist assassins played a role in the development of both the labor movement and the modern surveillance state. In chapter 4, I argue that in response to al-Qaeda, the United States reconceptualized borders and began governing through data. This case was constructed using government documents, newspapers, and interviews of twenty-two policy makers, experts, and privacy advocates.

I conclude by summing up the argument, drawing comparisons between the cases, and looking forward. I address the rise of the Islamic State, implications of the War on Terror for privacy, the fate of the current "liberal international order," and the future of the state. The future of the state in an increasingly globalized and transnational world and the future of global order are at an inflection point. The study of international relations is heading into an uncertain few decades (though when was it not?), and many disciplinary foundations need to be questioned. I hope that this book contributes to that effort in some way. I start by laying out what a practice theory of the state looks like and its implications for the transformation of the state and global order.

1

CHANGE AND CONTINUITY IN POLITICAL ORDER

My task is . . . to maintain the skin that keeps the law in place. Two laws in two places in fact.

—CHINA MIEVILLE, *THE CITY AND THE CITY*

This is a book about change and continuity. My critiques in the last chapter were not about overpredicting change or continuity but instead about their form. The globalization literature had (1) too much focus on erosion/reimposition and (2) little on which processes drive transformation. The state-transformation literature is too macro, and the war/economics/ideas debates cause scholars to miss important drivers of transformation. Transboundary processes drive the transformation of the state and global order by being illegible. This triggers a crisis that is solved when state agents develop new practices that draw new boundaries. There is clearly transformation here, but this transformation implies continuity. Because the state can transform, it remains at the center of politics.

In this chapter, I outline my theory of change and continuity in political order. The focus will be on change, because change is the driver of continuity; it is the reason why the state can persevere. First, I go deeper into my claims about the state being a series of boundary-drawing practices. In the process, I deal with two consequences of this theory: the state is multiple, and it exists amidst a series of unbounded flows. Next, I demonstrate that practice theories of the state have important implications for state transformation. They tell us that transformation is continuous. It happens at the margins or "from below." State collusion is as likely to cause change as state competition. Finally, scholars of state transformation should focus on case-specific configurations in explaining both change and continuity. The last part of this chapter then outlines my process of state transformation and the two mechanisms that structure my cases—shattering and reinscribing. I conclude by covering some weaknesses in this approach and talking about the next three chapters.

PRACTICE THEORIES OF THE STATE

Practice theories of the state and state transformation avoid the pitfalls I outlined in the state-transformation literature. They move scholarship beyond the machinations of political elites. They create space for state collusion to drive transformation. They get us beyond the war/economics/ideas debates that have shaped the field. They work up to the macro level, recognizing the continuous, dynamic nature of order and transformation.

There is a large literature that has addressed one or more of these problems and come up with similar answers to my own. These scholars often pitch themselves as combining the Marxist[1] idea of disaggregating[2] the state with the Weberian[3] recognition of its importance,[4] or as using field theory[5] and governmentality[6] not as alternatives to the state but as tools to make sense of it. Practice state theories also derive from the ways in which studies of the global South and globalization create paradoxes—the state is receding and overrun, yet more important than ever.[7] This section is about aggregating those arguments and clearly laying out the resulting vision of the state. For the rest of this section, I want to highlight two important elements of this vision of the state—practices and boundaries. I will also discuss one important implication of each: practices demonstrate how the state is made by multiple agents; boundaries demonstrate the role of global flows. Implications for state transformation will be taken up in the next section.

PRACTICES

The state is a series of practices. Practices are defined here as *habitual, patterned actions that both constitute the social world and its inhabitants and structure possible future action.*[8] This reflects an emphasis on process over stasis. As Bueger and Gadinger argue, "Practice theorists hence prefer... 'ordering,' 'structuring,' and 'knowing' ... [to] ... 'order,' 'structure,' or 'knowledge.'"[9] Rule is not constructed with a single "event," i.e., a peace treaty, a diplomatic mission, or a law passed in a legislature. It is constructed and maintained as actions become repeated often enough to become practices. Over time, these patterned actions become habitual or unthinking. As Hans Joas explains, action and perception are "anchored in an unreflected belief in self-evident given facts and successful habits."[10] When we brush our teeth or turn a knob to open a door, we do not debate the positives and negatives and make a calculation on whether or not we should undertake these actions. Nor do we debate whether they are appropriate or how they are attempts to solve some problem. We just do them. Habits are important because, as John Dewey argues, "[they] economize intellectual as well as muscular energy... freeing thought to deal with new conditions and purposes."[11]

Practice theory rests on the belief that action is the fundamental ontology of social life.[12] Without "doing," there is no doer. Without performing the functions that define them, states do not exist. How do we know that the United States exists? Is it because we can visit the White House or Capitol? Because of a map? Because of the titles of our leaders? Or is it because those of us who are citizens pay taxes to it, vote in its elections, and abide by its laws? If the Department of Treasury stopped performing the day-to-day tasks that it is assigned, would it exist? Would it not just be a building with a bunch of people in it?

Practice theory assumes that the state is performed, "order is always shifting and emergent.... Construction is never complete. Objects, structures, or norms, then, exist primarily in practice."[13] The state is a practice, a process, it is to be investigated and not reified.[14] It should be mentioned that these ideas are not new: Machiavelli argued that a principality needed constant maintenance,[15] while David Hume argued that political behavior was rooted in habit.[16]

Practices constitute the social world by helping us to create "conceptual maps" of what is possible and not possible, doable and not doable in both a normative and "best practices" sense. To understand any decision, we need to focus on historical context. Even in cases such as those highlighted in this project, where practices no longer "work," what is possible depends on what came before (previous practice) and/or what is currently happening (other, ongoing practices). New actions are not taken from a menu of all possible actions, and all options are not open to actors, because they either have not or cannot conceive of doing them in the practice-constructed context in which they find themselves. Therefore, it becomes hard for relevant actors to imagine alternatives unless forced to do so. In chapters 2–4, we see that in each case the relevant states doubled down on shattered boundaries because they could not think outside of their conceptual maps. In other words, practices construct the reified knowledge that we, as humans, need to think, to reason, to solve problems.[17]

Conceiving of the state as a series of practices has important implications for transformation. If the state is never formed, then it is always changing. Thus, incremental and constant change should be prioritized over major events. Such events are often just the moment when we realize or see the consequences of long, unfolding processes. World War I was the culmination of decades of interstate rivalry, World War II of the upheavals of the 1920s and 1930s, and decolonization of a series of localized battles that were resolved in locally contingent ways. And often the effects of these events are determined by later events: that World War I would lead to passports, for instance, is due to labor conditions and propaganda of the deed. Major events as turning points are at best simplifications of complex, multiple processes that overlay each other.

PRACTICES ARE PERFORMED BY A MULTITUDE OF STATE AGENTS

Once we accept that the state is a series of practices and we begin to look for those practices, it becomes apparent that they are undertaken by a multitude of actors. In the words of Iza Hussin, legibility comes from "many eyes, many optics, many voices."[18] When the focus is on boundaries and the margins of rule (see below), this becomes even more apparent. Many of these actors have even been traditionally characterized as private or non-state.

This is why I use the term "state agent" instead of "state." The practices that construct the state are undertaken by actors as varied as heads of state, Pinkertons, bureaucrats, and tax collectors. In chapter 2, I talk about the end of peacetime privateering in the colonial Atlantic sometime in the late seventeenth century. Prior to this, men like Henry Morgan—of Captain Morgan fame—were state agents! Morgan sailed with a letter of marque to attack ships from England's enemies and rivals. After his sea-raiding career was over, he became lieutenant governor or Jamaica. This is a far cry from the golden-age pirates of the early eighteenth century. Filibusters who engaged in "unauthorized" military expeditions often ended up as state agents. Pinkertons acted as state agents in the American West. The East India Company is another example. State agents are those that can act in the name and interests of the state. Sometimes "can" means legally and legitimately, other times it just implies they have the means to. Furthermore, they cannot be determined out of context.

Every agency or person who acts in the name of the state, whether formally or by contract, has some leeway to act in their own interests. Sometimes such groups (sea raiders, filibusters, etc.) have simultaneously worked against the state. This freedom is encoded in political science as deeply as studies of bureaucratic politics[19] or a simple reading of principal-agent theory. Yet it is often forgotten in IR. According to Kimberly Morgan and Ann Orloff, states encompass "multiple institutions, varying forms of interpenetration with civil society, multiple scales of governance, and multiple and potentially contradictory logics.... To understand states, we must both disaggregate and reaggregate."[20] Their metaphor that the state has many hands is apt. While this draws on traditions of assemblages or governmentality, the claim here is that states are important actors to be explained, not theorized away. Such a position, especially when paired with a focus on boundaries, opens up new possibilities for state transformation.

This is often reflected in the numerous modifiers the state, or some chunk of it, has received: carceral, surveillance, administrative, patriarchal, welfare, etc. A move to thinking about states as (or at least embedded within) empires buttresses this claim. Matthew Norton claims that the "circulation of goods, peoples, services and ideas [in the seventeenth-century Atlantic] is the [British] empire."[21] Thus, merchants, pirates, and smugglers, etc., were agents whose transactions drew the boundary between state and empire as much as, if not more than, those in London. In the pirate case below, colonial governors often acted autonomously to either rein in or profit from sea raiding. This not only was a problem but could influence when and how boundary-drawing practices developed. The same goes for police departments in the anarchist case and intelligence agencies in the al-Qaeda case. Solutions, and thus state transformation, were not always directed by the central government and often took place without its knowledge or blessing.

BOUNDARIES

In studying the state, we should prioritize practices that draw boundaries, as boundaries distinguish the state from other polities.[22] Scholars from across the social sciences have argued that social life is defined through the distinctions and categories created to make sense of the world.[23] Boundaries are lines of political significance that "decide which issues, activities, and practices fall within [the state's] authority realm—the political—and which lie in the provenance of non-state [or other-state] authority."[24] Boundaries create the Janus-faced nature of the state—inside/outside, international/domestic, community/anarchy—creating a need for scholars to problematize them.[25] Sovereignty is the practice of drawing boundaries around exclusive political authority.

Focusing on boundaries is not the study of two-level games, which assume a boundary and look at how the two spheres of politics interact.[26] The approach in this study is not about interaction between preconceived actors but instead transaction[27] between continually recreated and reinscribed actors. As Jackson and Nexon argue, "It is somewhat problematic to consider the way in which the state project operates 'domestically' without considering how it operates 'internationally,' and in particular to pay attention to the ways in which the operations of the project constitute this demarcation."[28] R. B. J. Walker echoes this thought: "The Cartesian demarcations between inside and outside, 'Us' and 'Other' . . .

[permit] ... the theory of international relations to occur as a discourse of community and anarchy in the first place."[29] The state is separated from society, but the emphasis is on the processes of distinction and creation, not their result.

Boundaries set the state apart from other types of polities.[30] For instance, universal systems—such as the medieval Catholic Church or many dynastic Chinese empires—claim all to be within their reach and therefore have no boundaries.[31] Empires are predicated on the relationship between center and periphery, a relationship that is often personal and is usually based on some form of tribute.[32] Buffer zones—such as those between fifteenth-century Italian city-states[33] or between nineteenth-century Southeast Asian kingdoms[34]—exist between small polities in areas where boundaries are not drawn. Overlapping systems break up the inside/outside dichotomy of sovereignty into multiple insides and outsides, similar to the heteronomous order of medieval Europe,[35] or some scholars' vision of a globalized future.[36] Of course, any real-world polity can contain elements of multiple ideal types.[37] For instance, the Soviet Union could be characterized as both a state with clear boundaries and an empire in its relations within the union and the Warsaw Pact.

The most obvious type of boundary is a physical one that delineates state authority. These are the borders[38] found on a map, such as the forty-ninth parallel or the Rio Grande, which separate the United States from Canada and Mexico, respectively. However, conceptual boundaries are even more important. For instance, the very idea behind distinguishing "domestic politics" and "international politics" as opposed to simply "politics," owes its purchasing power to state boundaries.[39] Similarly we can see distinctions between "society" and "state," "public" and "private," "citizen" and "alien," "in-group" and "out-group,"[40] among others. Timothy Mitchell argues for the state as a "structural effect," separated from society so as to rule it.[41] This necessitates boundaries that are drawn by the practice of ruling and are reinforced through the creation of "order" as a means of dispelling "chaos."[42] Territorial borders, then, are actually just a subset of conceptual boundaries, dependent upon knowledge practices such as the development of mapping[43] or the concept of linearity.[44]

No particular boundary is a necessity for the state. It is not a list of boundaries that separates predetermined realms but a polity that creates such realms from what it would otherwise recognize as chaos. What those boundaries separate in any particular time and place is contingent and must be determined historically. Boundaries are numerous and do not change simultaneously. Nor do boundaries exist wholly separate from one another. Take the border that separates India from Pakistan. In one sense, we could see the border that encapsulates India from its neighbors (or the sea) as singular. In another sense, the border between India and Pakistan could be thought of as a singular segment of India's border. In yet another, the boundary between India and Pakistan that runs through Kashmir could be characterized as a single border separate from others.

Boundaries are manifest in habitual actions that create our conceptual maps of the world, not by drawing lines on a map. An example from the narrative on golden-age piracy in chapter 2 can help to demonstrate this. This narrative focuses on an imaginary line drawn in the Atlantic that separated Europe from its colonial enterprises in that region. This line was supposedly drawn by Pope Alexander VI in 1494 as part of the Treaty of Tordesillas to separate the New World into Spanish and Portuguese realms.[45] By the early eighteenth century, it became a layering boundary that separated the states of Europe from their colonies.[46] So while "the line" dates back to the late fifteenth century, it was not this act that drew its eighteenth-century incarnation. Instead, a series of practices—the protection of trading lanes, low levels of direct colonial governance, and the use of peacetime privateers—did.[47] To focus on when and where a boundary was drawn misses how that boundary is made meaningful, why the boundary was drawn where it was, and its larger consequences.

BOUNDARIES AND UNBOUNDED PROCESSES

The circuits that Norton argues constructed the British Empire demonstrate that the state exists amidst of series of global or unbounded flows. Mitchell's argument that the state is an "effect" tells us that the state is not simply the container of politics but instead situated amongst a series of flows and practices. Bounding alters, halts, and redirects some of these flows but it can never address them all. This highlights the relational aspects of the state and points to processes that are occurring to create, undermine, and work outside it. Unbounded flows—made transboundary with the presence of the state—are the substance upon which the state is formed. These claims are also present in both transnational history's turn away from methodological nationalism[48] and claims in political geography that mapping and cartography are processes of making the state legible.[49]

The flows and circuits in which the state is situated can be broken into those "above" and "below" the state.[50] Below the state we see the non-state, transnational processes that are often associated with globalization: crime, terrorism, finance, trade, migration, ecological degradation, etc. Since the state is about bounding politics, transboundary flows can be problematic. However, they do not necessarily erode the state or merely make it one amongst many in a global assemblage. Transboundary processes have always existed as both problems and opportunities for states. Furthermore, any particular state's existence depends on the existence of all states, thus transboundary threats are not threats to a single state but to the institution itself. This is why we see transformations in global order.

Above the state, we see supranational and regional organizations such as the United Nations (UN), the European Union (EU), the World Trade Organization (WTO), the Organization of American States (OAS), etc. Additionally, the empire turn in the social sciences and history[51] reminds us that the states can be embedded in,[52] or interact with,[53] other types of polities. Obviously, as demonstrated above, many transnational and global flows not only do not challenge the state, they can be amplifying and constitutive as well. Boundaries are not primarily restrictive so much as they are exercises in distinguishing one thing from another. However, processes that cannot be distinguished, that do not flow in predictable ways, that do not make sense, fundamentally challenge states. This is especially true when they also provide a violent threat like the cases in this book.

IMPLICATIONS FOR STATE TRANSFORMATION

To describe the state as the practice of drawing boundaries does not guarantee change nor does it describe how change happens. Many practice theorists emphasize the difficulty of change.[54] Practices are about habits, and habits are hard to break. Similarly, a focus on process does not necessarily mean change. Processes, especially those rooted in habit, are less brittle than stasis and thus impervious to certain types of change. This becomes more pertinent when we take disaggregation into account. If the state is multiple, then habits need to be broken not just among multiple people but in people that inhabit different worlds. Thus, one could argue that change—and especially change directed from "the center"—is harder to enact and less complete than previously realized.

But state transformation is about change. In this section, I outline four implications of practice theories of the state for state transformation: (1) transformation is continuous, (2) transformation can be collusive, (3) state transformation can take place at the margins or "from below," (4) the literature on state transformation should focus on case-specific configurations. These are not either/or with more traditional approaches but "also." Competition, for instance, can still cause transformation, but so can collusion, and often the way in which one matters depends upon the other.

All orders take work to maintain, and they are constantly reaffirmed through habitual actions undertaken by myriad agents. If this is true, there is suddenly a proliferation of opportunities for state transformation. Since the state is comprised of hundreds of boundaries (or more), redrawing any particular boundary may not seem like radical change. But over time, as new boundaries add up, change becomes perceptible. States are constantly changing and, in the words of George Steinmetz, "never 'formed' once and for all."[55] The claim here is not that major events are unimportant; the War of Spanish Succession, the First World War, and 9/11 all play important roles in my cases. Instead, I make two interlocking claims. First, what often looks like a turning is actually observers recognizing changes they had not previously seen. Second, the way in which any event or process actually impacts transformation is through more local processes, such as how states have dealt with transnational violence. For instance, it is true that immigration restrictions and decreased movement took hold across the world following World War I. As I show in chapter 3, this was in part due to something happening much earlier—propaganda of the deed. Fingerprints, *portraits parlés*, and early immigration restrictions were already happening prior to the war and were necessary parts of what happened after. Yes, the war was important, but the way in which it actually mattered depended on the boundaries drawn to combat propaganda of the deed.[56]

Much of the state-transformation literature focuses on state competition. Research focusing on war or economic competition, even on their ideational components, does this. But practice theories allow for the possibility that state transformation happens in conjunction with other states to deal with actors such as pirates, anarchists, and terrorists. Cooperative action does not necessarily mean formal cooperation, as often conceptualized in IR.[57] While that happens, it is more common to observe something more akin to collusion or diffusion, where other states aid or repeat the actions of a "successful" state. The threats in the chapters below are transboundary. No single state can or did defeat them. Instead of state vs. state, it is state vs. other. Furthermore, states exist in part because of the recognition of other states; sovereignty is as much a diffused practice as any other. This also helps us to scale up from state to global order. Collusion, cooperation, or copycatting turn the practices of one state into practices constructing global order. Whether it is ending peacetime privateering in the early eighteenth-century Atlantic, regulating border regimes in the early twentieth century, or intelligence sharing through the Five Eyes in the twenty-first century, states have worked together to solve the problems that transnational violence poses. In the face of globalization, this aspect of state transformation should be a focus for scholars, yet it is largely ignored.

State transformation can also happen at the margins of the state or global order. These margins are where the cases in this study take root: the colonial Atlantic, the working-class quarters of European cities, the rugged terrain of Central Asia. For different reasons, none could be considered consolidated parts of their contemporary global or regional orders. As a consequence of relying on major events and state competition, scholars of state transformation have been too focused on the actions of the center. But a focus on boundaries, "many hands," and global flows means that state transformation can come from below. For instance, many scholars have begun to point to the non-Western origins of the "Westphalian" state.[58] Other scholars have pointed out the role that indigenous rulers,[59] peoples,[60] and natural forces[61] have played in the construction of borders outside Europe. This scholarship shows that the center is constituted through power relations with the margins and is as dependent on them for its existence as on recognized centers.

Finally, moving beyond war, economics, and ideas as causes meant taking a configurational approach rooted in historical context. This avoids the pitfall of attempting to find the one variable or cause, such as war, economics, or ideas, that drives the state by focusing instead on processes. Yes, violence is the focus of all three cases in this book, but I expressly claim that factors ranging from capital flows to migration, social movements, communication, pandemics, ecological degradation, etc., could be sources of transformation. This is not a bellocentric account because I am not defining the state to be about war making or violence, as bellocentrists do. As Friedrich Nietzsche observes, "Only something that has no history can be defined."[62] The state has a history, one this study is hoping to elucidate. Friedrich Kratochwil has argued that the state does not need to "have a clearly identifiable trans-historical core, but possess a certain 'family resemblance.'"[63] A trans-historical core calls for specifics such as bureaucracy,[64] international recognition,[65] nationality,[66] or the ability to marshal economic[67] or coercive power.[68] If one focuses on something like the welfare state and standing armies, erosion and/or reimposition are more visible than transformation. The welfare can rise and decline, but this does not mean that the state is doing so as well. Conversely, "family resemblances" necessitate analytical generality where specifics—which practices? what boundaries?—are "something we must go to history to discover."[69] A better approach is configurational. War, economics, and ideas work side by side as we look for practices of boundary drawing. Major events and local processes weave together. This is what I turn to in the next section, a process of state transformation and the two mechanisms that drive it.

ONE PROCESS OF STATE TRANSFORMATION

The question that I have not answered thus far is, "How does state transformation happen?" Two mechanisms drive transformation—shattering and reinscribing.[70] These are ideal types,[71] and they will not be found in their pure form anywhere. The point is not to test them but to use them to analyze previously overlooked instances of transformation.

While practice theorists inspired by Bourdieu often prioritize continuity, those with a grounding in pragmatism[72] highlight change and creativity.[73] Pragmatists argue that social change takes place in specific problem situations when habits no longer help actors to make sense of the world.[74] Hans Joas argues that "all human action is caught in the tension between unreflected habitual action and acts of creativity." He creates the following model of social change: habit/practice shattering of habit creativity in solving problem new habit/practice. Creativity "is performed within situations which call for solutions, and not as an unconstrained production of something new."[75] These solutions come from "the diffusely problematic quality of the action situation as a whole."[76] In other words, an actor's definition of a problem, dependent on their own conceptual maps, determines which types of solutions are possible. The problem situation in which practices are no longer useful is the shattering, and the creative solutions that turn into new practices that draw new boundaries are the reinscribing.

SHATTERING

Shattering happens when the practices that draw boundaries are no longer useful. In each of the cases below, shattering happens to one or a few boundaries at a time. In these moments, a crisis arises that goes beyond damage done and lives lost. The state becomes powerless; the distinction between it and society, alien, etc., no longer functions. Not the entire state, mind you, but instead some of the practices that construct it. Think about a major event in your own life (e.g., a breakup or a job loss). Your entire life was not thrown upside down; if you lose your job, you're likely to still have the same friends, have the same family, enjoy the same hobbies and foods as you did before. Nevertheless, it feels like your life is upside down because you cannot go on as you had. One can only detect a crisis in a particular problem situation by looking at the way in which a particular threat is articulated.[77] It is possible that in an identical situation happening to a different set of actors a problem situation would not be identified as such.

Let's break shattering down. First, the practices and boundaries at hand are responsible for the episode of transnational violence: so long as they exist, so does the threat. Second, the episode of transnational violence is able to inflict some level of material damage. For instance, the Earth Liberation Front contains many of the same elements as al-Qaeda with respect to shattering (anti-system, potential for transnationality, use of violence, hard to track) but has never caused a big enough nuisance for state agents. It is impossible to say how much damage a priori—fewer Americans die from terrorism than from shark bites, but the latter is not considered a major threat—but some level of damage is necessary to scare people. Third, the episode of transnational violence also creates a crisis of legitimacy for the state by preventing state agents from fulfilling their claims.[78] This is often tied into the fourth element: transnational violence is illegible to the state. It is instructive to return to illegibility with the theoretical framework flushed out.

The conceptual maps created by boundaries attempt to make legible what is otherwise illegible. However, as Scott notes, these maps do not "successfully represent the actual activity of the society they depicted . . . they represented only that slice of it that interested the official observer."[79] So there are parts of any legible process that remain illegible, not to mention whole processes. Given that the state exists amongst transboundary flows, there will always be processes that could, potentially, trigger a crisis through their illegibility—the problem is baked into the cake.

For our purposes, an illegible process is not one that state agents can never make sense of—such a process is vanishingly rare—but instead one they cannot make sense of using current conceptual maps or boundaries. Let's take the hunt for Dzhokhar Tsarnaev, one of two perpetrators of the April 15, 2013, Boston Marathon bombing. Following a gunfight that killed Dzhokhar's older brother (and accomplice), Tamerlan, the suspect escaped. The police response was to cordon off an area and thoroughly search it. This led to images of militarized police searching streets, houses, and basements in suburban Watertown, Massachusetts. The problem was, Dzhokhar Tsarnaev not in the cordoned-off area.

In this example, state agents used their power as they knew how, but no matter how many places they searched or what tools they used, they were not going to find Tsarnaev. In that moment, he was illegible. Tsarnaev was eventually found by a resident named David Henneberry, who went to investigate some padding that was out of place on his boat.[80] Henneberry's residence was only a few blocks outside the cordoned area. Assuming Tsarnaev stayed in place or was only able to move slowly (he was bleeding), he would have been caught eventually. Illegibility is not a natural property of anything, nor does it last forever. But the police would not have found Tsarnaev using their chosen coercive search methods. He was instead found by some guy who checked on his boat. This demonstrates (1) how illegibility happens no matter the technical expertise or power deployed and (2) that illegibility is rooted in the situation.

A threat could be illegible if the action itself makes little to no sense. This is apparent when speaking of blowing up a café in the late nineteenth century or flying planes into towers. However, in the piracy case, the act of sea raiding had been common for centuries. That was not the problem. Similarly, a threat could be illegible because the justifications are alien to contemporary political discourse. Again, both the anarchists and jihadists meet this criterion. I argue that golden-age pirates did as well, but I recognize that this case is made difficult by the pirates' illiteracy, which has provided us with few reliable materials. However, what really matters in these cases is the way in which the threat cannot be understood using current conceptual maps. Piracy did not stop after pardons; bribes of land and status to famous pirates were ineffective; piracy did not follow patterns of interimperial rivalry like it had for decades; naval power was an insufficient salve. So long as the practices that constructed the colonial Atlantic of the late seventeenth century persisted, so would piracy. Business as usual made piracy worse. This is the concept of illegibility I am using.

Finally, shattering is often driven home through failed attempts to defeat the threat. These early attempts—whether they be the use of pardons for pirates, public executions for anarchists, or regime change interventions in the War on Terror—are tied to previous boundaries. In many ways, the failure of these attempts drives home the idea that current practices, boundaries, and conceptual maps are inadequate. This may not be a necessary part of shattering, but it is present in each case.

REINSCRIBING

It is in those moments when early attempts to defeat a threat are judged inadequate that the process of reinscribing begins. When old boundaries are no longer operable, state agents need creative solutions. Shattering overlaps with, and creates avenues for, reinscribing. These solutions are dependent upon the creation of new conceptual maps that make a subset of previously unthinkable actions possible and previously common actions unthinkable. States may lose some capacity, legitimacy, or authority in one arena but gain elsewhere. This process *reinscribes* boundaries by alleviating crises and making illegible threats legible. The state is once again an entity that helps actors get along in the world. Though still a state, it has changed.

Crises can only be articulated by the actors involved. The same goes for any solution. Different articulations of crisis lead to different solutions and different future courses of action. There is no single "answer" to piracy or even golden-age piracy. It depends on how the problem or crisis is recognized and defined in the situation. This is especially true when problems are defined by aggregates like societies or states; there is always room to frame the problem and therefore create possibilities for solutions. The consequences of this point in each case and possible future cases will be taken up again in the conclusion.

Creativity means that state agents bring "something objectively new into the world."[81] This means new practices drawing new boundaries providing new conceptual maps. In order to be "new," these boundaries must be drawn by actions previously unthinkable. This does not mean that every part of said actions must have no historical antecedents. Solutions depend heavily upon both the constraints and possibilities of previous experience and concurrent habits. Rather, they create realms of state action that, prior to the shattering, were not a part of the conceptual map.

The way in which the Atlantic colonies were drawn closer to the state, as demonstrated in chapter 2, was new and creative, even if some aspects of the policies had historical antecedents. There were passports in the past, but the idea that the state would provide all prospective travelers with a passport (and therefore control who and what crossed their borders) was unthinkable in the late nineteenth century. That state agents would have the ability to track people across their own borders and sift through large amounts of metadata without specific court orders was not thought possible or legitimate. It was not an arena where the state claimed authority. Each action is creative not because its components are new, but instead because the context and use of those elements are new; state agents create novel realms of state authority even as old ones die.

Unlike what critics of pragmatism have long stated,[82] this is not simply a case of adaptation and instrumentality. Such theories take agency away from actors and have them choose new policies from a menu of options, usually based on predetermined criteria of effectiveness.[83] This is what might be called the rationalist-efficiency argument. Such an argument denies that new actions can lead to new actors. Instead it claims that already existing actors decide to undertake new policies, but otherwise stay the same. They also deny actors the creativity embedded in pragmatist social theory.

Instead, an actor's actions are creative, preserving what Joas calls "situated freedom."[84] Order takes work and is derived from the "situated accomplishments" of the actors.[85] Means and ends are not as self-evident as they may appear to be, with the exception of situations that Dewey refers to as "work," where goals are externally set. Typically, goals become clear only as we choose the means of our actions. In the words of Hans Joas, "Only when we recognize that certain means are available to use do we discover goals which had not occurred to us before."[86] In other words, goals are not something preset; they come about as we discover the means of action that are available to us in any particular situation. There are situations where the goals themselves develop depending upon actor experience. Drawing colonies closer to the metropole was not the goal of anti-piracy efforts. The context changed, then it became a goal.

Dewey calls these situations "play,"[87] and they form the backbone of many of the most important political processes, including state transformation. As a result of the Second World War, the winning states became much more concerned with the type of regime ruling other states. Part of this is due to the resulting Cold War (so not the war itself), but part of it was the belief that fascism was one trigger for the conflict. Fascism and communism needed to be stamped out. In many ways the war did shatter previous practices, and caring about regime type was one goal that was discovered as a result. It was part of reinscribing after the conflict. This demonstrates both the point above about goals and how my framework brings major events and local processes together to explain state transformation.

For a final example, I will turn briefly to a creative response from chapter 3: fingerprinting. New technologies are a common explanation as external stimuli to political change in rationalist-efficiency arguments. Fingerprinting technology developed as part of a larger eugenic project to identify people with predispositions to crime and deviant behavior.[88] However, it only proliferated when police officers learned of its utility in the process of preventing and punishing propagandist attacks. Fingerprinting did not exist as a choice in police work until a real-world problem shattered existing boundaries and it became a solution for reinscribing them. If fingerprinting proved so effective and the technology to implement it already existed, why was it not utilized earlier? Some may claim trial and error. But this would not explain why the early choices made in combatting propaganda of the deed—treating anarchism as the crime, brutality against anarchists, show trials and executions—adhered so closely to past practice. Trial and error happen in the context of new understandings triggered by shattered boundaries. Finally, we get back to the idea underlying this and most rationalist arguments: governing actors are ontologically separate from the governing that they do. If true, then new policies do not change the actors. However, there is little reason to assume an actor exists separate from their actions. It is unverifiable and, at best, an assumption. If order takes work to maintain, changes in the work reinscribe the order. Technological developments are not an exogenous force determining policy choice but instead part of the process of policy choices that become available (or not) based on the conceptual maps of relevant actors. Rationality, then, is not the starting point for social analysis but instead a learned and contextualized behavior.[89]

CONCLUSION

In China Mieville's novel *The City and the City*, quoted in the epigraph to this chapter, two rival city-states—Beszel and Ul Qoman—occupy the same geographical space. Next door may be another state, with your state again on the other side of that. What separates them is the ability of the citizens of each to "unsee" aspects of the other—to live life as if they are wholly in a single polity as opposed to physically inhabiting two. Unseeing is the law—Ul Qomans cannot even think of heading next door for a cup of coffee if next door is in Beszel—but it is built on habitual participation of the cities' respective citizens. The boundary is as conceptual as physical and built on practices carried out by myriad actors, from heads of state to police to citizens. The same is true for the modern state writ large. In order to understand the effects of transnational violence on state transformation, we need to conceptualize the state as multiple, produced by the practices that draw boundaries, and existing amongst transnational or global flows.

New practices create new boundaries, and new boundaries mean new states. The state is preserved—continuity can be observed. Yet, there has been change. The state persists as the dominant actor because it can transform. Whether one sees change or continuity depends on where and how one looks at the problem. But in order to see continuity and move beyond erosion and reimposition, we need to understand how transformation happens.

In turn, this means a shifting global order. If global order is the conglomeration of patterned relationships and actions by states and the state is defined by what it does, then states doing new things means a change in global order. This change may be imperceptible from one thousand feet, but enough change does eventually make for a meaningful difference.

The argument in this chapter has its limits. First, I do not claim that this is the only process through which transformation happens, nor do I claim that it is the only process of state transformation derived from practice theory. While I believe that the processes of shattering and reinscribing are useful in a range of other cases, it is inevitable that transformation happens through other processes as well. The changes outlined below could trigger other changes. There are also changes that can happen through learning or cultural exchange.

I do not claim to have vanquished traditional accounts of state transformation. "War made the state and the state made war" can be a useful way to think about state transformation in some instances. I do claim that the degree to which it is useful is overstated. Finally, this approach to state transformation does not lend itself well to 300–500-year-long studies of state development. Transformation is too common and happens in too many places and times to be easily digested in such a way. This may strike some as too complex of a theory, but then again, the social world is complex, and too much simplification inhibits our understanding of it. Whether this is a feature or a bug is in the eye of the beholder.

What follows are three case studies of state transformation triggered by transnational violence. I have already described the cases in the introduction, but here I wanted to discuss their layout. In addition to an introduction—which sets out the case and alternative explanations—and a conclusion, each case will be broken into three sections. The first will outline the relevant boundaries and the practices that construct them to provide historical, geographical, and cultural context. It will also outline how relevant boundaries played a role in the rise of each episode of violence, setting the table for the next section on shattering. This section will cover the material damage caused by the episode of violence, the crisis of legitimacy it caused, and its illegibility, not necessarily in that order. It will end with a description of failed attempts to defeat the threat that drove home the shattering. The last section will cover reinscribing, demonstrating how creative solutions to a concrete problem led to new practices that drew new boundaries, creating new states. This final section will also discuss the ways that global order changed as a result of state transformation.

2

THE GOLDEN AGE OF PIRACY AND THE CREATION OF AN ATLANTIC WORLD

This chapter is the first of three cases demonstrating that transnational violence can drive political transformation by forcing the development of new practices that draw new boundaries. In this case, the ideal typical boundary to be interrogated is one drawn in the early modern Atlantic that marked "Europe" or the "state" off from the "Atlantic colonies" or the "empire," hereafter referred to as "the line." This boundary was drawn through a configuration of five practices: (1) direct protection of ships on trading lanes claimed by a state, (2) warfare and rivalry over trading lanes, (3) economic patterns of extraction, (4) the enforcement of "no peace beyond the line" via the use of privateers to attack rivals during nominal times of "peace" in Europe without warfare ensuing, and (5) low levels of involvement in colonial governance. By the middle of the eighteenth century, the line no longer helps us to understand the colonial Atlantic, with the colonies pulled much closer to the metropole and warfare ensuing in both realms concurrently. I argue that the golden age of piracy was instrumental in this change. In other words, the practices constructing the state changed as a result of the golden age of piracy.

The golden age of piracy is neither a common reason given for the dissolution of the line, nor is it cited as a factor in state transformation. In fact, the disappearance of the line is often not thought of as state transformation. This makes dealing with alternative explanations tricky: few scholarly treatments are making the connections below. Additionally, there are multiple claims being made in this chapter: why the golden age of piracy started, why it ended, why the line was erased, even claims on the significance of erasure such as the causes of the American Revolution and England's role in eighteenth-century continental warfare. To deal with all of these in one place would be cumbersome at best. Alternative explanations and the larger configurations (of which piracy was a part) responsible for outcomes of interest are covered in the narrative below. What I want to do is address a few macro-processes that a) play a role in the outcomes listed above and b) are popular explanations for them. This approach is repeated in the next two chapters as well.

Some scholars point to the revolutions as cause for the end of piracy and state transformation in the region.[1] However, these revolutions (in the United States, Haiti, and across Latin America) took place almost a century after the events in this chapter. Transformation is never finished, and there is nothing here to dispute the importance of the "revolutionary Atlantic"; it does not play a causal role in this narrative. The same goes for Janice Thomson's claims about the end of private violence,[2] as it happened in the middle of the nineteenth century.[3] However, Thomson claims that piracy was a natural outcome of privateering and therefore does not distinguish between this era of piracy and others. This means that she cannot account for the end of the golden age nor the period from 1730 to roughly 1800, when wartime privateering did not lead to outbreaks of piracy in peacetime. My response to Rodney Bruce Hall's claims about Westphalia conditioning colonial politics was covered in the introduction.

This leaves three interrelated processes: the rise of the slave (or triangular) trade, the change from an extraction-based to a trade-based colonial economy, and the rise of England. All three play important roles in the rise of piracy, the end of piracy, and the state transformation that resulted. These processes make the line untenable because of piracy, they force state agents to deal with piracy as a problem, and they factor into the consequences of the fight against piracy. My claim is that the impact of these macro-processes was conditioned by the golden age of piracy and the campaign to defeat it. This will be demonstrated in the narrative below.

This chapter is split into three sections. First is a section on the line and the practices that drew it. It makes the case that the line, combined with shifting economic circumstances, created the conditions for the golden age of piracy. The next section will deal with how golden-age pirates shattered the practices that drew the line. The section is split into four parts—the material consequences of piracy, piracy's challenge to the legitimacy of state and empire, the illegibility of piracy, and how early attempts to combat piracy merely reinforced the line, the very boundary making piracy possible. Before the conclusion, there will be a section on reinscribing covering the successful actions undertaken to defeat piracy and how they played a role in state transformation.

Two further notes before proceeding: First, what follows is focused largely on threats to and the response of England. England had become the dominant actor in the Atlantic, with the most to lose from piracy and the most to gain by its demise. Additionally, most pirates were English and used England as their rhetorical bogeyman. Piracy was certainly a problem for the French, Spanish, Dutch, and others, as will be discussed below. However, England provides the best demonstration of what happened. Second, the assumption here is that the "state" existed as locus of politics by the early eighteenth century. I am not explaining the supposed development of the state from some other type of polity but instead its continued transformation.

"NO PEACE BEYOND THE LINE"

The line was a boundary separating state and empire. Empires are best defined by core-periphery relationships characterized by indirect rule and heterogeneous contracting.[4] Thus, empires can be conglomerations of political actors ranging from settled states or populations to chartered companies[5] and semi-cores[6] held together "not by formal allegiance to a mother-country but by economic, strategic, political, or cultural links that varied greatly in strength and character."[7] There is, ideally, little to no contact between peripheries, a "hub and spoke" system.[8] This allows imperial agents to contain resistance, preventing its spread across the empire. States are distinguished by integration within boundaries, empires by ruling through difference.[9] Empires are rooted in different logics from states.

However, there is no reason that any particular polity must follow one logic. From the seventeenth to early twentieth century, European colonial empires could be characterized as empires with states at their core—what may be called a state-empire hybrid polity.[10] These polities have boundaries that separate the realm of state and empire, layering sovereignty.[11] The line as it existed in the late seventeenth and early eighteenth centuries is one of these boundaries—a conceptual one separating state, Europe, and integration from empire, "the New World," and difference.[12] Therefore, boundary-drawing practices are exclusive to states, but the seventeenth- and eighteenth-century Atlantic empires included elements of both ideal typical states and empires. So, while piracy and the response to it took place in colonial spaces and alongside imperial dynamics of rule, we can still highlight dynamics of state transformation. The inverse could be true in this or other cases.

The origins of the line date back to fifteenth-century disputes over New World jurisdiction between the Portuguese and the Spanish. However, the identity and position of the line were and remain quite vague. It has been argued that it is simply the Tropic of Cancer,[13] the Tropic and a "prime meridian passing through Ferro in the Canaries" set at the Treaty of Cateau-Cambresis in 1559,[14] and the equator, among others.[15] It began as a way to demarcate Spanish and Portuguese spheres of influence, then to protect Spanish claims in the New World from French and English traders and explorers, and finally as a layering boundary separating state from empire. The meaning of the line mutated beyond its original purpose.[16] It should also be said that there is some skepticism of its existence. It is true that there is little official recognition of the line in peace treaties, and its shifting placement means it was often more of a political tool than something that organized politics. However, in war and peace and in daily routines, the politics of the Atlantic were separated from those of Europe.

While there tended to be little official recognition of the placement of the line, its function at this time was clear: what happened beyond the line was recognized to be "behind God's back."[17] As Oliver Cromwell quipped, "everyone could act for his own advantage in those quarters."[18] On one side of the line were the affairs of Europe, on the other were colonial affairs. In this situation, warfare could happen in the colonies without breaking out in Europe (but the reverse did not prove to be true). The line also patterned trade behavior, as joint stock companies only developed for trade on the other side of the line, not with other Europeans.[19]

POLITICAL ECONOMY OF THE LINE

The line had meaning due to the type of economic goods that colonies provided.[20] In this period, the major value of colonies lay in their ability to fill state coffers with precious metals as directly as possible. Gold and silver were the most sought-after properties, prompting Spain's incursions into South America and Mexico, where there was gold and silver, rather than into North America, where there was little. By the sixteenth century (and into the early eighteenth century), Spain claimed all territory—land and sea—south of the Tropic of Cancer by right of discovery. The French, English, and Dutch understandably did not recognize such claims. Yet, it wasn't until 1624 that the English had a permanent settlement in the West Indies, and 1635 for the French.[21] Thus "no peace" was maintained by the Spanish, who saw everything beyond the line as their territory, and by other colonial powers because it was the only way to access Spanish bullion and trade with Spanish settlements.

Colonial governors were given wide latitude of action: control over non-trade policy in a colony, unsupervised colonial courts, rights to collect tribute from natives—the encomienda system[22]—and the ability to commission privateers on their own authority. This was because most colonies functioned as ports from which precious raw materials were shipped to the metropole (common for Spanish colonies), a trading post or fort to protect sea lanes, or a settlement of religious exiles (common for English North America). In none of these cases were local issues important to the state. Colonies were not independent, but state control over day-to-day activities was loose, especially in colonies with few valuable raw materials.

Authority was claimed, and recognized, over sea lanes in the name of trading rights. While ocean space was not to be possessed, it did become a site for interstate competition and the exercise of power.[23] Hugo

Grotius believed that states had the ability "to take Possession or Jurisdiction only over some Part of the Sea."[24] His arguments for free navigation were against claiming jurisdiction over the entire sea; his problem was monopoly, not possession. He was actually reinforcing standard practice through reform.[25] The major threats at sea were the activities of rivals. Therefore, recognizing it as a site for competition became standard practice, and disagreements over trading lanes proved to be a legitimate casus belli.[26]

Warfare over trading lanes and extracted goods such as gold and silver was often conducted by privateers. Privateers were equipped with a "letter of marque" provided by a state or colonial government, allowing them to undertake predation in its name. The most famous privateers, often called buccaneers,[27] of this age were considered patriots, heroes standing up to enemies in the great wilderness of empire. This was a narrative that dated back at least as far as Francis Drake's publication of his adventures in 1589 and continued through stories by Henry Mainwaring, Henry Morgan, William Dampier, and Henry Every, among others. The tales proved quite popular with the public.[28] As one contemporary Englishman opined, "The privateers of these parts . . . theire bodys are habituated to this country, they knowe each place and creeke, know the mode of Spanish fighting, townes being never so well fortified, the numbers being never so unequall, if money or good plunder be in the case they will either win it manfully or dye coradgiously."[29] Many privateers were able to use this language for their own benefit. In an autobiographical song, Henry Every claimed, "French, Spaniard and Portuguese, the Heathen likewise / He [Every] has made a War with them until that he dies."[30]

If privateers were viewed as a threat, it was because they were an arm of a rival state's power. In an account by one seventeenth-century Spanish engineer taking part in an anti-privateering mission, the nationality of the pirates captured was constantly repeated: "The number of English dead was six"; "On 10 September an English ship was sighted"; "These English pirates were taken back to the mainland."[31] Privateers tended to raid with their fellow countrymen. There was a French privateer base on Tortuga and an English one on Port Royal, Jamaica. Privateers with the sponsorship of England would attack French, Spanish, and Dutch trading ships, while privateers with French sponsorship would attack

English, Spanish, and Dutch trading ships, and so on. It should be mentioned that the nationality of pirates did not always match that of the sponsoring state (with which they were identified), and crews were often multinational. This competition went beyond times of war, though it was expanded during periods of official hostility to include times of peace. The use of privateers during peacetime constituted the idea that "there is no peace beyond the line," i.e., peace agreed upon by states after wars on the continent did not apply to the colonial, international sphere.

It was common for privateers to go beyond their mandate to undertake unsanctioned actions, blurring the line between "pirate"—a legal term for someone engaging in unsanctioned sea raiding[32]—and "privateer." State leaders tolerated this so long as the enterprise was beneficial. As Lauren Benton argues, "letters of marque ... could be broadly interpreted to permit attacks on a wide range of targets."[33] For instance, Henry Morgan strayed beyond his letter to sack Panama City. One observer commented that Morgan's men "committed many ... cruelties. They showed little mercy, even to the monks. ... Nor did they spare the women, except for those who yielded themselves completely."[34] Frustrated, the English appointed Sir Thomas Lynch to enforce the Treaty of Madrid—which ended hostilities between the British and the Spanish in the Americas—and clean up privateering in Jamaica. Morgan was captured and sent back to London for punishment, but upon his arrival he was knighted and awarded the position of lieutenant governor of Jamaica. The English may have thought Morgan a morally deficient outlaw and they may have wanted more control over Jamaica, but his services were deemed a beneficial resource for the state in its competition with rivals in the colonial Atlantic. He was not a threat.

CHANGING POLITICAL ECONOMY AND THE PROBLEM OF PIRACY

The economic patterns of sixteenth- and seventeenth-century colonies facilitated a competition for and extraction of raw materials in the colonies. However, as the seventeenth century progressed, colonies came to provide agricultural, and even some manufactured, goods.[35] This created a demand for workers, which was filled by the rising number of slaves available from West Africa. Trade, not simply extraction, became the chief source of colonial value, provided by the growing mercantilist economic system. This was due in part to English attempts to profit from its Atlantic colonies due to Spanish policies of no peace and recurring yellow-fever epidemics.[36] England's rise as a naval superpower was built in part on this shift, as North American tobacco and cotton, West Indian sugar, and West African slaves replaced Central and South American gold and silver as the goods of choice. However, these changes were not solely due to England's rise, as French colonies saw similar shifts, and local merchants and actors looking out for their own interests played a role as well.

As economic and colonial interests changed, patterns of colonial rule were slow to adapt. Here is where the macro-processes discussed above begin to play a role. However, there is little reason to assume that, in a vacuum, seventeenth-century boundaries would have been forced to change, or change in the manner that they did, because of England's rise or new economic patterns. While the mix of new economic patterns and old patterns of colonial rule did not determine the change to come, they created tensions in the state-empires of that period that were critical to piracy's golden age.

Trade functioned best in peace, and it became harder and harder for state agents to justify continuous warfare beyond the line to other states, merchants, and their own treasurers. Attempts to enforce peace beyond the line started in the middle of the seventeenth century with the allowance of a grace period—ignored in Morgan's case—of nine months after the signing of a peace treaty. In the 1670s, England began to tell colonial governors that they could not undertake measures of war without London's blessing, and in 1689 all West Indian governors were barred from issuing letters of marque.[37] The Board of New York, a renowned privateer haven for much of the century, called "privateer" "a soft name for pirates" in 1698.[38] In the 1680s and 1690s, colonial officials were appointed with specific mandates to clean up piracy. One of these men was Henry Morgan, who claimed that privateering and piracy interfered with trade interests.[39] Nonetheless, the practice continued, as the crown had few avenues for disciplining colonial governors. Jamaican governor Archibald Hamilton gave out letters of marque to privateers under the guise of fighting piracy well into the eighteenth century.[40] In addition, privateering was still used extensively in the Atlantic by European states in wartime well into the nineteenth century.[41]

The attempts to stop sea raiding between the Nine Years' War (1689–1697) and the War of Spanish Succession (1703–1714) is best encapsulated by the saga of Captain William Kidd. Kidd, a renowned privateer in the ongoing war,[42] took a commission from King William to capture pirates and attack French shipping in 1696.[43] While on his mission, he performed largely the same actions he had on previous commissions, even going beyond his letter of marque to attack merchant shipping. He soon discovered that his actions had been termed "piracy" while he was at sea. One of the ships he captured, the *Quedagh Merchant*, was owned by Abd-ul-Ghaffur, an important figure at Indian mughal Aurangzeb's court. Since the East India Company (EIC) was experiencing a historic downturn in profits, Aurangzeb was able to pressure the company to do something about "English" piracy. Kidd soon became the unsuspecting poster boy of the EIC's anti-piracy campaign. Kidd learned of his predicament while still at sea and decided to return to New York, where one of his financiers, Richard Coote, Earl of Bellomont, had been made governor with a mandate to end the colony's reputation as a pirate haven.[44]

However, upon Kidd's return, Bellomont, whose Whig faction in London had fallen out of favor, turned him in. Bellomont told Kidd, "I set myself a rule never to grant a pardon without the King's express leave or command."[45] Bellomont told the authorities in London that "I had an account that he was certainly turned pyrate,"[46] and that "there has never been a greater Liar or Thief in the World than this Kidd."[47] Kidd was arrested and sent to London for trial on charges of piracy and the murder of his gunman, William More. Kidd claimed he had "French passes" for the *Quedagh Merchant*, meaning, that his letter of marque covered his actions, but they were being kept from him by his benefactors. In a letter he sent to the judge before his trial, he claimed that he was "made a pirate."[48] Henry Morgan strayed from his letter of marque and was knighted. Just a few decades later, Kidd did the same and was hanged.[49] Similar fates befell other pirates of the era, including Thomas Tew,[50] John Quelch,[51] and Henry Every,[52] though the last was never apprehended.

A changing political economy and static governance, i.e., the line, created nearly perfect working conditions for pirates. As historian Marcus Rediker puts it, "The sailor knew . . . the Atlantic was a big place, that the empires were overstretched... These circumstances created openings from below."[53] There was open land for bases in Madagascar, the many capes on the Carolina Shore, the Bahamas, and other small Caribbean islands. The situation also provided markets because pirates and privateers alike found welcome buyers in Atlantic colonies, especially in North America. It was piracy money that kick-started a shift from an agricultural to seafaring economy in Bermuda in the 1690s.[54] One English official remarked that "the Pirates themselves have often told me that if they had not been supported from the traders from thence [New York, Pennsylvania, and Rhode Island] with ammunition and provisions according to their directions, they would never become so formidable, nor arrived to that degree that they have."[55] This was not a major problem so long as these privateers were serving England's interests. Once this stopped being the case, the openness of colonial markets to pirate goods became a problem, because it gave pirates an outlet to get rich off what was now illegal plunder.

A common reason given in the historiography for the rise of golden-age piracy is the drawdown of naval forces following the Treaty of Utrecht in 1714. This follows an economic view of piracy as being determined by supply and demand. After the war, the English navy went from roughly fifty thousand sailors to around fifteen thousand, creating a large group of men with sailing experience and no work. A number of early pirate captains, such as Henry Jennings and Benjamin Hornigold, were former privateers who, while willing to attack French and Spanish ships illegally, "refused to take and plunder English Vessels."[56] This has led some IR scholars who have dealt with piracy to focus on the link between privateering and piracy as a major causal claim.[57]

While I do not deny that the war gave a kick start to this wave of piracy, the numbers do not bear it out as the cause. Many wars ended, but there was only one golden age of piracy. With an influx of thirty-five thousand unemployed sailors at the end of the war, Rediker estimates that only about four thousand or five thousand men went "upon the account" during the entire period, and only fifteen hundred to two thousand in the years 1716–1718.[58] Those not connected to the war include famous captains such as Bartholomew "Black Bart" Roberts[59] and Calico Jack Rackham. Pirates tended to come from preexisting freebooters and ship mutineers. And even if the situation gave the golden age a kick start, the opportunity for plunder still had to be there. The major causes of the golden age of piracy were the change to a mercantilist economy in the Atlantic and patterns of rule that had yet to catch up with this new reality. As long as the line existed, so would pirates.

SHATTERING: "ROBBERS, OPPOSERS, AND VIOLATORS OF ALL LAWS HUMANE AND DIVINE"

During the War of Spanish Succession, Spanish treasure fleets were deemed too vulnerable to sail to Spain. In early 1715, a fleet was loaded up with roughly £12 million of gold and silver and took sail to Spain. However, a hurricane hit the fleet, and it was wrecked off the coast of Florida. Within a few weeks, word was out about the wreck, and freebooters from across the West Indies went to the wrecks to dive for precious metals. One observer claims that he saw twenty-five ships from Jamaica and Bermuda at the site while passing by. Jennings and Hornigold used Jamaican commissions as a cover to dive on the wrecks.[60] They also found a new outpost that would become the major pirate base of the early parts of the golden age of piracy—New Providence in the Bahamas. When the gold dried up, they found themselves outside of society and willing to start attacking ships.[61]

A spate of piracy was foreseen following the Treaty of Utrecht. First, the understanding at Utrecht was that it would set up a "lasting peace in America," making it safe for trade.[62] The run-ins with Kidd, Every, and others in the 1690s told colonial officials that piracy was still a problem. Without the war, piracy may have been squelched earlier. Yet, colonial officials had no idea what was coming, both in terms of scale and in type. Immediately after the war, the Spanish authorized privateers to attack French and English ships trespassing beyond the line.[63] The golden age of piracy was a crisis for European Atlantic empires that would shatter the practices that drew the line. Shattering comes down to three things— enough material damage to matter, a challenge to state legitimacy, and the illegibility of the violence itself. While sea raiding was not an illegible action—it was expected—the way in which sea raiding took place and the justifications for it were illegible. Finally, failed attempts to combat piracy were drawn from previous practices. Their failure underscores both the challenge to state legitimacy and the illegibility of the threat.

MATERIAL CONSEQUENCES OF PIRACY

It is estimated that roughly 2,400 English ships were taken between the years 1716 and 1726 by pirates, more than the privateering ventures of any state during the recent war (1703–1714), without the concurrent gain in privateering booty. The triangular slave trade, crucial to budding colonial agriculture, was interrupted repeatedly by pirates to the tune of £204,000 worth of damage in 1720 alone, at a time when the average outlay of a venture was £3,000[64]—or £66,180,000 in 2018 value as a share of GDP.[65] The disruption to trade took money directly out of state coffers in the form of stolen treasure. These numbers do not reflect losses to French, Dutch, or Spanish shipping.

Pirates proved adept at concentrating attacks. Edward Teach, aka Blackbeard, halted shipping to and from Charleston for more than a week in 1718 in response to the capture of his former shipmate Stede Bonnet.[66] Black Bart Roberts paralyzed trade to the West Indies in 1721 and took an £80,000 prize off the coast of Brazil.[67] The Grand Banks Fisheries off the coast of Newfoundland lost more than fifty English and French fishing boats in 1720.[68] Philadelphia had its entire trade halted for a week in 1722. Virginia and Maryland merchants complained that in 1717 pirates had cost them £300,000.[69] The year 1720 had the lowest volume of slaves shipped during a year of peace. As might be predicted, the downturn in piracy in the late 1720s correlates with a 25 percent increase in the number of slaves shipped across the Atlantic.[70]

This contributed to a period of stagnation in trade. Rediker points out that "there was zero growth in English Shipping between 1715 and 1728, a prolonged period of stagnation between extensive periods of growth."[71] This is borne out in table 2.1.

While the data in the table is admittedly spotty, some trends can be discerned. First, we see that the trade numbers in each column tend to grow or decline in correlation: years with high entries tend to be years with high clearances, and so on. Second, looking at total clearances, we see a small boom in 1713 as the War of Spanish Succession was winding

TABLE 2.1 English Trade (000 Tons), Entries and Clearances, 1710–1758

Year	Entries			Clearances		
	Total	England	Foreign	Total	England	Foreign
1710				311	244	67
1711				324	266	58
1712				356	327	29
1713				438	412	26
1714				479	445	34
1715				426	406	20
1716	49			456	439	17
1717	47			429	414	15
1718	69	354	5	445	428	17
1723	93			420	393	27
1726–28	21			457	433	24
1730		422				
1737		404				
1744		269				
1751	80	421	59	694	648	46
1758	13	283	30	526	427	99

Source: Ralph Davis, *The Rise of the English Shipping Industry in the Seventeenth and Eighteenth Centuries* (London: Macmillan, 1962), 26.

Note: Entries are goods entering port through customs; clearances are those leaving.

down. However, from about 1715 until the data fades away in 1726–1728, we see a leveling off, then much higher numbers in the middle of the century. Finally, if we look at English entries, we see a jump between 1718 and 1730/1737. If we put these three trends together, it stands to reason that trade leveled off during the golden age of piracy. While piracy was probably not the only cause of stagnation, the evidence mentioned above would seem to argue that it played its part. However, even if it was not the case that piracy played a role in the stagnation of trade, the lack of trade growth itself deepened a sense of crisis, which, combined with the aforementioned widespread piratical activity, led state agents to define piracy as a crisis and take action accordingly.

Piracy also threatened to tear apart the peace recently agreed at Utrecht. For this reason, Jennings's and Hornigold's "patriotic" decisions to exclusively attack Spanish and French ships were a major problem for the English.[72] The problem got bad enough that the lieutenant governor of Virginia, Alexander Spottswood, complained that pirates were "committing depredations and acts of hostility upon the Spaniards and other nations in amity with his Majesty,"[73] while one Spanish official claimed that such acts were "deviating from the publick faith."[74] These attacks took place at a time when the Spanish were seen as a major problem in the Bahamas and elsewhere,[75] eventually leading England into the War of the Quadruple Alliance in 1719.[76] In addition, there are reports that English ships would be attacked "by mistake" under the guise of legitimate attacks on Spanish ships.[77] Such confusion only made colonial letters of marque more untenable.

PIRATES AS ILLEGIBLE ACTORS CHALLENGING STATE LEGITIMACY

The pirates of the golden age are unique in the history of sea raiding.[78] I have already demonstrated how the sea raiders of the sixteenth- and seventeenth-century Atlantic were state agents. For all intents and purposes, the same was true of the Barbary Corsairs at the turn of the nineteenth century.[79] Other "waves"[80] of piracy were tied to, or took advantage of, national liberation movements, like in the Latin American[81] and Greek[82] wars of independence in the early nineteenth century. Sea raiders in the nineteenth-century Malay world fought Dutch, Spanish, and English colonial rule, though piracy was often portrayed as a natural defect of the people.[83] Multiple waves of piracy acted as their own polities.[84] Twenty-first-century piracy is often cast as a criminal enterprise for economic gain brought on by political dissolution.[85] However, sea raiders in Mindanao[86] and the Gulfs of Aden[87] and Guinea[88] claim to be defending local interests. All of these waves of piracy can be made legible. They are either amplifying state power, part of local resistance, or a criminal enterprise. This cannot be said about the pirates of the golden age. They were not working for any empire. They were not part of a local political resistance. And the "piracy as criminal" narrative was developed in response to them (see below).

Sea raiding in the early eighteenth-century Caribbean was not simply an economic problem; trade was viewed as a major arm of statecraft. It became an important area of competition and was used to fill state coffers and pay off debts incurred during almost constant warfare. Colonies, especially in the Atlantic, had become prized for trade. State and the economy were intertwined in the early eighteenth century, with the rise of free trade capitalism still to come. Capitalism often sets government or politics as "public," something foreign and often in tension with "private" economic exchange. However, mercantilism sees the latter as an arm of the former. If the state could not protect property rights, its utility to those it claimed to rule would dwindle significantly. In addition, pirates proved a challenge to state authority. They began to develop an egalitarian shadow society full of adventure, riches, and merriment (see below). Both the pirates and the English pitted them against God, country, and labor. The presence of these pirates challenged state claims to legitimacy and authority in their colonies, especially in an era of mercantilist trade. This is why plunder at sea was more threatening than other types of robbery or crime, even in England. It struck at the legitimating principles of the state-empire.

Raiding at sea was not new or surprising, but the political claims pirates made were illegible, and piracy made little sense to those in power. While all pirates in all eras are concerned with economic gain through plunder,[89] golden-age pirates made proto-anarchist political claims. They fought for a way of life that they could not enjoy within society and openly rebelled against the idea of state control. One pirate by the name of Joseph Mansfield said at his trial that "love of drink and the lazy life [had] been stronger motives for him than gold."[90] To Mansfield, becoming a pirate was about a lifestyle that he could not claim within the confines of English and colonial society. Pirate captain Sam Bellamy went even further in claiming that "I am a free prince, and I have as much authority to make war on the whole world, as he who has a hundred sail of ships at sea, and an army of 100,000 men in the field."[91] One of Bellamy's crew claimed at his trial that they were acting as "Robin Hood's men."[92] Bart Roberts claimed that raising the black flag meant that one declared "war against the whole world."[93] William Fly claimed before his execution that the English had hung many "honest fellows,"[94] while Charles Vane's crew regularly drank to the "Damnation of King George."[95] To the pirates, power and God did not determine legitimate authority; the true criminals were the state, the navy, and the merchants.

Pirates claimed to have come "from the seas" and to have "sold their nation."[96] For instance, early captains who refused to attack ships from their own nation soon gave way to captains who did not care whom they attacked. Benjamin Hornigold's refusal to attack English ships resulted in problems among his men, causing him to lose an election to Bellamy for control over his ship.[97] One observer was shocked to find that Roberts's crew "seem much enraged at Bristol [an English port] men . . . whom they hate as they do Spaniards."[98] Pirates, knowing they challenged state legitimacy by interrupting trade, also made shows of burning or sinking ships and throwing goods overboard. For instance, Roberts sailed into Trepassey Harbor in Newfoundland and found twenty-two ships docked there. He decided that he only wanted one of them and burnt the other twenty-one.[99] Opposing the authorities was just as important as riches.

Pirates of the golden age were networked and tended to stick together. Markus Rediker has shown that 90 percent of active pirates from 1716 to 1726 came from one of two lineages.[100] This provided something of a community. In many ways, that community was progressive in how they organized themselves.[101] This can be illustrated in the apocryphal tales of the pirate island Libertalia, located near Madagascar, where each man had an equal share of all plunder.[102] That this was a story pirates told of themselves demonstrates that they had politics beyond economic gain. There is also evidence that, at least early in the period, pirates saw themselves as part of a larger movement.[103] For instance, Blackbeard made a point of terrorizing New England on the eve of the trial of Sam Bellamy's crew in Massachusetts.[104] One English official observed that pirates "already esteem themselves a community, and to have one common interest."[105] In addition, this "community" also tended to be multiracial[106] and accepting of homosexuality[107] and female leadership,[108] at least in comparison to the society it reviled. There was also a strong Jacobite (supporting Stuart claims to the English throne) element, making it a strange political mélange.[109]

The articles of Black Bart Roberts's crew read: "Every man has a vote in the affairs of moment; has equal title to the fresh provisions, or strong liquors, at any times seized, and may use them at pleasure, unless a scarcity make it necessary, for the good of all, to vote a retrenchment."[110] While pirate captains may receive a slightly higher share of plunder than others on the ship, the exact amount was open to vote, while many privileges, such as use of the cabin, were shared.[111] This stands in contrast to the navy. For instance, the ranking officer got most of the spoils from the capture of Blackbeard's ship, though he was not present at the fight.[112] His sailors got very little. Merchant ships were no better. It is not surprising that many sailors saw piracy as a viable option. Pirates had a vision of a better world they began to create aboard their ships. As Rediker remarks of the pirate William Kennedy, he was "not only a rebel ... not only a force of destruction against the slave trade; but a seafaring storyteller, and one with ideas, even a political philosophy that was not ... an imitation of 'the legal government' but rather a critique of it."[113]

The choice to "go a pyrating" was often a response to the execrable treatment of sailors on merchant and naval ships. Many sailors were impressed into duty, and conditions aboard ships were cruel. Sailors ate little, and what they did eat was usually rotten. They were whipped and punished repeatedly, disease was rampant, and, after all of this, many went unpaid. In the words of contemporary essayist Samuel Johnson, "No man will be a sailor who has contrivance enough to get himself into a jail; for being in a ship is being in a jail, with the chance of being drowned. ... A man in jail has more room, better food, and commonly better company."[114] This sentiment is captured in one pirate's response to a merchant captain who claimed he was deficient: "You son of a bitch, you starved the men and that it was such dogs as he [the captain] as put men on pirating."[115] To many, the life of a pirate, while short, was certainly preferable to that of a merchant seaman (often very short as well).

At his execution, Daniel Macarty claimed the "Pyrate's life to be the only life for a man of any spirit."[116] Roberts rejected the life of a sailor, claiming that "a merry life and a short one shall be my motto."[117] Indeed, when pirates attacked a ship, it was the captain who faced their wrath, unless his crew was able to speak well of him. It was uncommon for pirates to impress the sailors on captured ships. Roberts was quoted as asking "who was willing to go, and who not, for he would force nobody."[118] Such practices undermined claims of captured pirates that they were forced onto the ship, which would have spared their lives under English law.[119] There were, however, exceptions for men with practical skills. For instance, Roberts's men impressed a tailor,[120] and Bellamy's crew told Thomas Davis, "Dam him, they would first shoot him or Whip him to Death at the Mast" before letting him leave, "because he was a Carpenter."[121]

Pirate attitudes toward death and hell also made their actions illegible. Blackbeard claimed that he "came from Hell."[122] One observer was astonished when told that instead of being captured, pirates would "all go merrily to Hell together."[123] Another bragged of not being afraid of "going to the devil by a great shot." Many attempted to blow up their own ships when all looked lost, hoping for "a brave blast to go to Hell with" while cheering their own destruction.[124] To some, this attitude toward death made some sense; it was a way of coming to grips with their likely end. A pirate's life was short, and this way they could exert control over its conclusion. One report had pirates saying that they would not be going to "the River of Thames to be hung up in Gibbets a Sundrying as Kidd."[125] The fate of Kidd was a lesson—they could not work inside the system and consequently must overcome any fear of death. This had the bonus consequence of scaring the authorities. Even captured pirates often proved defiant. Thomas Morris's only regret upon the gallows was that he "was not a greater plague" to the Bahamas. John Gow broke the rope at his hanging and immediately climbed back up the gallows to be hung a second time. Reports of the trial of Roberts's men in 1722 described their walk to the gallows: "None of them, it was observed, appeared to be the least dejected"; William Fly "walk'd to the gallows without a tear."[126] It was also popular among pirates on shore to enact a "Mock-court of judicature to try one another for pyracy."[127]

Legitimate authority lay in the crown, which in turn was granted power by God. Claiming authority from another source was not only blasphemy but dangerous and illegible to colonial and state officials. In addition, piracy did not follow previous patterns of predation, making it hard to make sense of what was happening. That this resulted in shattered conceptual maps is reflected in the language these officials used to talk about pirates. First, piracy caused panic. From the beginning, many calls came into London asking for more men and ships. Virginia governor Alexander Spottswood wrote that "the number of pirates has increased since and there is now no conceivable force that will serve to reduce them."[128] Another complained that they had become "so formidable" that it would be hard to combat them.[129] The *Boston News Letter* reported that they "so intimidate our sailors that they refuse to fight when the pirates attack."[130] One admiral complained that for all ships going into the capes of Virginia, "it goes for granted they were chased by pirates, I see daily instances of it."[131] Piracy was not simply a nuisance or a set of romantic tales; it had real-world consequences for the statesmen, sailors, and merchants of the day.

Panic soon led to overheated rhetoric. Colonial officials tried to paint the pirates as the enemies of humanity, the villains of all nations, opposed to God, country, and labor. Everything that pirates did was a sin.[132] They were the "dregs of mankind, and then they will appear blaspheming their creator, coining of oaths, embrewing their hands in innocent blood, and racking their hellish invention for unheard of barbarities."[133] One official complained that "piracy is a thing of so heinous a nature and of so pernicious consequence."[134] Another called pirates "Varmints."[135] Famed colonial puritan minister Cotton Mather called them "Sea Monsters"; a description of pirates during one attack said that they descended onto ships "like a Parcel of Furies."[136] To the victim of one attack, their speech was comprised solely of "Cursing, Swearing, Dam'ing, and Blaspheming to the greatest degree imaginable."[137] One judge remarked that pirates acted "without any pretense of authority other than that of their own private depraved wills. . . . [They were] robbers, opposers, and violators of all laws humane and divine."[138] However, foremost pirates were *hostes humani generis*,[139] enemies of humanity. In 1699, the British Parliament passed the first Act for the More Effectual Suppression of Piracy—prior to this, piracy law was governed by the Offenses at Sea Act, passed in 1536 by Henry VIII[140]—calling pirates *hostes humani generis* and setting the pirates outside of state and society.[141]

The narratives developed by both the English and the pirates cast the pirates as being against the state itself. They were outside of society, against authority, and made claims that were rendered illegible in the state-empire system of the eighteenth-century Atlantic. If they had fit within common narratives of criminality and privateers, colonial officials would have used those narratives. But golden-age pirates did not. In this way they are as akin to al-Qaeda as they are to contemporary piracy.[142] The pirates of the golden age created a crisis that went beyond monetary losses; it struck at the heart of the state, empire, and society by challenging the line and the boundaries that created colonial rule. That pirates made exotic claims about acting under their own authority is at the crux of the challenge: the authority of God, country, and property were rejected. Pirates could not be accommodated or defeated within contemporary boundaries.

FAILED ATTEMPTS TO COMBAT PIRACY

All of this is brought together by the failure of early attempts to combat piracy—overwhelming naval power and pardons. Such attempts only served to reinforce the boundaries that made piracy such a problem. This demonstrates a lack of understanding on the part of colonial officials while opening up the space for the reinscribing detailed below.

The earliest attempts to defeat piracy involved placing many naval ships at sea. That naval power was the deciding factor against piracy is a popular claim in the historiography.[143] While state power was certainly a factor in piracy's downfall, it does not play nearly the role many historians claim. For instance, in 1700, during a time of peace, England had more naval sailors in the Caribbean and Atlantic than there were pirates, yet the heart of the golden age was still to come. The French found that the ships they sent to combat piracy during the golden age were no longer in good enough shape to do the job by the time they reached the Caribbean. By the 1730s, there was little in the way of armed ships *of any kind* off the North American coast, and yet piracy did not return.[144] Nor did it return off the coast of Newfoundland despite a twenty-year period beginning in 1725 when the coasts were not patrolled.[145] However, this was certainly the favored strategy of colonial governors and officers early in the period.[146] For instance, because "trade in these parts is thereby in great danger," the governor of the Leeward Islands requested "one Fourth Rate & two Fifth Rate Men of War be ordered to these Seas to suppress the Pirates & protect the Trade."[147]

While naval strength did prove decisive at times—it was a naval mission that killed the prolific Roberts[148]—it was not specifically a show of force that was critical but how force was used. Naval power in the earlier parts of the golden age tended to be used to guard ships directly or flood the sea. The Atlantic Ocean was viewed as a contested but controllable space. While possibly effective against rival states and their privateers, naval power proved ineffective against piracy, not least because naval ships tended to be quite cumbersome and unable to chase pirates into shallow waters.[149] In fact, it was often locally organized ships that chased pirates away, such as when Governor Robert Johnson and slaver William Rhett took the offensive after Stede Bonnet disrupted South Carolina's slave trade in 1718. Merchant men had fewer sympathies with pirates than the impressed sailors of the Royal Navy.[150] The use of naval power was a continuation of existing practices that predictably failed. The sea, and in particular trading routes, were seen as the places to protect (the first of the five practices listed in the introduction to this chapter), not the land from which pirates came and sympathetic publics resided. Without control of land, piracy could flourish, but with it, naval ships eventually became unnecessary to protect trade during peacetime.

Another common approach adopted by colonial states early in this period was the giving of crown-approved pardons.[151] King George in 1717 issued a pardon for all pirates who would accept. This proved unsuccessful; most pirates either ignored the pardons or accepted them and continued looting. Blackbeard accepted a pardon that came with land in North Carolina, a title, and the hand of a local aristocrat's daughter only to go back upon the account a few months later.[152] Charles Vane accepted a pardon after an unsuccessful attack and then proceeded to continue attacking ships that same week.[153] Many pirates even mocked the government and ripped their pardons to pieces upon receiving them.[154] Members of Roberts's crew "often ridicul'd and made a mock at King George's Acts of Grace."[155]

The failure of this policy makes a certain amount of sense. When men are rebelling against the state, why would they tie their fate to these forces by accepting a pardon? They wanted to be outside of society, not gain status within it. In addition, many who accepted pardons ultimately found it hard to re-assimilate and returned to piracy. Pardons were the mirror image of the letter of marque (tied to privateering, the fourth practice listed in the introduction). In the latter, the monarch gave the pirate the opportunity to pursue future plunders; in the former, the monarch gave him the opportunity to be forgiven for past plunders. Either way, plunder was sanctioned by the state. Pardons were doomed to fail because they did not change the conceptual maps of state agents, which made possible the practices of colonial governance allowing piracy to flourish in the first place.

There were some success stories. For instance, Benjamin Hornigold accepted a pardon and became a useful weapon against pirates sailing in and around the Bahamas, much to Governor Woodes Rogers's "great satisfaction."[156] However, the failure of the pardons became apparent to those governing the colonies.[157] Governor Hunter of New York remarked that "we have found by experience that their money spent and no merchant willing to employ them, they generally return to their former course of life."[158] More colorfully, Walter Hamilton, governor of the Leeward Islands, remarked to the Council of Trade and Plantation, "your lordships may now plainly perceive how little acts of grace and mercy work on these vermine."[159]

The use of both naval power and pardons was ineffective in large part because they were part of the practices that drew the line. This is when the shattering is complete: when state agents realize that the way in which they habitually exercise authority is insufficient to quell that crisis. The boundary was shattered, and space opened up for creative solutions to the concrete problem of golden-age piracy.

REINSCRIBING: PEACE BEYOND THE LINE

The golden age of piracy ground to a halt in the years from 1726 to 1730. Its end is usually dated either with the English capture of Captain William Fly in Boston in 1726 or with the French capture of Olivier La Buse in Southeast Asia in 1730.[160] Pirate attacks between 1726 and 1730 were few when compared to the previous decade, and after 1730, attacks dropped even further. How did this happen? I have argued above that it was not due to the issuing of pardons or greater naval strength. I should also say that it was not because of a more favorable economic climate. As noted above, trade picked up after the end of the golden age, and less piracy led to more trade and more labor-market opportunities, not the other way around. England's rise and changing economic conditions are background causes in this—it was England that worked to make the sea safe for trade—but new practices to defeat piracy were how they did this. Colonial officials hit on three solutions. First, there was a change in law, both in substance and procedure. Second, policy against piracy was standardized. Third, a propaganda campaign against pirates in the colonies was undertaken. These actions demonstrate transformation taking place at the margins, through cooperation/collusion between states, and as a function of creative actions. It led to reconfiguring the layered sovereignty of the colonial Atlantic and reinscribed the state.

COURTS, DIRECT CONTROL, AND PROPAGANDA

The 1699 Act for the More Effectual Suppression of Piracy created the conditions for the practice of universal jurisdiction—where any state, as a member of humanity, could try pirates. Pirates were legally extricated from the state and citizenry; an English pirate could see justice in French courts with no repercussions. Indeed, it was France who caught one of the greatest pirates of the later stages of the golden age, Ned Low, and sentenced him to death, with English acquiescence, despite his English ancestry. While universal jurisdiction may seem like a violation of sovereignty, state agents saw it as in their interest, increasing their own authority and control. Matthew Norton argues that state power "depended on the ability of state agents to engage in an extended, coordinated pattern of performances that construed piracy as a distinctive social object, defined by violent state repression."[161] A line was drawn around citizenship that left pirates outside of state protection.[162]

That *hostes humani generis* and universal jurisdiction have been part of settled piracy law for centuries means that piracy became, after the golden age, a problem that was legible to the state. It is not that state agents were able to make sense of all pirate actions and claims, but instead that they were able to make sense of them in order to defeat them. But this did not happen with just the passing of a law. The original intent of the 1699 act and its harsh punishments for piracy was to scare potential pirates away from a life of sea raiding. Given the defiance and black humor with which many pirates treated death, it is unlikely that this happened. Where the law did prove effective was in taking pirates out of the sea: there were 418 hangings for piracy from 1716 to 1726.[163] That means about one in ten who went upon the account met their fate on the gallows.

But piracy did not stop. The act was renewed in 1701, 1715, and 1719, even as pardons were given out. If the law had been effective, why continue to renew it? The problem was not the law itself, but its implementation. The law became more effective when England began establishing vice-admiralty courts in its Caribbean, West African, and North American colonies to try pirates.[164] Before this period, all pirates were tried in London or in local colonial courts. The former meant transporting pirates back across the Atlantic—an expensive, slow, and arduous process. The latter were designed to try colonial crimes, not those, such as piracy, classified as against England and English shipping.[165] When pirates were tried by colonial courts, they tended to be acquitted due to friendly juries, many of whose members profited from the plunder. Governor Woodes Rogers of the Bahamas claimed that "the inhabitants here are such their [the pirates'] friends that I fear that I shall be forced to receive them at all hazards."[166] Robert Ritchie claims that "local jurors recoiled from hanging a man for something many of them did not view as a crime."[167]

The extension of vice-admiralty courts—presided over by English judges and under the aegis of England's court system—into the colonies dissolved the choice between a long, expensive journey to London and the risk of acquittal at the hands of a friendly jury. It also standardized piracy law throughout the empire. The problem of how to try pirates was recognized as early as "piracy" became a problem distinct from privateering in the 1670s. There were early attempts to establish admiralty courts in Jamaica in the 1670s and 1680s.[168] Local courts felt that they could not claim jurisdiction over the sea,[169] and frustrations with having to ship pirates to England were common in the 1690s in the East Indies.[170] However, as one would expect in an empire, this process was not uniform, and there were still many problems and uncertainties. Kidd was shipped to London from Massachusetts—where Bellomont was also governor, and which was not allowed to execute pirates[171]—for his trial in

1699. There is evidence of regulations about which pirates ought to be sent to England in the 1690s,[172] meaning some were not. In 1718, the Council of Nevis complained "of pirates, that we have not any power of jurisdiction whereby we might proceed to trye them."[173] As late as 1720, the admiralty had questions about what to do with the plunder taken from pirates.[174]

Colonial resistance is one reason extending the admiralty court system took so long. Colonial councils and their publics did not want their judicial systems subverted. For instance, a vice-admiralty court's decision to execute John Quelch and members of his crew provoked a lot of local anger in 1704.[175] Similarly, the Council of Virginia pushed Governor Spottswood, often virulently anti-pirate, to accept only county courts when dealing with piracy as opposed to crown courts.[176] The use of vice-admiralty courts was creative in the sense that it was not part of the habitual actions that constructed colonial governance. It was also emblematic of two larger shifts wrought by the war on piracy. First, the use of English judges meant that England had taken greater control over colonial policy in a way that it had not done previously. Now, there was an enforced uniformity of law on pirates. Second, trying pirates in the colonies led to the spectacle of hanging pirates in the colonies, whence many pirates originated and where they were therefore held in much higher esteem.[177] This leads us into the next two "solutions" in defeating piracy.

As English courts were established, colonies came ever closer to direct rule. While the colonies were still treated differently than the state core, the contracts between hub and spoke changed in ways that gave the hub more direct control over this aspect of the spoke's business. This challenged the line. Governors were appointed who complied with British policy on piracy, and those who did not were replaced. This happened in New York with Benjamin Fletcher during the Captain Kidd affair,[178] in Jamaica in 1716,[179] and most effectively with the appointment of Woodes Rogers as governor of the Bahamas in 1718. The Bahamas were a largely ungoverned set of islands following the destruction wrought by the war of Spanish Succession. They did not provide economic value in seventeenth-century terms, but as the eighteenth century wore on, their importance grew because of the islands' "conveniency for trade."[180] The port of New Providence had been the major pirate base of the golden age's early years, and the sorry state of the island became an issue for other colonies.[181] It had housed (in)famous pirate captains such as Benjamin Hornigold, Henry Jennings, Stede Bonnet, Sam Bellamy, and Blackbeard. Rogers found seven hundred pirates there upon his arrival.[182] He claimed, "I was at that time [of my arrival] too weak to bring them to a trial for most of the people here having led the same course of life."[183] The admiral of the HMS *Phoenix* opined that the islands' inhabitants "seemed more inclinable to assist than to reduce" pirates.[184] However, Rogers was given a mandate and the policy latitude to clean up the colony. He scattered the pirates within a year by taking responsibility not only for New Providence but also for the many small islands and coves that became pirate safe havens.[185]

Colonial charters, a relic of the previous era that gave permission to form a colony under the power of the crown, were threatened or even revoked if piracy was tolerated. In the Bahamas, the lords proprietor forfeited their claim because they "had not 20 years then past taken any care for the security of the said islands."[186] Defeating piracy meant more than applying force and a stern judicial hand. It meant giving the pirates nowhere to go. All English colonies in the Atlantic needed to be accountable to England for a growing set of standardized goals toward pirates, even if methods were open to discretion. The governor of New York could no longer be friendly to pirates while the governor of Virginia attempted to eradicate them. There were still, of course, largely ungoverned areas, but these areas became fewer and harder to live on as time went by. The idea that a colony such as the Bahamas would be claimed by the British crown but left ungoverned because it did not provide any tangible economic benefit would have seemed strange in this new system, even as it was the reality a mere decade before.

The third prong in this "war on piracy" was a propaganda campaign leveled against pirates in which they were depicted as the lowest sort of humans. This happened as access to print media expanded in the colonies and around Europe. Printed trial records, broadsides, sermons, and novels narrated piracy, while "newspapers brought deep sea piracy into colonists' homes."[187] However, instead of the patriotic narratives of the seventeenth century, sea raiders were now described in much harsher tones, while victories over pirates were celebrated. For instance, Blackbeard's demise was inscribed in stories that "sold wonderfully," one written by none other than a young Benjamin Franklin.[188] Beyond piracy, newspapers also reported on the trade boom that brought goods colonists once relied on pirates to provide. As historian Mark Hanna puts it, "The information revolution deconstructed the image of the pirate as a social bandit."[189] Importantly, the rhetorical campaign against piracy took place in the colonies. As discussed above, colonial inhabitants had a rather favorable view of pirates. Pirates had been considered engines of economic well-being in the colonies, where they provided cheap goods and/or treasure. In previous decades, they even acted as local protection against enemy navies. Since piracy existed in some measure because it had access to markets, that access had to be closed.[190]

This was done partly by taking control of colonial policy. Another major piece of this strategy was portraying pirates as outside the cornerstones of society; they became "instigated by the devil." It was remarked of Ned Low's crew that they were "Devils in carnate [sic] . . . [providing] the liveliest picture of Hell."[191] In a Christian society, this was meant to taint pirate goods and turn public opinion. Of course, as detailed above, the pirates themselves were complicit. Not only did they embrace their image as hell-bound demons, but, as we get closer to the end of the golden age, ever desperate pirate captains began to attack targets of value to the colonies. This marks a move away from their egalitarian, progressive views—they were inching ever closer to the savages they were portrayed to be. As Hanna argues, "Rifts that once divided private and royal colonies or London imperial administrators and colonial leaders dissipated, as they all become victims of piracy."[192]

Low was one pirate captain known for his cruelty. His former quartermaster recounted at trial that "in the Bay of Honduras he murdered forty-five Spaniards in cold blood" and was once so mad at the captain of a captured ship that he "cut off the said Masters lipps and broiled them before his face; and afterwards murdered the whole crew being 32 persons."[193] The *New England Courant* ran a series tracking Low and his barbarities from 1722 to 1723.[194] This made the British propaganda campaign much easier. Eventually the colonists turned against pirates. As Daniel Macarty said on the gallows in the Bahamas, "[there was a time when] many brave fellows on the Island would not suffer him to dye like a dog ... [but there was] too much power over their heads ... [for anyone to] attempt any Thing in his Favour."[195] In Philadelphia, there were complaints of pirate behavior on land in 1720.[196]

The importance of this campaign, however, was not necessarily its decisiveness or even its effectiveness, both of which are debatable. Instead, it confirmed that colonists were not living beyond the line but were instead English subjects, albeit without all the attending rights. In order to cast pirates as *hostes humani generis*, the bond between colonist and pirate needed to be broken. Breaking this bond meant renegotiating the colonial contract to bring the colonist closer to the state. The propaganda campaign itself did not change this, but its presence demonstrates that the colonies needed to be under the control of the state in order for piracy to be defeated. Of course, piracy itself did not end at this time. There were intermittent attacks throughout the eighteenth century, but these pirates were cast as criminals, not as threats to the state.[197] The golden age of piracy had ended, and piracy in the Atlantic was not a major problem for European states until the turn of the nineteenth century, but for different reasons and with different consequences.[198]

Each of the three actions described above were creative in the sense that they brought something new into the world. They resulted from the shattering of existing practice and ultimately reconfigured the conceptual maps of early eighteenth-century states. Each also solved the problem of piracy as it related to the trade upon which the state and the economy were built. This second claim is not to say that each one actually solved the problem, though they all helped. Even more importantly, they were viewed as having solved it and therefore each became a part of the new boundary that was drawn as a result of the war on piracy.

Cooperation between states was another feature of the fight against piracy. A willingness among European powers to work together to rid the seas of piracy was signaled early; Article 2 of the Treaty of Utrecht in 1714 contained a clause to combat piracy.[199] This came from recognition that the enemies to trade were increasingly not state agents but pirates. It was in every trading state's interest to eradicate piracy and protect trade. This is reflected in the legal coordination necessary to make universal jurisdiction reality. Allowing other states to prosecute one's own citizens if they were accused of piracy shows that this was a problem for all states. Still, there were complications. Pirates knew how to play off state rivalries.

Many English pirates give their ships Jacobite names like *Queen Anne's Revenge* (Blackbeard) and the *Royal James* (Stede Bonnet). This invoked sympathies from many in France and Sweden. For instance, pirate Alexander Dalziel was able to get a state pension in France and was only arrested in Scotland on his way to Sweden to serve the government there.[200] The French did not protect their ships until 1718,[201] keeping pirates in business with easy targets. After England stopped giving blanket pardons in 1719, the French continued their amnesty policy. This made French colonies like Martinique safe places for pirates chased by other countries.[202] Coordination on such issues was vital.

A lot of cooperation happened at lower levels of interaction. For instance, French and English colonies banded together to fight piracy.[203] Similarly, Admiral Channeler Ogle was given the following instructions in addition to his mission to chase and attack Roberts crew: "In case you should meet with on the coast of Africa any ships of war fitted out from France against the pirates, and you find that the joining them may more effectually contribute towards the suppressing of them, you are in such case to do the same, and to act in concert with them."[204] English insistence that all colonies fight pirates soon diffused through the French and Spanish empires.[205]

THE CONSEQUENCES OF COMBATTING PIRACY

Universal jurisdiction, vice-admiralty courts, the end of peacetime privateering, more direct control over colonies, and anti-pirate propaganda campaigns were not just tools used by static actors to defeat a threat. They changed how states functioned. It is important here to reiterate that while we are talking about colonial spaces and imperial dynamics we are seeing practices exclusive to the state and state transformation. First, the seas began a transition to a truly open space, the "great void."[206] As Thomson states, "the absence of sovereignty over the oceans is not a timeless feature of the international system but something that emerged in the course of the eighteenth century."[207] As Gabriel Kuhn has argued, policies against pirates turned the sea from a smooth space, i.e., contested and ungovernable, to a striated space, i.e., ordered, regulated, and open for trade.[208] The sea was not naturally open—it took practices to open (or close) the sea. The goal was, in the words of the leading judge for the High Court of Admiralty Leoline Jenkins, to protect English citizens and interests from piracy, "even in the remotest Corners of the World."[209] In order for the sea to be made safe for trade, the state had to directly rule the territories surrounding it. The pirates of the golden age drove this lesson home for those conducting colonial policy. For English sailors, the line was effectively moved to the equator, where it was said to demarcate the pacific: a land so far away as to be politically uncontrollable.[210] Essentially, the North Atlantic became a "European lake." That said, attempts to claim jurisdiction over the oceans in other parts of the world did not cease until sometime in the nineteenth century.[211]

Because piracy was defeated and the oceans opened up, the world was once again safe for Atlantic trade, which grew in leaps and bounds starting around 1730. Not only did trade bloom once again in its aftermath, but this episode was crucial in the development of a tight-knit "Atlantic World." The concept of such a world is a common one in the historiography.[212] Studies have proliferated that look not just at the French colonial economy or the British Empire, but also at the Atlantic economy and the politics of the Atlantic as a whole. There is also a plethora of evidence of a society developing in this space, such as the standardization of goods between French and English trading cities and the interimperial relations necessary to suppress slave revolts.[213] This was often performed by local leaders and merchants,[214] the state's "many hands." The creation of a political Atlantic happened at some point in the late seventeenth and/or early eighteenth centuries, and piracy played a vital role in this process by forcing states to cooperate and take greater control of colonial governance and policy. Indeed, other forces, ranging from England's rise to the growth of trade to political developments in the colonies, played important roles that should not be forgotten or understated; the "Atlantic World" is about more than tying colonies closer to states. However, the development of the "Atlantic World" owes quite a bit to the consequences of combating piracy in the early eighteenth century.

The consequences of this new boundary reverberated elsewhere. Colonial trade was a major part of Britain's rise to power in the eighteenth century,[215] and trade boomed after piracy was finally dealt with. Many within both history[216] and IR[217] emphasize the connection between trade, imperialism, warfare, and the state in the eighteenth century. These connections even had implications to states that were not active in the Atlantic. For instance, Britain's vast trade surpluses and sound fiscal position allowed it to lend money to Prussia, a landlocked state. This money was integral to Frederick the Great's military successes against Austria and France on the continent, especially during the Seven Years' War (1756–1763). Patterns of mercantilist trade and colonial governance were deeply tied into the broader patterns of international politics that characterized the eighteenth century, and those patterns of trade were shaped by the war against piracy.

Similarly, while war in the colonies usually followed war on the continent, the opposite was not the case before this period. After piracy, the idea of "no peace beyond the line" no longer held in the Atlantic. Colonial conflict could lead a state into war in Europe, as was the case with English entry into the War of Austrian Succession, known in England as the War of Jenkins' Ear, in 1742.[218] Colonies were also treated differently in peace treaties before and after this period. For much of the seventeenth century, warfare at sea was "essentially a contest about the maritime lines of communication."[219] This is reflected in the Treaty of Utrecht, signed in 1714, two years before the peak of piracy's golden age. England gained control of a single port, Gibraltar, and won the *asiento*, a series of trading rights in Spanish colonies.[220] However, the War of Jenkins' Ear was fought over control of territory in Spanish colonies, and England won great territorial concessions as the victor of the Seven Years' War in 1763. Colonial territory had become prized during this period, and the campaign against piracy played a role in this development because it drove home the importance of controlling land in order to control the sea. Yes, shifting economic conditions, ecological barriers to conquest,[221] and the outcome of the era's multitude of wars were important. But piracy was also important in shaping the effects of these macro-processes.

Yes, there was still some separation, and abolishing the line created new tensions in the empire. Few colonial governors or officials in either London or the extended empire thought that fighting piracy would change how the empire functioned. They just wanted to get rid of piracy. As a result of their actions, however, colonists did not have the same rights as those living in England but still had many of the same responsibilities. Furthermore, some practices, such as slavery, were banned in England but not in the colonies;[222] a boundary was still drawn around them, layering sovereignty. New York was not a part of England proper as Manchester was, but its relationship to the core had changed.

This would become one of the major reasons for the rebellion of thirteen of England's colonies a half-century later. I should be clear here. The claim is not that the golden age of piracy caused the American War of Independence, though such claims have been made on the basis of the revolutionary spirit of those working in the maritime Atlantic.[223] Instead, the argument here is that the campaign to defeat piracy in the early eighteenth century played an important role in creating the tensions between empire and state that would allow for the conditions in which such a rebellion could arise. Contracting was less heterogeneous and rule more direct, shifting the balance between difference and integration. It might be accurate to say that, in 1730, it was just as likely that England's North American colonies were on a path toward becoming a part of England proper as it was that they would ultimately rebel. Much happened in-between to allow for and cause that particular outcome. That we know what happened should not be taken as a reason to claim too much. What is important here is that while the new boundaries solved England's piracy problem, they also put pressures on its Atlantic empire. The tension between state and empire, difference and integration, remained.

Change, not control, is the operative word. State agents drew new boundaries; they exchanged attempted direct control over trade routes for control of land to make the sea safe for trade. English state agents took actions that made rule more direct and contracting more homogeneous. These tilted the scales toward integration, and one could certainly see this as the state expanding, as it taking more control. Such a view is incomplete for two reasons. First, while greater control was taken over land, less direct control was exercised over the sea. This development matters for the reasons outlined above. Second, even if we are to grant that the English state gained more authority, more control, doing so did not necessarily bode well for its long-term outlook. It lost its North American colonies a few decades later, and other states that followed suit lost influence in the Atlantic even quicker than that. This isn't the story of the state's inexorable march to controlling the world—that story probably should not be told—instead it is the story of state agents reinscribing the state to deal with a crisis by redrawing the boundaries.

CONCLUSION

Historians have dated the end of "no peace beyond the line" to around 1740[224] or 1750[225] and have often pointed to developments in law and economics. My argument is that the practices that constructed "no peace" and "the line" as a whole were shattered by piracy and, while economic and legal processes were important, their end cannot be told without this episode of transnational violence. Pirates exploited the disconnect between the rise of mercantilist trade, the lagging of governance structures in dealing effectively with this emergence, and the practices of warfare and colonial rule during that period to cause a crisis for states at the core of early eighteenth-century Atlantic empires. It challenged the mercantilist trading system, it directly affected the coffers of state-empires, and it challenged the idea that the state-empire hybrid polity could provide security to those it claimed to rule. Their political claims were illegible. They did not act as sea raiders, even illicit ones, did in the recent past. This is reflected in the ways in which early attempts to deal with the threat—namely, naval power and pardons—were ineffective. Pirates shattered the practices that constructed the conceptual maps of colonial officials.

In order for piracy to be brought under control and the Atlantic to be made safe for trade (and thus legitimize imperial rule), the state-empires of the time had to take creative actions. Piracy was defeated by extending the state judicial system out into the colonies, standardizing policy goals across the empire, and from a propaganda campaign that cast those living in the colonies as part of the state and cast pirates as *hostes humani generis*. The upshot of these actions was that state agents now focused on controlling land (not sea), pulled their colonies closer to themselves, and ended the line as a politically meaningful boundary. In other words, how the state was practiced changed so that piracy was no longer a threat.

That the golden age of piracy drove state transformation is missed by a literature that is too macro, too focused on competition and formal institutions. This case demonstrates state transformation happening at the margins of empire, through the actions of varied agents needing state cooperation to discipline a transnational threat. State transformation does not end here. What happened in this case was transformed over time. This bring us to the next two chapters: two more cases demonstrating how transnational violence drove transformation, starting with anarchist propaganda of the deed and the development of both the labor movement and the modern surveillance state at the turn of the twentieth century.

3

"PROPAGANDA OF THE DEED," SURVEILLANCE, AND THE LABOR MOVEMENT

At the turn of the twentieth century, Anarchists practicing "propaganda of the deed"—a theory that actions, not words, would spark the revolution—created a crisis for state agents with a series of assassinations and bombings.[1] Five heads of state (or their consorts) were assassinated between 1894 and 1901: French president Sardi Carnot, Spanish prime minister Antonio Canovas, Austrian empress Elisabeth, Italian king Umberto, and U.S. president William McKinley.[2] The Portuguese king was assassinated in 1908, and another Spanish prime minister in 1912. The Russian tsar was killed in 1881 after many failed attempts, and there were numerous assassinations of prominent Russian officials.[3] There were three attempts on the life of the kaiser and another on the Spanish king at his wedding. In 1893, Alexander Berkman almost killed Henry Clay Frick in Pittsburgh,[4] and a bomb exploded on Wall Street in 1920. In 1900 there were unsuccessful attempts to assassinate the prince of Wales in Brussels and the Persian Shah in Paris.[5] In addition to Umberto's assassination, Italy experienced numerous peasant revolts led by anarchists.[6] The period also saw numerous attacks at landmarks, public cafés, opera houses, and apartment buildings frequented by the bourgeoisie. There were eleven bomb explosions in Paris between the years 1892 and 1894.[7] Similar patterns developed in Spain around the same time. There were bomb explosions in Belgium in 1892, 1894, and 1897, two explosions in Italy in 1894, and another in Portugal in

1896.[8] One attempt on the kaiser was undertaken while he was in Cairo, and there was propagandist[9] action in Latin America, Asia,[10] and Australia.[11]

Like golden-age piracy, propagandist violence forced state agents to redraw conceptual boundaries. Propaganda of the deed challenged the practices that drew two boundaries. First, a boundary between public and private excluded anarchist (and other) ideas from the public sphere. This boundary was supported by the following practices: (1) a focus on ideas, as opposed to actions, as the threat and (2) use of show trials and public executions to enforce this and demonstrate state power. As a result, anarchists of all stripes, not just those practicing propaganda of the deed, were often the subject of brutal repression. States that proved successful in the struggle managed to redraw the public/private boundary in order to open political space to allow anarchist ideas. This was a step to more democratic regimes that funneled anarchists into more acceptable channels, such as the burgeoning labor movement instrumental in winning the eight-hour workday, standardizing unions, and ultimately the development of the welfare state.

The other important boundary for this case was an international/domestic boundary that allowed for the untracked movement of people and goods across borders. Three practices produced this boundary: (1) unregulated or little-regulated movement of people and goods exemplified in few restrictions and the abolishing of passports in the first half of the nineteenth century, (2) uneven policies on exile and extradition that resulted in some states (Italy, Spain, Russia) exiling undesirables while others (England, Switzerland) gave them protection, and (3) a decentralized police force incapable of tracking targets. In response, state agents altered extradition practices. New methods of policing culminated in large databases on criminals and citizens, presaging the growth of the modern surveillance state. This led to the creation of passports and immigration restrictions, giving states greater control of who and what crossed borders. Borders did not shift on a map, but their practical significance changed.

Before getting to the narrative, I wanted to address competing explanations for (1) the rise of anarchism and propaganda of the deed, (2) the end of propaganda of the deed, and (3) the state transformation that resulted. My claims are (1) that industrialization caused tensions between the two boundaries listed above that opened space for propaganda of the deed, (2) that allowing anarchist ideas into the public sphere, crushing anarchist violence, and finding ways to track anarchists ended propaganda of the deed, and (3) this resulted in a strong labor movement and the development of the modern surveillance state. There are four processes or events that scholars often point to when discussing these issues: globalization, industrialization, the revolutionary movement, and World War I. Each plays a role, but the role that they play depends in part on how propaganda of the deed was defeated. Each will be taken in turn.

The "second wave"[12] of globalization taking place concurrently with propaganda of the deed was built on imperialism.[13] It resulted in a period of unprecedented free trade and migration. It is also reflected in two of the practices listed above. In many ways, anarchism was a product of, and a force for, globalization. It was avowedly anti-imperial, with a global imagination not always found in the wider revolutionary movement. It took advantage of the spread of ideas and peoples to challenge states and empires. As anarchist Giuseppe Fornara claimed, "For us there are no frontiers, the bourgeois are the same all the world over."[14] This direct assault would create the crisis of legitimacy outlined below. Scholars also point to the end of globalization as a cause of the surveillance state. John Torpey points to the rollback of laissez-faire economics and a desire to regulate labor,[15] and others highlight the nativist backlash to major demographic shifts brought by decades of migration.[16] However, propaganda of the deed played a role in nativist sentiment during the period.

Industrialization was important for the rise of anarchism and propaganda of the deed in two ways. First, the resulting inequality and poor living conditions for factory workers created grievances that led to anarchism and anarchist violence. It also provided an opportunity. Industrialization and globalization are intertwined; industrialized goods and technology drove globalization, even as the global markets fueled industrialization. Both processes are important to the story below, but propaganda of the deed conditioned, at least in part, their consequences for state transformation.

Propaganda of the deed was part of a wider revolutionary movement. As described in the next section, disagreements in this movement molded the anarchism of assassins and *dynamiteurs*. In turn, propaganda of the deed and its failure had a major impact on the rise of

Marxism within the movement following World War I. Maybe more importantly for this case, scholars point to splits within anarchism for the end of propaganda of the deed.[17] There was certainly a lot of internal debate on the effectiveness of bombs and assassinations.[18] Increasingly, other anarchist methods—especially anarcho-syndicalism—proved more effective at helping workers.[19] Others have argued that the rise of radical nationalist movements took the sting out of anarchism.[20] One example is the failure of the anarchist movement to gain a foothold in Russia following the 1917 Revolution.[21] However, these choices were heavily influenced by opportunities created by new practices. Finally, Jay Feldman argues that fear of bolshevism led to passports. This was true, though anarchism was a more common justification.[22]

Finally, World War I is a popular explanation for both the end of propaganda of the deed and the creation of the surveillance state. Barbara Tuchman claims that the war gave states something larger than assassinations to ponder;[23] Alex Butterworth claims that a brutal interstate war crushed anarchist hopes;[24] Carl Levy argues that the war ushered in a new tide of nationalism that led radicalism in a different direction.[25] However, attacks had begun to tail off prior to World War I, and then continued well into the 1920s. There was no discernable break caused by the war. After the war, the fear of anarchism was strong enough to justify immigration restrictions and passports (see below). Additionally, much of the literature on universal passports—a key part of the modern surveillance state—places emphasis on the war.[26] As Mark Salter remarks, "With the outbreak of World War I, there came a bureaucratic-governmental need to track combatants and verify deserters."[27] It also led to a need to track and identify spies. Like with industrialization and globalization, however, the campaign against anarchism conditioned particular consequences. The details of how these events (industrialization, globalization, the wider revolutionary movement, and World War I) configure with propaganda of the deed to produce state transformation are covered in the narrative below.

The chapter will unfold as follows: First will be a short section on the origins and development of both anarchism and propaganda of the deed within the wider revolutionary movement. Next is a section demonstrating how attempts to control the public sphere and free movement led to propaganda of the deed. This is followed by a section on shattering that will place the material damage described above into a context where propaganda of the deed created a crisis because it challenged state legitimacy and was illegible to relevant state agents. The penultimate section will cover the solutions state agents arrived at to defeat anarchism and how these reinscribed the state. Finally, I will conclude with a summary and a short discussion of propaganda of the deed, Marxism, and totalitarianism.

ORIGINS OF ANARCHISM AND PROPAGANDA OF THE DEED

Those I call "propagandists" were usually lone-wolf actors. They were not a part of some centralized network or a coordinated anarchist conspiracy. Their connection lay in a set of philosophical ideals and an epistemic community that transcended borders. Rhetoric and practical knowledge on how to make bombs or evade capture circulated through meetings, papers, and pamphlets.[28] While those committing violence were often disconnected and highly local, the propaganda of the deed was transnational in its common affinities and ideas. Since those ideas were anarchist, it is impossible to talk about propaganda of the deed without talking about anarchism.

Anarchism was the leading radical movement worldwide prior to World War I.[29] Industrialization gave anarchists cause and means. In Europe, at least, the movement largely consisted of craftsmen and rural peasants threatened by economic changes.[30] Industrialization had brought with it the technology, embraced by anarchists,[31] not only to make weapons such as dynamite, but also to spread their ideas through pamphlets and mainstream newspapers.

Anarchism was part of a larger revolutionary movement, including socialist and communist strands, that gained traction as industrialization created large disparities in wealth and opportunity. This created an underclass ripe for revolutionary zeal, what many christened the "social" or "labor" question. To many, both inside and outside the movement, revolution seemed inevitable. Madame Hennebau, from Émile Zola's novel *Germinal*, mused on "the red vision of revolution that on some somber evening at the end of the century would carry everything away. Yes, on that evening the people, unbridled at last, they would make the blood of the middle class flow."[32] This discontent exploded in 1871, when members of the Parisian working class took control of the capital for three months, until the French state was able to muster enough troops from the countryside to crush the rebellion. It did not recede for the rest of the century. The bombings and attacks covered in this chapter took place in an environment where authorities were on the alert for revolution.

The revolutionary movement agreed on the evils of capitalism and private property, but they clashed on questions of hierarchy and the state. While Marx was always insistent that the state was merely the accumulation of the interests of capital, anarchists—led by Pierre Joseph Proudhon and his protégé Michel Bakunin—argued Marxists were re-creating the state in the name of communal property, founding a dictatorship of the proletariat. To anarchists, centralized authority of all stripes enshrined property and was the cause of society's ills.[33] As propagandist Émile Henry would remark at his trial, "Socialism changes nothing about the current order. It maintains the authoritarian principal."[34] The anarchists focused on transnational rebellion as opposed to the socialists' national solution.[35] With the feud spilling "into open warfare" in the 1870s and 1880s,[36] the two factions separated, as much rivals as comrades.

The origins of the anarchist movement itself can be seen in three touchstone moments: the 1871 Paris Commune discussed above, the Haymarket Affair, and the assassination of Russian tsar Alexander II. On May 4, 1886, a bomb was thrown at a protest in Chicago, injuring sixty-seven police officers and killing eight.[37] The police arrested eight anarchists, none of whom had thrown the bomb. They were convicted and sentenced to death (only four saw the gallows). The accused loudly proclaimed they were on trial for "believing in a better future."[38] Anarchists saw the bomb as a conspiracy to crack down on Chicago's growing anarchist community, while the authorities saw the trial as justice.[39] On March 13, 1881, after many failed attempts, three members of Norodnaya Volya[40] assassinated Alexander II, ironically the man responsible for freeing Russia's serfs. The assassination signaled to the anarchist community that action was possible after the failure of the commune, and aborted regicides in Russia, Germany,[41] Italy, and Spain. Russia reacted by repressing and/or exiling subversives, creating a European diaspora of Russian revolutionaries that formed the base of the broader movement.

The question for the anarchist became how to start a revolution without hierarchical organization.[42] Marxists could argue that industrialization was a necessary component of the "movement of history" while creating armies and political parties tasked with bringing about the revolution. The anarchists were ideologically restricted in this sense, arguing that "the emancipation of the workers will be made by the workers themselves."[43] The theorist or activist could only attempt to provoke this spontaneous act. Anarchists held that science backed both revolution and their ideal society and thus believed the masses would revolt if knowledgeable of the situation. While the proliferation of anarchist presses demonstrates the importance of "propaganda of the word," many maintained actions would spark the revolution.

The idea of propaganda of the deed was developed by thinkers such as Élisée Reclus, Errico Malatesta, and Piotr Kropotkin.[44] Italian socialist Carlo Pisacane claimed that "ideals spring from deeds." Carlo Cafiero, citing Pisacane, argued for "permanent rebellion, by work, by writing, by dagger, by gun, by dynamite."[45] In its earliest incarnation, propaganda of the deed—a phrase attributed to Paul Brousse—emphasized peasant revolts such as the one in Benevento, Italy, led by Cafiero and Malatesta in 1877.[46] The assassins and *dynamiteurs* of the period were a derivation of this idea. To these men, a bomb could enlighten the proletariat, demarcate enemies from friends, and ultimately spark the revolution against the bourgeois state and usher in the anarchist utopia.

Propaganda of [or by] the deed became a part of how both anarchists and state agents narrated the threat. Charles Gallo, who threw a bottle of vitriol into the Paris Stock Exchange in 1886, proclaimed at his trial that he intended to carry out "an act of propaganda by the deed for the anarchist doctrine."[47] French art critic and anarchist Félix Fénéon claimed that "anarchist attacks did much more for propaganda than 20 years of pamphlets from Reclus and Kropotkin."[48] Even anarchism's enemies used the term. A 1902 *Arena* op-ed lamented an "insane propaganda of the deed," while a *Washington Post* columnist demonstrated its logic by claiming that the assassin of Empress Elizabeth "might cause all who impoverish the populace to tremble and shiver."[49]

INDUSTRIALIZATION, GLOBALIZATION, AND PROPAGANDA OF THE DEED

Propaganda of the deed challenged two different boundaries: (1) a public/private boundary where state agents attempted to control speech in the public sphere and assert themselves through violence and (2) an international/domestic boundary where borders were open, demarcating only the lines between governments. Above, I mentioned five practices pertinent to the construction of these boundaries: (1) public trials and executions, (2) attempts to control ideas in line with a conservative nationalism, (3) decentralized police forces, (4) unrestricted movement of goods and peoples, and (5) liberal, uneven immigration and exile policies. This section will discuss these practices, the boundaries they created, and how they facilitated propaganda of the deed.

To the ruling classes, authority was thought to be a part of human nature, and the state provided it, whether through custom or "merit."[50] Those who went against this authority were termed the "enemies of humanity."[51] The response was often to use force, or at least the appearance of force, to control speech and the movement of ideas. The Paris commune and Haymarket demonstrate the use of force. Political dissidents were often subject to public trials and executions that verified the power of the state. In addition, there was little control over the movement of people across borders. As Jensen states, "The era's fundamental belief in liberalism proclaimed that labor, as well as goods and capital, should be as free as possible to flow around the world."[52] For much of the nineteenth century, there were no passports and people could move rather freely across Europe without harassment or questioning.[53] Only Russia and the Ottoman Empire required passports for entry. In fact, their purpose was often to protect upper-class travelers.[54] Additionally, extradition policies were haphazard at best.[55] Standard practice was to banish undesirables from the home state without cataloguing them or alerting other states. Russian mass exile may have kicked off the anarchist movement in Europe. Italian mass exile led to Italians becoming the chief purveyors of regicide. This may seem like a case of no boundaries, but there were boundaries demarcating state jurisdiction. They just did not reflect what happened to people, goods, and ideas.

These practices construct nineteenth-century nationalism. Rejecting the nationalism of the French Revolution, the nationalism of state actors was a way to utilize people as tools for standing armies, as economic cogs, and staffing colonial governments.[56] This produced apathy toward what the people did, where they went. While it would contribute to the squalor and brutality that created the revolutionary movement, it was also a justification for free movement and lax extradition policies. It is important to note I am not claiming that a conservative nationalism created the practice, but that we can speak of a conservative nationalism only when we consider practices.

When combined with industrialization, the practices that drew these boundaries would facilitate the growth of propaganda of the deed in two ways. First, attempts to control the public sphere through force made it hard for state agents to understand the threat. I cover illegibility in the next section and focus here on the prosecution of the wrong people for the wrong crimes. Relevant state agents thought the crime was the idea challenging their rule. As a result, anarchy drew their focus, and a "war on anarchy" was all but declared in name, like the "war on terror" a century later. Italian author Ettore Zoccoli called anarchism "the most important ethical deviation that may ever disturb the world."[57] *Harper's Magazine* called it "the most dangerous theory that civilization has ever had to encounter."[58] U.S. president Theodore Roosevelt proclaimed, "Anarchy is a crime against the whole human race."[59] George Bernard Shaw remarked that anarchism and criminality had become synonymous.[60] The target was not the assassin, the bomb thrower, or the propagandist, but anarchy—the set of ideas that argued against hierarchy.

The problem was that not all anarchists were propagandists. Most anarchists rejected this manifestation of propaganda of the deed, preferring some combination of a more traditional propaganda by the word and syndicalism (see below). When bombings first garnered international attention, many anarchists, including Kropotkin, denounced them. Most representative were those who denounced the acts but understood the impulse. As one anonymous but widely distributed pamphlet claimed, "We hate murder with a hatred that may seem absurdly exaggerated . . . [but] the guilt of these homicides lies upon every man and woman who, intentionally or by cold indifference, helps to keep up social conditions that drive human beings to despair."[61] However, the distinction between anarchists and propagandists was either ignored or unknown to authorities and the general public. The average citizen in Paris, Madrid, or London had little reason to fear the anarchist bomb; it was meant for the bourgeoisie.[62] Prosecuting the idea led to trials of sympathetic intellectuals and made sure that states were not able to take advantage of the splits within anarchism.

Second, increasing industrialization made the combination of controlling ideas and public brutality on one hand and free movement on the other untenable. State attempts to control the content of speech in the public sphere became increasingly unsuccessful as the material and conceptual tools needed to enter it became more accessible. I have discussed how industrialization and globalization created the grievances that led to anarchism and the wider industrial movement. But they also provided the opportunity for propaganda of the deed (and anarchism in general) to flourish through the movement of peoples, goods, and ideas. Anarchism was a truly global movement, active in Eastern Europe, East and Southeast Asia, Africa, and across Latin America.[63] In an era where internationalism and imperialism were indistinguishable, anarchism was a force in the former and against the latter: "Artificially formed Empires, constructed and held together by force ... [the anarchist] regards as miserable shams."[64] Its transnationality within Europe and the propensity of officials and publics to blame it on "foreigners" (often Eastern European Jews or Southern Europeans) provided challenges to the openness that fueled the internationalism of the era.

While propaganda of the deed was mostly limited to Western Europe, the United States, and Argentina, it reflected this transnationality. This meant it was well positioned to take advantage of the movement of goods, people, and ideas, while also undercutting attempts to control the public sphere through force. The growth of mass media allowed anarchist actions to be broadcast to a wider audience. It was said of the French propagandist Émile Henry that "the bombs of Barcelona hypnotized him."[65] A poor man in Italy learned of the execution of a French anarchist and decided to exact revenge against the French president in Lyon. A Polish immigrant in the United States heard of the treatment of an American-born Italian anarchist and decided to assassinate President William McKinley. Police brutality became public knowledge. When

Spanish treatment of anarchists in the Montjuic prisons could lead to anarchist bombings in France and rallies in London, there was a problem for those attempting to maintain order using these methods. A number of states, notably England and Switzerland, became places of political shelter for exiles. In 1894, Paris police believed that they had just missed apprehending documents detailing an "international anarchist plan," because the papers were sent to Madame Brochet, a sympathizer in Switzerland.[66] Such a lax system of border control benefitted the propagandists. As the Spanish duke of Arcos complained, "the anarchist agitator who is driven out of one country by the authorities finds lodgment in another."[67]

While state practices had yet to adapt, propagandists could take advantage in order to attack the state. Gérard Chaliand and Arnaud Blin sum up the situation nicely: "The very gradual emergence of democratic freedoms allowed malcontents to broadcast their demands on a scale that had previously been unthinkable. Yet, the winds of freedom blew weakly... thus legitimizing such protest movements."[68] The control of ideas and public executions were not able to coexist with the increased movement of peoples, goods, and ideas that were a result of industrialization. The reason for this was propaganda of the deed. The effects of the macro-processes of globalization and industrialization were determined by practices developed to solve concrete problems. Thus, the entire system itself was under threat. The process of shattering began as what had previously been habitual actions for state agents needed to be rethought and conceptual boundaries redrawn.

SHATTERING: "THE ANARCHIST ASSASSIN MURDERS SIMPLY AT HAPHAZARD"

As noted in the introduction to this chapter, in the thirty-five years prior to the Great War, Europe was beset by a series of bomb attacks and assassinations by those labeled "anarchists." Contemporary criminologist Arthur MacDonald reported that there had been fifty-nine attempted assassinations of political leaders from the United States, the UK, Russia, Germany, Austria, Spain, France, and Italy between the years 1897 and

1902.[69] Of course, the number of attacks and the damage they caused are only a part of the story. There have been many other instances of assassinations and bombings by the Euro-American left outside of this period—usually by Marxist-Leninist groups such as the Red Army Faction and Weather Underground. The interwar period witnessed more assassinations of political leaders by anti-colonialists than propaganda of the deed.[70] In England, Fenian separatists were more deadly and numerous than propagandists.[71] And of course, the most famous assassination of the age, that of Archduke Franz Ferdinand, was by Gavrilo Princip, a Serbian nationalist. Yet, it was propaganda of the deed that provoked a crisis for the state itself. This is because states found themselves not only powerless to stop attacks but unable to make sense of them. This caused a crisis of legitimacy. Anti-colonial attacks in Ireland, the Balkans, Algeria, and elsewhere were destructive but legible. They wanted—or at least were interpreted as wanting—their own state. Propaganda of the deed was illegible. The anarchists or propagandists came to be considered the most devious of criminals due to the surprising nature of their attacks, adding to the sense of terror. Propagandists could be hiding anywhere, they could be anyone. They could be under the bench of a carriage waiting to strike or sipping coffee at a café that was about to explode. They had no central figure, and their dealings were conducted outside of the public eye. This led many to overstate the anarchist threat and tie it to anxiety about the second wave of globalization—ignoring native anarchists[72] in favor of an international conspiracy led by Jews and immigrants.

CONSPIRACY

All sides saw the conspiracy as fitting their own interests. Conspiracy theories helped secret police gain funding and autonomy; they had an interest in framing all attacks as anarchist. They even had a hand in some attacks (see below). Italian officials argued that "in every country the adherents and centers of propaganda and of organization of the anarchist sect maintain relations with all their alliances in other nations."[73] The Spanish ambassador to Rome claimed that attacks "in Barcelona have their origins in, if indeed they don't obey, an international anarchist impulse."[74] One German correspondent claimed that "the anarchist element is so mobile that even if a plot were destroyed today, tomorrow another one would be formed."[75]

The media was willing to amplify these concerns, and attacks, trials, and plots were front-page news and took up a lot of column space. The *Evening News* claimed that eight thousand anarchists were present in London in 1894,[76] despite only five hundred French anarchist exiles entering England during the peak years of the 1880s and early 1890s.[77] Of course, many anarchists were all too happy to play along. This shared interest came together in the coverage and production of trials. During trials, many propagandists prioritized persuading and scaring the public to saving themselves. Giuseppe Fornara freely ventured his unrealized plot to blow up the London Stock Exchange, exclaiming, "I want to kill the capitalists!"[78] During the trial of famed propagandist Ravachol, his friends circulated a pamphlet that claimed that the bourgeois make "of this man a monster in the eyes of satisfied egoists and the indifferent who do not want to see that it is they who created him."[79]

Conspiracy theories helped anarchists scare the public. For instance, anarchists were put on trial for a failed plot in Walsall, England, in 1892. A telegram of support was sent to the defendants from the "United Anarchists Groups, London."[80] The letter caused a panic because of the belief that reprisals were imminent from these "united groups." If the anarchists were united, who knows where they would attack next! However, the letter was sent by a single man, Thomas Cantwell, editor in chief of the anarchist newspaper *Commonweal*. The whole panic was fueled not by good intelligence but instead by a prior belief in a large conspiracy that made the use of the term "United Anarchist Groups, London" a threatening one.[81] But so long as the public remained scared, police forces received resources and papers were sold.

Finally, as anarchism become associated with globalization, conspiracy theories were often pinned on minorities and immigrants. Claims of an anarchist conspiracy in England had anti-Semitic roots connected to the influx of Jewish immigrants following Russian pogroms. Historian Alex Butterworth has even gone so far as to trace the origins of *The Protocols of the Elders of Zion*—a fabricated Russian text purporting to outline Jewish plans for world domination—to attempts to pin the anarchist conspiracy onto Europe's Jewish population.[82] In the United States,

Italian immigrants and exiles were categorized as anarchists. While both countries had "native" anarchists, they were not taken seriously by the authorities.[83]

ILLEGIBILITY AND ILLEGITIMACY

The rise of conspiracy theories reflects the illegibility of propaganda of the deed. It starts with the anarchist idea. One observer remarked that "every other class of political assassin has at least some definite, tangible object in view. He commits murder because he seeks to remove some particular ruler, or a member of some particular governing party or body. The anarchist assassin, however, murders simply at haphazard.... They exploded bombs in a theatre in Barcelona which was filled with innocent men, women, and children, none of whom were connected with the government."[84] While independence movements made sense, the propagandist justification for violence was nonsensical to elites and state agents. Misunderstanding was widespread; a briefing on the extradition of the propagandist Théodule Meunier from England to France claimed that anarchists were not interested in "a new form of government, but general destruction."[85] For their part, the propagandists claimed that they were killing their enemy, the bourgeois. For instance, Giuseppe Fornara claimed at his trial that he had attempted to blow up the Royal Exchange in London because "there were many bourgeois and capitalists there"; he "wanted to blow up the capitalists and the middle class."[86]

Propaganda of the deed was also illegible because it was hard to follow. Attacks seemed to come from nowhere. A January 1894 column in the Spanish periodical *La Lectura* summed up the mood:

> Explosives are on the order of the day in the Chambers [of parliament], in the disorder of the night in the theaters; they hang as a menace over the entire bourgeoisie, without respecting the poor worker if they encounter him in passing, and there is no person who does not worry about dynamite, nitroglycerine, *panclastinas*, and detonators.... Modern explosives have come to upset everything: ideas and property and social relations.

> The lowliest wretch in the worst social rubbish heap [*pudridero social*] holds a threat over the entire society, like a horde of barbarians showing their monstrous heads over the frontier. The result is that the least becomes the first, if not by power, by terror.... Satan has made himself a dynamiter and tries to be equal with God, and threatens his shadow [on earth].[87]

There are two things to keep in mind here. First, the anarchists are said to be against "ideas and property and social relations." Their actions struck at the heart of state legitimacy. This is reflected in suggestions that propagandists are "barbarians," "monstrous," and "Satan," echoing the *hostes humani generiis* rhetoric of the early eighteenth century. Similar to golden-age pirates, anarchists were denounced as having "inhuman designs"[88] or as being "wild animals."[89] At this trial, publisher Johann Most was denounced as a "malicious and evil disposed person and unlawfully, maliciously, and wickedly contriving, intending, and attempting in defiance of all principles of morality and good government to justify the crimes of assassination and murder."[90] Roosevelt's declaration that anarchy was the greatest threat of the age fits nicely with this rhetoric.

Second, it definitely shook state agents that "the lowliest wretch in the worst social rubbish heap" could threaten them. Thus, the act was viewed as cowardly because propagandists would not face up to their enemies. This demonstrates how the surprising nature of attacks facilitated the crisis. One German correspondent claimed that "the anarchist element is so mobile that even if a plot were destroyed today, tomorrow another one would be formed."[91] The anarchist act, especially the use of dynamite, was illegible as it had not been seen before. Anarchist justifications made no sense in contemporary political discourse. Finally, contemporary boundaries made it hard to see where attacks were coming from.

Anarchists also threatened state legitimacy. While we risk oversimplifying when claiming that the nineteenth-century nationalism was used for the purposes of the state, it does capture something important. This was a period where man's nature was a popular explanation for social phenomena: the criminal had a "look."[92] People were of "races," and "scientific" theories like eugenics became popular.[93] Political elites believed that it was in the nature of the common man to follow their lead; in return they would provide protection from the deviant. Propaganda of the deed complicated this picture because it presented a clear alternative version of social organization, and because the usual tools for handling security threats were ineffective. Its adherents proved too decentralized, too hard to separate from the populace and too willing to sacrifice their own lives for the cause. This failure to stop anarchist bombings and assassinations chipped away at state claims as the provider of security. Why countenance hierarchy if it cannot protect you? Propaganda of the deed was a threat to *the* state, not merely a particular state or regime. It forced states to redraw boundaries to make sense of and defeat the threat. Those that did not adapt, notably Spain and Russia, saw grave consequences for their ruling orders as anarchists played important roles in the Russian Revolution and the Spanish Civil War.

FAILED SOLUTIONS TO PROPAGANDA OF THE DEED

The eventual "solutions" to propaganda of the deed took years to come to fruition; in the meantime there were many ineffective strategies tried by governments, police departments, and intelligence services. Understanding these strategies tells us how these agents drew state boundaries. I will go over three strategies: repression, the use of secret agents, and international cooperation. The immediate response in most states was to step up police work and prosecutions, "a mass of draconian 'anti-terrorist' legislation, summary executions, and a sharp rise in torture."[94] While this lead to the successful prosecution of particular culprits, it did not prove effective in stemming the tide of attacks. As U.S. senator George Frisbee Hoar warned his colleagues, "the [anarchist] assassin is willing to give his life to accomplish the result. There is your trouble."[95] As detailed above, propagandist trials became media events and served as a platform for the accused to spread their gospel. The damned became martyrs and heroes to those who felt crushed by the combination of industrialization and nation building. Additionally, prosecuting a movement leader such as Piotr Kropotkin or Errico Malatesta failed to separate the idea from the action. In the end, each execution tended to be answered by a "revenge" response by another propagandist.

Attacks in France in the early 1890s demonstrate this claim. In 1891, authorities arrested and tortured striking miners in Clichy.[96] One of their friends, François Claudius Koenigstein, alias Ravachol, set off a series of bombs in the residences of the convicting judge and attorney, causing injuries but no fatalities. The police arrested him while he was bragging of his deeds to a waiter at the Café Very—though his execution was for prior crimes.[97] At his trial he proclaimed, "My object was to terrorize so as to force society to look attentively at those who suffered."[98] He was carried to the guillotine proclaiming "Vive l'anarchie!" and he became a patron saint of the anarchist movement, inspiring songs[99] and the term *ravacholisier*, meaning "to wipe out an enemy."[100] In revenge, a man named Théodule Meunier exploded a bomb at the Café Very on April 25, 1892, killing the proprietor.[101] On November 8, 1892, the police discovered another bomb in the Paris office of a mining company. They defused it and took it to the nearest police station, where it unexpectedly exploded, killing six officers.[102] On December 9, 1893, Auguste Vaillant detonated a bomb inside the Chamber of Deputies, causing multiple injuries but no fatalities. Vaillant mentioned Ravachol at his trial in 1894 before being sentenced to death.[103]

In response, the Chamber of Deputies passed the *lois scélérates* or "wicked laws,"[104] severely cracking down on anarchism. Vaillant's execution brought many threats of revenge.[105] A few months later, a man named Pauwels phoned in suicides in two different apartments rigged with explosives, killing the investigating officers.[106] On February 12, 1894, Émile Henry set off a bomb in the Café Terminus, injuring twenty and killing one. Henry confessed not only to the Terminus bombing but also to the bomb that had gone off at the police station fifteen months prior. At his widely published trial, he spoke eloquently of Vaillant and Ravachol[107] and defiantly exclaimed, "Go ahead and cut off my head, you may as well.... Others will come after me."[108] As he was executed, he was heard screaming a muffled "Courage, Comrades! Vive l'anarchie!"[109] Henry became yet another hero of the movement, the "Saint-Just" of anarchism beheaded by the French state.[110] In June 1894, a young Italian named Sante Caserio fatally stabbed French president Sardi Carnot. A few days later, Carnot's wife received a letter addressed to the "widow Carnot" that contained pictures of Ravachol and Vaillant and the words "He is avenged." The Paris police began arresting people for "incitement to hatred of the bourgeoisie,"[111] but attacks continued. It got so bad that a scare in a Paris theater in 1894 led to multiple deaths due to screams of "Les anarchists! Une bombe!" when scenery crashed backstage.[112]

Similar cycles of copycatting and revenge also played out in Spain. In 1892, a peasant uprising in Jerez led to the garroting of four young men. One of the men, before being choked to death in public, got out the words "avenge us." The resulting demonstrations in Barcelona led to mass arrests. In 1893, a man named Pallas threw a bomb at the Spanish minister of war, General Martínez, killing one soldier, five bystanders, and the general's horse (though leaving the general unscathed). At his trial, Pallas talked about revenge for the Jerez "murders." When he was sentenced to death, he yelled out "Agreed! There are thousands to continue the work!"[113] Before his death, he proclaimed that "vengeance will be terrible!" A few weeks later a bomb went off in the Teatro Lyceu in Barcelona, killing fifteen and causing mass panic. The government's reaction was swift and devastating, rounding up anyone associated with anarchism and/or socialism and torturing them at the infamous Montjuic prison just outside Barcelona.[114] A man by the name of Santiago Salvador admitted to being responsible for the bombing of the Lyceu as revenge for the death of Pallas. Within days, another bomb went off, killing two more people. In 1896, Michele Angiolillo assassinated Prime Minister Canovas, leading to more torture of anarchists through 1897. All told, anarchism—which had deep social roots in Cadiz Province—would remain a potent political force against the ruling regime into the 1930s.[115] Repression only had the effect of, in the words of the Duke of Arcos, "scattering their forces."[116]

Italian repression made the problem of peasant revolts more acute. Russian repression only led to a mass exodus of anarchists and other revolutionaries in the 1880s while doing little to end violence there. A tough U.S. immigration law passed after McKinley's assassination did not stop anarchist attacks, nor did the Espionage Act of 1917.[117] In fact, they only embittered the anarchist community, playing a role in the postwar surge of propaganda of the deed in the United States.[118] It seemed that wherever repression of anarchy and anarchists was used as a tactic, it was unproductive at best and often backfired. One German official opined that suppression only created "a multitude of smaller groups whose surveillance could not be managed with the same reliability."[119]

With one exception (see below), official multilateral cooperation also proved unfruitful. The 1898 Rome Conference, convened after the assassination of the popular Austrian empress by an Italian, included all of the major states. Its biggest official achievement was the agreement of a legal definition of "anarchism"[120] and an agreement to change the "attentat" extradition clause, refusing political exile to those suspected of killing, or attempting to kill, a head of state. However, none of the agreements from the Rome conference were put into legislation. England did not even sign the final draft of the agreements. Following McKinley's assassination, another meeting produced the 1904 St. Petersburg Protocol, aimed at creating official channels of communication between police departments. However, it was not signed by the UK, France, or even the United States, who saw it as an unnecessary measure pushed by Russia and Germany to interfere in their respective political processes (and liberal rights). In particular, the English rejected the Russian proposal to make anarchism itself a crime.[121]

Diplomatic cooperation often took a back seat to secret agreements between police departments. For instance, the Russian police force (Okhrana) had a bureau in Paris, the British Special Branch cooperated with Okhrana against the wishes of the UK parliament, and Italy set up a network of secret agents in cities across Europe and North America to spy on Italian emigrants. This was ineffective as well. The state with the largest international secret police, Russia, never rid themselves of anarchist agitation during the time of the tsar. Often, secret police actions contributed to the anarchist movement. For instance, a widely read anarchist journal, *La Révolution Sociale*, was operated by the Paris police.[122]

Attempts to infiltrate anarchist groups were unproductive. Much of the secret police action was centered on London's Club l'Autonomie.[123] Founded in 1887, it became a focal point for foreign governments fond of blaming England for their anarchist troubles.[124] One German correspondent claimed that "it is ridiculous to allege that the English police are carrying out any sort of surveillance at all on the anarchists who reside in London."[125] The club attracted a lot of spies. Scotland Yard first detective Patrick McIntyre recalled, "I know, of my own knowledge, that a large minority of those frequenting the place were in the service and pay of Continental Governments."[126] A French inspector remarked, "I realize why political squads never find any anarchists.... Most of the anarchists are informers."¹²⁷ Of course, the fear that propelled the use of spies was rooted in the conspiracy theories developed to make sense of an illegible threat.

Secret agents were also used as agents provocateurs. The goal was to instigate bombings to either foil the plot or alert the public to an international conspiracy.¹²⁸ In 1894, a supposed anarchist attempted to kill Belgian king Leopold. The attack was to be used as an excuse for greater funds for the Special Branch of Scotland Yard. Subsequently, it was revealed that the man who had carried out the attack, Baron Ernst Ungern-Sternberg, was in the pay of the Russian Okhrana's infamous chief Peter Rachovsky. It was also revealed that English Special Branch officers were known associates of the accused.¹²⁹ His cover was blown when upon his arrest he asked for a Monsieur Leonard, Leonard being the maiden name of Rachovsky's wife.

Thus, the line between agent and anarchist was blurred. An Italian infiltrator in London named Gennaro Rubino used Italian funds to start an anarchist press.¹³⁰ Upon being revealed as a secret agent by his anarchist friends, Rubino decided to prove his worth by using a gun he got from the Italian government to kill King Leopold of Belgium. The attack failed, and Rubino was captured. The whole episode was a major embarrassment for the Italians and stalled future cooperation.¹³¹ An Italian named Michele Angiolillo was the one who assassinated the Spanish prime minister Antonio Canovas after the French anarchist community shunned him as a suspected spy.¹³²

Police shenanigans became the stated reason why the English rejected cooperation attempts by the Russians, Italians, Germans, and Spanish.¹³³ In the words of one English official, "In my opinion no good could result from Spanish detectives coming over here to study the system adopted by the Metropolitan Police."¹³⁴ One English official noted to the Italians that their actions "seriously aggravate the danger they are designed to check."¹³⁵ The English even began to believe that the most dangerous anarchists were those, like Rubino and Angiolillo, whose spying was uncovered by the anarchist community. In several instances, threats were invented just to get a reaction from the English.¹³⁶ However, secret policing efforts did have a lasting effect. The files of the Russian Okhrana were studied by the Nazi Schutzstaffel (SS), the American Central

Intelligence Agency (CIA), and the Soviet Komitet Gosudarstvennoy Bezopasnosti (KGB) with an eye toward copying their tactics.[137]

Extradition and exile policies did not help either. It was uncommon for continental states to alert others when anarchists were expelled. This was something England complained loudly about, calling it an "international discourtesy to a friendly power."[138] The French were accused of "wanting to funnel toward England the dregs of the Society."[139] Russia, Germany, and Spain provided no lists of those expelled, while the French, Italians, and Belgians provided lists a month or more after expelling anarchists.[140] The English complained they had no idea whom to look for when they arrived.[141] For instance, the Belgian police waited weeks after expelling an anarchist named Jaffei to tell the British of his possible arrival. At that point, one British official opined that it was only their "good fortune to spot him" that allowed them to take precaution.[142] These actions—repression, extradition and exile policies, and agents provocateurs—did little but reinforce old boundaries, attempting to cover up the problems in porous borders by extending state reach across them.

REINSCRIBING: THE "UNIVERSAL EYE"

The first wave of policies undertaken to counter propaganda of the deed was not only ineffective but, in most cases, backfired. The methods states had at hand were ill-equipped for the job. As one observer put it, "Attempted suppression of anarchism by governments has been [a] great failure."[143] This forced them to come up with new ideas and new tactics—tactics that were not only "successful" but also creative in that they brought something new into the world. As a result, they had the effect of drawing new boundaries and reinscribing the state. I argue that practices were established that ultimately played a role in two major developments in twentieth-century politics: the labor/progressive movement and the rise of the modern surveillance state. Decoupling the idea of anarchism from the propagandist act meant less repression of anarchism.[144] This eventually funneled anarchist energies toward the less destructive and increasingly legitimate pursuits of syndicalism and the labor movement.[145] Similarly, centralized police forces and the collection of biometric data led to the creation of the modern surveillance state, which was in turn necessary for the institution of universal passports and the tightening of borders.[146] These practices redrew public/private and international/domestic boundaries. Surveillance replaced more direct forms of control as the domestic sphere opened up and the international sphere closed down. This section will cover these instances of state transformation, beginning with allowing anarchism into the public sphere.

ACCEPTING ANARCHISTS

As outlined above, the first reaction to propaganda of the deed was the repression of anarchism. However, as Jensen notes, "Repression only convinced many anarchists that legal activity was pointless."[147] Once again, events in France in the 1890s are instructive. President Carnot's assassination led to the arrest of known anarchist agitators and intellectuals. In the resulting "Trial of Thirty" that lasted from August to October of 1894, these men were tried as one group for conspiracy. However, evidence was so flimsy that even a jury sympathetic to the prosecution acquitted most of them, including all of the intellectuals. Unlike previous episodes, there was no response to this very public trial. Instead of repressive tactics and sham trials making the problem worse, the French realized that allowing the peaceful activists and intellectuals to operate led to fewer attacks, if they could be separated from the propagandists.[148] Of course, many anarchist intellectuals were all too happy to distance themselves from those conducting assassinations and bombings. While Ravachol's actions split the anarchist intellectual community across Europe,[149] most believed his sentence rested on his anarchist beliefs, not his crimes. However, Henry's bombing two years later was loudly denounced as immoral and ineffectual. Anarchist publicist Charles Malato said that Henry "struck a blow at anarchy,"[150] while literary critic Octave Mirbeau wrote, "A mortal enemy of anarchy could not have done more than Émile Henry."[151] The acquittal of prominent anarchists in the Trial of Thirty made them largely untouchable on precedent, so long as they were not associated with violent acts. The view that the trial was a sham gave anarchism an air of legitimacy. The French government learned to stop producing anarchist martyrs; it commuted an anarchist's death sentence in 1898 to life in prison and acquitted all four accused in 1905 of plots against the king of Spain and the president of France.[152] The days of being jailed and executed for being an anarchist were over in France; so was propaganda of the deed.[153]

From an early stage, England was prosecuting the violence as opposed to the idea. London had become a base for exiled anarchists, as the English were "not disposed to think of political refugees as dangerous,"[154] and because "to be an anarchist is not any offence to English law as it is to hold any other theory with regard to social or political questions."[155] England allowed anarchist publications in multiple languages.[156] The English police would arrest a publisher for inciting violence,[157] though anarchists excelled at not explicitly doing so. One British member of parliament (MP) called for the arrest of an anarchist editor for applauding an attempt at the Spanish royal family, to which the authorities responded, "Any attempt to prosecute would serve no purpose but to advertise the mischievous article."[158] It also refused to prosecute on continental terms. England resisted the extradition on grounds of anarchism of Meunier and Jean-Pierre François, the latter a supposed accomplice of Ravachol, and only relented when they were credibly charged with murder.[159] Continental authorities were critical of England's stance. As one observer noted, "It is a fact that many of the outrages which have taken place on the Continent were arranged beforehand in London, within the four walls of the Club Autonomie."[160] However, this was overblown, and England did not see many attacks within its borders. Its policy of separating idea from act allowed it to foil two attacks: one in Walsall in 1892[161] and a plot to bomb the Royal Exchange.[162] The lone attack, an 1894 bombing of Greenwich Observatory, only killed the man carrying the bomb, Martial Bourdin.[163] In the end, "England Alone [was] spared on account of her hospitality to the anarchists."[164] Kropotkin even supported England in the war.[165]

After the assassination of King Umberto I in 1900, Italy stopped passing laws directed at anarchists, and in 1901, interior minister Giovanni Giolitti instructed journalists not to sensationalize attacks.[166] One was free to speak anarchist ideas; only the bombings and assassinations were illegal. It also forced anarchists to defend their ideology publicly. The spate of bombings and a propaganda campaign that described anarchist as "enemies of humanity" turned public opinion against anarchism. This led to disillusionment with violence among the movement's leaders.[167] In fact, the majorities of the European publics had no idea about most anarchist beliefs despite the bombings.[168] Propaganda of the deed had failed.

At the same time, union liberalization brought many anarchists into the public sphere and further drove a wedge between different factions of the community. The labor movement created space for anarchists in the guise of syndicalism, while its successes prevented possible future propagandists.[169] States that liberalized labor agitation early, particularly the UK and the United States, saw less propagandist activity than others. As Richard Bach Jensen has argued about Italy, "Labour union and strike activity became available as a safety valve for proletarian energies."[170] While Germany had a politically repressive regime, the prominence of trade and labor unions in its growing industries spared it from attacks.[171] While the progressive movement in the United States coincided with the decline of propaganda of the deed in Europe, New Deal labor protections coincided with its decline domestically.[172] In each case at least one of two strategies were followed: greater opportunity for organizing labor and/or the end of prosecuting anarchism as an idea. As anarchists became detached from propagandist attacks and the public sphere was opened to anarchist ideas, conspiracy theories were harder to sustain, and states such as the United States and France came closer to achieving their liberal-democratic ideals.

By the end of World War I, many who were open to anarchist ideas now found it more effective to work through the system, which gave them bargaining power and greater political rights. Anarchists became fascinated with Britain's labor movements, with the influential anarchist publication *Pere Peinard* auguring for action in this area.[173] Anarcho-syndicalism, a militant anarchist movement that believed that unions and the labor movement could better the lives of workers,[174] began to take hold in the 1890s, picking up as propaganda of the deed began to wane over the next decade. The Trial of Thirty created space for anarcho-syndicalism, as after 1895 "the general strike became a pillar of revolutionary syndicalism" in France.[175] Italian anarchists followed suit. Many favored syndicalism because, unlike propaganda of the deed, it put anarchists in contact with the workers who were the revolution's vanguard.

Among those arguing for syndicalism were prominent anarchist theorists and publishers like Kropotkin and Émile Pouget.[176] Of course, many anarchists scoffed at efforts for the eight-hour workday and other union campaigns, claiming that it did not matter how long one worked if hierarchy remained.[177] Malatesta even called syndicalism a conservative movement.

To be clear, the state did not actively funnel anarchists into the labor movement: anarchists rejected propaganda of the deed and accepted syndicalism themselves. However, the conditions influencing whether or not they did so were dependent on state practices and boundaries that incentivized working within the system and rejecting propaganda of the deed. Nor did state agents or the bourgeois capitulate; the labor fights undertaken by the syndicalists and others were fiercely fought. Syndicalists themselves are responsible for few clear labor victories, though they provided the movement with a radical wing to play off in negotiations and public relations. Additionally, intellectuals like Kropotkin, Reclus, and William Morris became less dangerous once they began giving talks to the Royal Geographic Society and undertaking speaking tours in the United States. The state is no more than the actions it undertakes; a state with a more inclusive public sphere is a state with different democratic possibilities from one without. While the campaign against propaganda of the deed was not the only cause of the labor movement or the welfare state, each would have developed differently without it.

THE MODERN SURVEILLANCE STATE

The campaign against propaganda of the deed also contributed to the development of the modern surveillance state. Propaganda of the deed drove home the idea that citizens could not be directly controlled but that they could be tracked. This allowed for the closing down of borders in the form of immigration restrictions and universal passports. Recent developments have made surveillance a popular topic in history and the social sciences.[178] In addition to the explanations covered in the introduction above, the historiography also points to the provision of national welfare[179] and a desire to track colonial subjects[180] as explanations for the rise of the modern surveillance state. Finally, other scholars have focused on the international conferences and agreements that led to the standardization of the passport.[181] These arguments are incomplete. The rise of the modern surveillance state depended upon many factors concatenating in specific ways in particular states. Propaganda of the deed was one important factor. The campaign against propaganda of the deed influenced the development of the surveillance state in three ways: (1) key practices developed to directly combat propaganda of the deed or were dependent upon such measures; (2) propaganda of the deed was the justificatory device for new practices; and (3) propaganda of the deed fueled the larger nativist discourse of the 1920s.

Repression and violent action did not quell propaganda of the deed. Jensen argues, "The extreme measures of the Italian and Spanish were in part the frustrated reactions of the government and police to difficulties in tracking down and identifying terrorists."[182] Eventually police began to centralize operations and develop new techniques. At the end of the nineteenth century, police forces were decentralized, with little communication between localities. This meant that efforts were not coordinated and resources were wasted, as reflected in the secret police machinations around L'Autonomie noted above. For instance, it is claimed that there were five agents in the same anarchist meeting in France in the early 1890s.[183] This facilitated the use of agents provocateurs and the attempts of Spain to let other countries do their police work for them. This changed as a result of propaganda of the deed. The U.S. Federal Bureau of Investigation (FBI) was created in 1908,[184] boasting three hundred agents on the eve of the Great War whose main concerns were white slavery and anarchism.[185] The French created a special organization to centralize intelligence following the events of the early 1890s.[186] Germany attempted to follow suit in order to combat "anarchists and other social revolutionaries," though resistance from southern German states delayed the implementation of any such organization.[187] While early tactics left much to be desired, centralized police forces were necessary for coordinating policies, cooperating across borders, and directing funds.

While ineffective in developing law and diplomatic measures to combat propaganda of the deed, Rome and St. Petersburg inadvertently strengthened international police cooperation. At the Rome meetings, British metropolitan chief Howard Vincent claimed that anarchism was "wholly a matter for international police communication."[188] Vincent himself led closed-door breakaway sessions between various police officials attending the conference. It was these sessions that proved the most lasting impact of the conference as they shifted the issue form one of great power politics and international law to one of "expertise and professionalism in police institutions."[189]

There is evidence of Greek police obtaining information from Italian counterparts as late as 1913 by citing a cooperative agreement signed at the Rome conference.[190] Hungary and Germany began to exchange names and photographs of those expelled, echoing the future development of *portraits parlés* and passports (see below). The Netherlands, Luxembourg, Spain, Italy, Serbia, Bulgaria, and Austria-Hungary all made similar agreements with each other. St. Petersburg, like Rome, allowed for deeper connections between participating police departments. Slowly, police cooperation went from covert actions and secret meetings to professional agreements made by competent bureaucrats. Jensen states that these acts made police cooperation "official and systematic to a degree it had never been before. Because of this, the system promoted by the Final Act of Rome and reinforced by the St. Petersburg Protocol can now take its rightful place as a major precursor, perhaps the first, to the creation in 1923 of an authentic international police organization [Interpol]."[191] To pull this off, there had to be international communication and centralized databases. In short, state agents needed the capability and authority to monitor citizens.

The biggest advantage of centralization, however, was that it allowed for the creation of databases and a change in technique. In the late nineteenth century, police started to utilize biometric methods of identifying criminals. Originating from the work of Cesare Lombroso, an idea took hold that criminality was a condition whose "victims" displayed certain physical features.[192] Max Nordau built on Lombroso's idea of "degeneracy" to argue that ideologies such as anarchism, socialism, and liberated sexuality were actually signs of human regression.[193] Gaining even more traction was the work of Alphonse Bertillon,[194] best known for his criminal-identification technique called Bertillonage.[195] Bertillon advocated for the measurement and collection of arm lengths and ear sizes in addition to pictures of criminals. Craig Robertson argues that Bertillon "did not make use of an existing (social) identity; he used Bertillonage to produce a new identity."[196] Fingerprints supplanted Bertillonage in

Britain in 1901 as part of a series of reforms initiated by Francis Galton.[197] Anarchism was the chief justificatory device for fingerprint databases as far back as 1911.[198] Like Lombroso and Bertillon, "Galston's original interest was to locate deviance, risk, and threat in biometric facts."[199] Galston's work, like that of Bertillon, Lombroso, and Nordau, was part of a larger eugenic project. Even though their ideas would be discredited, their methods would lay the groundwork for scientific policing and the use of biometric data. The best characterization of these reforms may be Sir Arthur Conan Doyle's Sherlock Holmes stories.[200] Holmes's use of fingerprints, crime scene evidence, and logic epitomized the scientific approach to police work; such methods were another factor preventing Britain from experiencing the volume of propagandist attacks experienced on the continent. Britain's methods were soon copied elsewhere.

This new field of scientific criminality played a role in the centralization and professionalization of police forces described above. For instance, by the end of the 1890s, "a scheme for systematic political surveillance had emerged in Switzerland for the first time" to deal with its anarchist community.[201] There were seven international congresses on criminal anthropology between 1885 and 1911.[202] Furthermore, as fingerprints and ear-and-nose measurements would have to be catalogued to be of use, biometric databases were created. Soon *portraits parlés* were generated for anarchists with Bertillonage measurements, fingerprints, a description of skin tone and hair color, and even a portrait where possible. They were standardized in 1898[203] and were distributed by centralized police organizations, used by police on the ground, and shared across borders.[204] One French police chief celebrated them as a "universal eye ... unmasking criminals."[205] These changes would be integral in two important developments in combatting "propaganda of the deed": immigration restrictions and the advent of the universal passport system.

Immigration restrictions became a common response to the problem of propaganda of the deed. The United States, the affected country with the greatest levels of immigration, attempted to enact immigration restrictions and deportation laws for anarchists throughout the 1890s, but anarchist fear in the United States was regional, and the laws never got passed.[206] However, after McKinley's assassination, Congress amended immigration law in 1903 to bar from entry "anarchists, or persons who believe in or advocate the overthrow by force or violence of all governments, or all forms of law, or the assassination of public officials."[207]

However, the broad definition of "anarchist" led to the expulsion of the avowedly nonviolent and backlash from a public who valued free speech.[208] The British enacted the Aliens Act in 1905, its first law restricting immigration, in large part due to fears of immigrant anarchists.[209] Paul Knepper argues that taking "steps to rid Great Britain of 'these criminals' [anarchists] ... would enable the country to rid itself of many alien criminals of the ordinary type."[210]

After the war, immigration restrictions took a greater hold. For instance, immigration to the United States reached a high of 1.2 million in 1914. While it dipped during the war, it once again reached up over 800,000 as late as 1922, and stood at 706,896 in 1924. However, that year a sweeping immigration law went into effect, and immigration dropped to 294,314 in 1925 and down below 100,000 by 1931. It would stay there through the Second World War.[211] More specifically, immigrants from Italy, who bore the brunt of the nativist fear of anarchism, hit a prewar high of 283,738 in 1914, rebounded after the war to 222,260 in 1921, but dropped to 6,203 in 1925. Broad-based immigration restrictions proved more popular by not singling out any particular type of person or belief and proved effective, as radicalization usually took place prior to emigration.[212] In the United States, the Sacco and Vanzetti episode—where two Italian anarchists were charged (probably wrongly) with murder during a botched robbery in 1920[213]—demonstrates how closely tied anti-immigrant and anti-anarchist views were. Thus, immigration restrictions were popular even if they were not effective.

While immigration restrictions were put into place, passports also became common. That guarding borders was not thought a necessity at the end of the long nineteenth century is evidenced by England's complaints about agents provocateurs. The problem was not that agents from Spain and Italy were violating English sovereignty, but that they were so ineffective as to be making the problem worse.[214] They were welcome if they proved effective. Universal passports—where everyone traveling across borders needed documentation, even during times of peace—began to be used during the First World War and were codified in the early 1920s. As Mark Salter explains, "The passport not only prompts questions of immigration, nationality, globalization, travel, and belonging but also connects the individual to the realm of the international."[215]

In addition to these claims, we can also make a case that anarchism and the fight against propaganda of the deed played a role. I argue that the establishment of the passport was not possible without the measures taken against anarchism. The role of anarchism and propaganda of the deed dates back to the first attempts to institute passports. They appear on the agenda of European states in the 1890s as a response to anarchism. In 1894, Germany and Italy attempted to require passports from travelers from Switzerland, which had a large anarchist exile community. The measure failed due to concerns about the tourism industry, but the idea was planted.[216] Britain created a "black book" of known anarchist names to check the passengers lists on incoming liners.[217] And of course, biometric techniques were necessary to the first passports.

However, after decades of free movement, universal passports were not popular. For instance, all participants in the 1920 and 1926 League of Nations conferences declared a desire to do away with passports.[218] Therefore, they needed to be sold, and propaganda of the deed became one of the chief justificatory devices. For instance, the United States justified the implementation of entry restrictions during peacetime as means of keeping out "the undesirable, the enemy of law and order, the breeder of revolution, and the advocate of anarchy" or "anyone advocating . . . or teaching anarchy,"[219] and the British denied passports to "suspects, anarchists, and bolsheviks."[220] Passports were also justified using anti-immigrant sentiment and the fear of alien crime,[221] of which anarchist hysteria was a part. For this reason, while conferences were often held with the goal of easing transport and movement, in practice they standardized restrictions.[222] On the other hand, Argentina resisted using passports or immigration controls into the 1930s and experienced one of the biggest waves of propaganda of the deed in the 1920s, most infamously a series of bombs by Italian emigrant Severino Di Giovanni.[223] Making the end of propaganda of the deed a part of the justificatory framework of the institution of passports created the rhetorical space for passports to be taken seriously while coercing opponents with claims of national security.[224]

Passports depended upon the databases and police practices developed to keep track of subversives, of which the propagandists were often considered the chief threat. The *portrait parlés* was basically the inverse of the passport. Both included physical descriptions of the subject and information on nationality and even family and personal history.[225] However, instead of being in the hands of the police, the document was now on the traveler. Internationally shared databases were also necessary for a passport system, echoing the databases and information sharing that grew in the 1900s to combat propaganda of the deed. They were among the first incarnation of "big data." Surveillance had moved from the police identifying criminals to citizens having to prove their identity, and their movements were tracked without police effort.

The advent of the passport and other measures such as postal-service restrictions put the final nail in the coffin of the free movement of people and ideas, which was so important to the propagandists. As detailed above, this happened in conjunction with the opening up of the public sphere to include anarchist and other radical ideas. These "creative" actions had the effect of drawing new boundaries around state authority and thus were an important instance of state transformation. It was neither more nor less: state agents gave up some control over the content of political discourse but gained control over the movement of people and goods across borders. It was at best a lateral move for liberal governance and did not represent the erosion of state authority. Redrawing boundaries changed authority qualitatively but not quantitatively.

Before concluding, I want to cover one final consequence for the wider revolutionary movement. In the years following World War I, communism overtook anarchism as the most influential revolutionary ideology. While Soviet support was a major factor,[226] communism was simply a better fit for the less globalized and more nationalized postwar international order. State agents began to take worker welfare more seriously, even setting up their own unions.[227] Nationalist and communist anti-colonial movements expropriated anarchist rhetoric and found recruiting easier.[228] Finally, the transnational flows that were the lifeblood of anarchism dried up.[229] The campaign against propaganda of the deed played an important role in these processes. While not explicitly state transformation, this does place the consequences of propaganda of the deed into the context of the larger revolutionary movement.

CONCLUSION

Propaganda of the deed was an episode of transnational violence that caused a crisis for the state, especially in Europe and North America, at the turn of the twentieth century through a series of assassinations, bombings, and other attacks. The rise of propaganda of the deed can be traced back to the way in which the macro-processes of globalization and industrialization made it hard for state agents to both facilitate open borders and control the public sphere. As a result, these boundaries and the practices that drew them were shattered. Propagandist attacks were hard to make sense of, they were hard to track, their political claims were illegible, and they challenged state legitimacy on claims of security. Early attempts to combat anarchism—repression, public trials and executions, agents provocateurs, exiling anarchists—proved either ineffective or counterproductive.

As a result, affected states needed to find creative solutions, developing new practices that drew new boundaries. Allowing anarchism in the public sphere by divorcing anarchist ideas from propagandists facilitated the rise of syndicalism, strengthening the labor movement and ultimately building the foundation of the welfare state. In this environment, potential Ravachols and Henrys would be funneled into the system. New surveillance techniques led to the creation of new databases, revolutionizing the role of police forces, state surveillance and, in the form of passports and immigration restrictions, closing down borders to free movement. The two broad solutions work together, and surveilling anarchists made it easier to allow nonviolent ones into the public sphere. Both are key components of the twentieth-century European and North American nation-state. Neither would have happened as they did without the campaign to defeat propaganda of the deed.

Of course, the story told here is not nearly as uniform or clean as described. Each state developed policies that were unique to them, and not every state drew each boundary effectively. Spain and Russia, for instance, did not learn these lessons, and their ruling regimes paid dearly as attacks continued and anarchists were a part of the revolutionary parties in bloody civil wars. Of course, in both cases, the anarchists ultimately lost. Franco's fascists crushed the anarchists in Spain, and their Bolshevik comrades crushed them in Russia. Spain and Russia, eventually, demonstrate an alternative answer to propaganda of the deed and anarchism more generally: totalitarianism. Totalitarians like the communists and fascists were better equipped to run repressive regimes in an age of nationalism than the ancien régime, because they claimed to act in the interests of the nation and the people. This gave them the freedom found in popular support and newly developed surveillance techniques to ferret out dissidents. In both cases (the liberal Western states and the new totalitarian ones), a shared crisis caused new boundaries to be drawn, which would have resounding effects on political life throughout the twentieth century.

4

AL-QAEDA, THE WAR ON TERROR, AND THE BOUNDARIES OF THE TWENTY-FIRST CENTURY

In chapter 1, I argued that al-Qaeda's political claims and transnational character proved a challenge to the state. As a result of its violence, the United States and other affected states redrew boundaries. Attacks on "terrorists" or "extremists" by unmanned aerial vehicles (UAVs or, more popularly, "drones"), and the U.S. National Security Agency's (NSA) and UK's Government Communications Headquarters' (GCHQ) programs to track, collect, and analyze data have made al-Qaeda legible, making it possible to defeat them. These led to new conceptions of "citizen" and "alien" that decouple the citizen from their body and into a series of data flows. National security is extended into new territorial and conceptual jurisdictions. New boundaries are drawn in the incorporeal spaces where data is collected. Borders change from sites of exclusion to sites of collection. These developments lead to the assertion of the state into processes in which it had previously been absent—laying ground for a nationalization of the internet—even as we see state agents struggle to stop flows of people, goods, and information. Thus, al-Qaeda and the ensuing War on Terror drove state transformation.

I want to start by discussing three alternative explanations for the rise of al-Qaeda, the response to it, and the consequences thereof. First, many scholars have focused on al-Qaeda's religion when discussing the threat that al-Qaeda posed to the state.[1] As discussed in the introduction, al-Qaeda's threat is not dependent upon religion. Many other Salafi, let alone Islamic, extremist groups have not developed the worldview or utilized the tactics of al-Qaeda. They are more similar to anti-globalization movements than, for instance, Hamas. That the major anti-globalization terrorist group is Islamic has as much to do with contingent factors (bin Laden and al-Zawahiri's innovations) and historical processes (the Soviet-Afghan War, Western intervention, and the need for oil) as with Islamic teachings.[2]

Another major thread is globalization. Like in chapter 4 with propaganda of the deed, globalization plays a role in both the rise of al-Qaeda and its demise. How this episode of violence unfolds is important to understanding the consequences of globalization. Connected to globalization would be claims that technology explains the rise of drones and surveillance, and that al-Qaeda is superfluous. This is a version of the rational-efficiency argument addressed in chapter 2. Obviously, technology needed to be developed for flying robots and data surveillance to be used. However, as will be shown below, both drones and data surveillance existed prior to 9/11, and it took 9/11 and the War on Terror for them to be accepted by the national security community and the public. Furthermore, the need to identify and kill jihadists led to further innovation.

Finally, there are claims that drones and data surveillance are merely the latest development in the continuation of the national security state. Ian Shaw argues that drones and data surveillance are part of a decades-long attempt at global empire.[3] Christopher Fuller sees drones as the culmination of counterterrorism policy goals created in the 1980s.[4] It is true that drones and data surveillance, while creative, did not come from nowhere—they have histories. Government officials backed them. Those histories and advocates are important parts of the story. However, it took 9/11 for many important figures to warm to these techniques. New techniques and practices mean transformed states. Drones and data collection might have happened eventually, but they did happen with al-Qaeda and 9/11. That matters in how the state develops. Clearly all three explanations play some role, but the specifics are filtered through the way in which the United States and others found creative solutions to the concrete problem of al-Qaeda.

The narrative unfolds in four parts. First, I will cover the emergence of al-Qaeda and its goals. Second, I will outline the boundaries challenged by al-Qaeda and the practices that drew them. Like in the previous two chapters, I will argue that these boundaries provided space for al-Qaeda to thrive. The next section will cover the process of shattering, focusing on material damage, illegibility, the crisis of legitimacy, and how failed attempts to defeat the threat, namely the wars in Iraq and Afghanistan, forced the United States to devise creative solutions. The penultimate section will cover the two counterterror innovations—targeted killing/signature strikes and data surveillance—that are reinscribing the state. This section will spend some time dealing with the effectiveness of these measures to lay the groundwork for claiming that they have become practices and therefore draw boundaries. Even more importantly, there is a perception that drones and data are effective and therefore will persist as options moving forward. Unlike in the other two cases, the process of redrawing boundaries as a result of the War on Terror is still underway. For this reason, the end of this chapter is about forecasting possible futures.

This chapter draws on published government documents, news reports—including the *Guardian*'s 2013 archive of Edward Snowden reveals—and twenty-two interviews I conducted with national security professionals, think-tank experts, and privacy advocates. The interviews were very open, and topics varied across interviewees depending on their particular expertise and experience. There were a few objectives for the interviews. First, I wanted to gauge reaction to 9/11 and attempt to recreate what was happening in the national security world in its aftermath. Second, I wanted help in recreating the chronology of events. Third, I wanted to get reactions on the development, utility, and consequences of both targeted killings and data surveillance. The interviews provided a trove of background information that made this narrative possible.

AL-QAEDA'S POLITICS

Since al-Qaeda is a group driven by a particular interpretation of Islam, scholars have tried to gain insight into it through the Koran, Salafism, Wahhabism, and the writings of Ibn Taymiyyah and Sayyid Qutb (among others).[5] However, this does not identify what made al-Qaeda circa 2001 unique and threatening. Much of Qutb's writing was about creating a local community,[6] and his political actions targeted the Egyptian state. The organization founded in his image, the Muslim Brotherhood, is not really a "terrorist" organization. Probably the most famous violent arm of the Muslim Brotherhood, Hamas in Palestine, is tied to a state project. Little about Islam or Salafism leads one to understand al-Qaeda and the threat it has posed. The group developed out of the Afghan-Soviet War of the 1980s under the leadership of the son of a wealthy Saudi family, Osama bin Laden. Following the war, in which it got weapons, infrastructure, and other aid from the United States, it believed it had defeated the stronger superpower and wanted to take on the weaker one. Throughout its existence, it has partaken in the poppy trade, been a part of local political struggles, and even enjoyed state sponsorship from the Taliban. Yet, none of these actions really define it, as its major goals lie outside the realm of local politics and crime.

So what did al-Qaeda want circa 2001?[7] It has been said that they were looking to return to a tenth-century caliphate,[8] to institute Sharia across the world[9] or at least in the lands that belong to Islam, to get the United States out of the Middle East,[10] to end democracy and freedom as we know it,[11] and that 9/11 was a symbolic gesture to awaken the Umma.[12] Al-Qaeda have been accused of nihilism[13] and the intention of doing harm to, or even starting a war with, the United States,[14] and of looking for revenge.[15] Some feel that their goals were utopian and unrealistic: "They want to create a vacuum into which they think goodness and light will suddenly pour."[16] They were "incomprehensible."[17] A common media trope framed the fight as modern vs. premodern, enlightened vs. medieval.[18] Others argue al-Qaeda was a creature of modernity or postmodernity.[19] This was recognized by the 9/11 Commission report, whose authors mused that al-Qaeda was "more globalized than we were."[20]

Historian Faisal Devji argues that al-Qaeda's jihad was not political but ethical or moral.[21] Al-Qaeda created a global landscape that works beyond geography, cause and effect, "historical ideas and identities," and ultimately the state itself. Devji argues that "Osama bin Laden is indiscriminate in his invocation of domestic and foreign causes for the attacks of 9/11, thus erasing any distinction between the two and operating instead at a purely global level."[22] Cian O'Driscoll points out that al-Qaeda's members' "biographies often relate to a disdain for national boundaries ... [with] little connection with their homelands."[23] Further, Devji claims that the choice to attack the U.S. embassies in Tunisia and Kenya in 1998 "had nothing to do with their political or military status ... it depended on the presence of local, willing agents in the region."[24] Al-Qaeda was "not a territory-occupying organization."[25]

Bin Laden's rhetoric on Saudi Arabia and Palestine demonstrates this point. While al-Qaeda's leadership were angered by the presence of American military bases near the holy land in Saudi Arabia, these were symptoms of the larger problem: the global dominance of the secular, liberal state. Al-Qaeda have never really formed a localized insurgency to attack said bases. Similarly, bin Laden said that he would like to see Palestine "completely liberated and returned to Islamic sovereignty."[26] However, instead of a driving concern, it is often a recruiting tactic.[27] Bin Laden's number two and current al-Qaeda leader Ayman al-Zawahiri claims that "Palestine is the cause that has been firing up the feelings of the Muslim nation from Morocco to Indonesia. . . . In addition, it is a rallying point for all Arabs, be they believers or non-believers, good or evil."[28] Similar dynamics were also present when al-Qaeda has intervened in local struggles from Chechnya to the Maghreb to the Philippines.[29]

Devji's contention that al-Qaeda's goals were metaphysical, lying outside the realm of politics, is half-right. Al-Qaeda is quite political, only they are not recognized as such by state agents unable to make sense of al-Qaeda's claims on their own terms. We can see the distinction between al-Qaeda and, for instance, a Palestinian cause drawing on the same ideological foundation that was "finally legitimized within an order of intentionality dedicated to the establishment of a national state."[30] Al-Qaeda desired freedom, justice, wealth, and power, only "it wants them on its own terms," to "define the terms of global social relations outside the language of state and citizenship."[31] It is "envisioning a whole new map."[32] If al-Qaeda was attempting to field a battle on a metaphysical plane where boundaries as we know them are nonexistent, even engaging in the battle would be perilous for the state. According to Devji, the sphere of action is one occupied by Muslims, Christians, and Jews. There is to be no distinction, no boundary.[33] What must happen is for state agents to redraw boundaries, to develop new practices that can make al-Qaeda a "legible" problem. Devji is not the only one to notice this dynamic. Ayse Zarakol argues that al-Qaeda was "a direct threat to the international system."[34] Ronald Krebs and Jennifer Lobasz argue that al-Qaeda "threatens the very logic of inside/outside that sustains the modern nation-state."[35]

AL-QAEDA AND THE BOUNDARIES OF THE LATE TWENTIETH-CENTURY STATE

To begin to understand this threat, we need to look at the boundaries al-Qaeda's actions have shattered. These three boundaries are: (1) a world of bounded polities where all threats are narrated to have a local origin, (2) a legal, practical, and institutional boundary between domestic and international surveillance, and (3) borders as sites of exclusion. These boundaries made it harder to perceive the threat al-Qaeda posed to the United States and global order more generally, and it also hindered the response. This was exacerbated by the interplay between these boundaries and globalization. Globalization, and the technology behind it, made it harder to separate domestic from international or to use borders to exclude threats, and they made possible threats that are not tied to local struggles. Thus, al-Qaeda was able to take advantage of these boundaries to attack the United States. Each boundary will be taken in turn.

We start with the idea that all threats, even those labeled "transnational," emanate from local disputes, claims, oppression, etc. The United States has long dealt with transnational and international actors, but they could be interpreted as being rooted in local or national struggles. Anti-colonial, communist, and anti-communist movements were transnational, but they had strong national elements and could be engaged as such. The same goes for al-Qaeda in Afghanistan during the 1980s. The concept of the "West" developed after World War II was civilizational,[36] but the state system was foundational to the narrative and it was instituted by state centered institutions like NATO. All of these transnational movements had the state at their center. But al-Qaeda circa 2001 was so divorced from territory and nationality that it could not be treated this way.

At the turn of the twenty-first century, the term "transnational" often referred to the operations of a group—do they attack across borders? are they a network?—rather than their politics. Looking at recent history, this made sense. Hezbollah's attack on U.S. marine barracks in 1983 was legible because it emanated from the Lebanese Civil War. To John Poindexter, Ronald Reagan's national security advisor, "terrorism was a foreign problem."[37] Similar patterns develop for groups like Hamas and the Irish Republican Army, or the attacks backed by the Libyan government. Terrorism was believed to be largely state sponsored,[38] and the resulting threats "were things you managed via diplomacy."[39]

It was believed that al-Qaeda was no different, even if its claims were not fully understood. Bin Laden was not an unknown. The World Trade Center bombing of 1993, the attacks on U.S. embassies in Tunisia and Kenya, and the attack on the USS *Cole* all got U.S. attention. Knowledge of al-Qaeda was quite common in certain circles of the Clinton administration, especially around Richard Clarke, the National Security Council's (NSC) director of counterterrorism. However, in a 1995 speech, President Bill Clinton placed jihadist terrorism in the same category as state collapse and internal warfare in Haiti and Yugoslavia.[40] At the center of these actions is a conception of politics that is synonymous with the state and its local claims to authority.[41] There was little room to imagine politics outside of *the* state. Thus, it becomes a conceptual boundary delineating the political. The practices constructing this boundary may seem tautological: only threats connected to states were on the radar of policy makers and those working in national security. It had been this way for decades.

Many prominent national security people refused to take al-Qaeda seriously. Clarke commented, "I think if you ask most terrorism experts in the mid-1990s, 'Name the major terrorist organizations that might be a threat to the United States,' they would have said Hezbollah, which had a relationship with Iran. They would have said Hamas, which is a Palestinian group. Most people would not have said al-Qaeda. Most people wouldn't have known that there was an al-Qaeda."[42] Daniel Benjamin, who worked under Clarke, asserted that it was "a bridge too far"[43] for many departments because "Iran remained the counterterrorism community's top concern."[44] Chris Kojm claimed that al-Qaeda were not seen as a global player even following the 1998 embassy attacks.[45] The Bush administration was warned of the threat by Clarke when they took office.[46] Attempts to draw attention to the group were often dismissed. After retaliatory actions following the embassy attacks, Clinton was mocked for trying to "wag the dog"[47] to refocus attention away from his sex scandal. CIA director George Tenet was ridiculed for trying to drum up al-Qaeda's threat in the late 1990s. As one policymaker explained to me, "Zero Americans died from international terrorism in 1999. So make a budget case for why we should dramatically increase spending at the end of 1999."[48]

This even continued after the 9/11 attacks. To many officials, 9/11 was not a strategic surprise but a tactical surprise at a larger scale than expected.[49] Clarke sent a memo on September 4, 2001, to NSC director Condoleezza Rice that warned of "hundreds of American" deaths, an order of magnitude less than the attacks one week later.[50] However, as Bush administration official Phillip Zelikow stated, it took many officials "some time [to understand 9/11]. You notice that the almost immediate reaction of [Defense Secretary Donald] Rumsfeld and [Deputy Secretary of Defense Paul] Wolfowitz is to assume that this is somehow a state act and wonder whether Iran or Iraq might somehow be responsible for this."[51] The 9/11 attacks were not enough to shatter boundaries; old conceptual maps needed to be proven useless.

This boundary can be viewed as a baseline assumption for each of the next two. Pre-9/11, there was a clear distinction between domestic and international intelligence. This boundary was created by the following practices: (1) no sustained cooperation and intelligence sharing between those working in international and domestic agencies and (2) a separation for the protection of U.S. citizens from the Central Intelligence Agency (CIA) and the NSA. These led to stovepiping and prevented the intelligence gathering and analysis developed as a response to 9/11.[52] The failed project Able Danger demonstrates this effect. During the 1990s, Eric Kleinsmith, the head of the Information Defense Agency (IDA), made waves within the Defense Department by collecting open-source internet data and placing it in three-dimensional maps that could show hotspots of terrorist activities. However, data he collected on U.S. persons could be held only for ninety days before being discarded—not enough time for proper assessment. In addition, his data-collection efforts pulled up sensitive information not just on suspected foreign terrorists but also on U.S. citizens, including Defense Secretary William Cohen and future Secretary of State Condoleezza Rice. He ended up having to ditch the project altogether.[53] After his program shut down, it shifted to the consulting firm Raytheon, only to be shut down again on the same premises.[54] The lines between domestic and international intelligence were drawn in such a way as to make such surveillance practically impossible.

The FBI, who controlled a lot of domestic intelligence, needed warrants to gather information and focused on solving crimes rather than preventing them. The CIA and NSA did not need warrants for gathering information on non-U.S. persons and focused on prevention. As one former NSA official told me, "Nobody in the government at that time [prior to 9/11] had clear authority for what happens when one side is foreign and one side is domestic."[55] The lines between crime (domestic intelligence) and security (international intelligence) were drawn by the idea that politics was connected to nation-states, and its institutionalization made it difficult to connect relevant information.[56] As Lee Hamilton told me, "The law itself creates this difference."[57] However, there were, and still are, good reasons for the distinction, as "cordoning off of data is a protection mechanism for civil rights."[58] This argument is not one of folly but instead of how threats were recognized and dealt with.

Different spheres of intelligence demonstrated a belief that threats to national security came from outside of borders, the third boundary. Practices such as policing borders, border checks, the use of passports, and cargo inspections were meant to keep undesirable goods, peoples, and ideas from entering the country. For instance, NSA cryptological mathematician Michael Wertheimer's surprise was not at the attack but that the attackers had "been here all along ... plotting their attack within miles of the NSA's headquarters in Ft. Mead, Maryland."[59] He told me, "I was hired to do a job and I didn't do that job ... it was a blind spot."[60] As I establish in the last chapter, this has not always been the case. At the turn of the twentieth century, borders demarcated sovereign holdings, and the movements of the lower classes were deemed unimportant. Propaganda of the deed changed this. Regulation happened at the border, now a site of exclusion meant to stop certain people or goods from entering. Almost a century later, al-Qaeda shattered this boundary.

Bounding all threats into local struggles, boundaries between international and domestic intelligence, and borders as sites of exclusion were all in tension with newly developing global processes. Al-Qaeda utilized international news media to proselytize its attacks[61] and the internet to maintain a decentralized network for communicating propaganda and technical knowledge. They also took advantage of migration patterns and global travel to undertake attacks across the globe. They left their targets, including the United States, as "prisoners of the past."[62] This is similar to how propagandists were able to use mass media and new printing technology to publicize ideas and events, and how pirates took advantage of the flow of goods across the Atlantic. Habituated boundaries combined with major processes created the space for transnational violence to thrive and shatter those boundaries.

SHATTERING: "TODAY . . . OUR WAY OF LIFE, OUR VERY FREEDOM CAME UNDER ATTACK"

In addition to the 9/11 attacks, which killed 2,996 people in New York, Virginia, and rural Pennsylvania, the al-Qaeda network has been prolific. Attacks prior to 9/11 included the bombing of a Yemeni hotel, the World Trade Center, the U.S. embassies in Kenya and Tunisia, the Khobar Towers in Saudi Arabia, and the USS *Cole*.[63] In the years following 9/11, al-Qaeda have been linked with a series of bombings across the Muslim world, in Casablanca, Amman, Istanbul, Riyadh, Manila, Jakarta, and two in Bali, in addition to the assassination of Pakistani prime minister Benazir Bhutto in 2007.[64] During this time, al-Qaeda was also able to carry out high-casualty attacks in Madrid in 2004, London in 2005, and Paris in 2015. Al-Qaeda also inspired attacks by those with little to no formal connections to the organization, such as the 2013 Patriots' Day attack in Boston discussed in the introduction. Failed schemes— including the Bojinka plot to hijack twelve transpacific planes heading to the United States, an attempt to run a plane into the Eiffel Tower,[65] an attempt to detonate explosives hidden in shoes,[66] and the Christmas Day bombing[67]—add to the hysteria. Al-Qaeda has also taken part in local struggles in the Sudan, Somalia, Afghanistan, Chechnya, Bosnia, Yemen, Iraq, and Syria, among others.

DECLARING A WAR ON TERROR

That said, al-Qaeda shattered boundaries because they were narrated as a crisis. They were illegible, and they created a crisis of legitimacy. These are woven together and will be dealt with concurrently through the lens of U.S. rhetoric against al-Qaeda. Before doing this, I want to make two points about illegibility referring to what I have already discussed. First, al-Qaeda's metaphysical politics made little to no sense to policy makers stuck in a state-centric world. In fact, it still does not. This is a big reason why al-Qaeda was illegible for so long. Second, that al-Qaeda shares an intellectual and ideological tradition with so many familiar state-based movements may have exacerbated this problem. It was easy to see political Islam and assume something attached to the Muslim Brotherhood, Iran, Hezbollah, Palestine, or another local dispute. Making sense of al-Qaeda required not only novel thinking about politics but disconnecting political Islam from the state.

That the United States could not make sense of al-Qaeda and felt its legitimacy threatened is reflected in its rhetoric, which focused on al-Qaeda as a threat to the state. Krebs and Lobasz note that "the attacks of September 11 were, according to the dominant discourse, attacks on the nation-state, but this should hardly be treated as unproblematic or natural. These events could have been represented differently: for example, as attacks on the central symbols of the neoliberal empire, as crimes against humanity, or as crimes against innocents."[68]

That the threat posed by al-Qaeda was treated as different to any other in U.S. history was apparent in President George W. Bush's first public remarks following 9/11: "Today, our fellow citizens, our way of life, our very freedom came under attack in a series of deliberate and deadly terrorist acts."[69] Notice that the attack is not on the United States or upon those living in New York City or Washington, DC, or working at the World Trade Center or the Pentagon. It is against a "way of life" and "freedom," concepts that are manifest by, but larger than, the state. Just nine days later, this sentiment was displayed in greater detail in a speech to Congress announcing the War on Terror: "They hate our freedoms—our freedom of religion, our freedom of speech, our freedom to vote and assemble and disagree with each other. . . . This is the world's fight. This is civilization's fight. This is the fight of all who believe in progress and pluralism, tolerance and freedom."[70]

While there is no mention of the state itself as an institution under attack, it has been framed in such a way that core values and institutions are at risk. Remember that the pirates of the golden age attacked "god, country, and labor," and the propagandists were against "institutions and social relations." In each case, what was attacked happened to be the very ideals upon which the state was legitimated. Hence, in recognizing and creating a threat to these values, there is an implicit recognition of the state's legitimacy being under attack.

The threat was novel. Deputy Secretary of State Richard Armitage claimed that 9/11 created a "whole new world."[71] Deputy Secretary of Defense Paul Wolfowitz claimed that "the old approach to terrorism was not acceptable any longer."[72] In June of 2002, Bush stated that deterrence "means nothing against shadowy terrorist networks with no nation or citizens to defend."[73] The 2002 National Security Strategy (NSS) claimed new strategies were needed to combat a "shadowy network."[74] In 2006, Bush reiterated this point, with strong parallels to rhetoric on propaganda of the deed: "The terrorists who declared war on America represent no nation. They defend no territory. And they wear no uniform. They do not mass armies on borders or flotillas of warships on the high seas. They operate in the shadows of society. They send small teams of operatives to infiltrate free nations. They live quietly among their victims. They conspire in secret. And then they strike without warning."[75]

Bush's predecessor, Bill Clinton, had framed terrorism similarly. In his remarks following the bombing of the Alfred P. Murrah Federal Building in Oklahoma City in 1995, Clinton remarked that it was undertaken by "forces that threaten our common peace, our freedom, our way of life."[76] Following U.S. retaliation for the embassy attacks in Kenya and Tunisia, he stated that "America is and will remain a target of terrorists precisely . . . because we act to advance peace, democracy, and basic human values." At stake was the "ongoing struggle between freedom and fanaticism."[77]

The nascent narrative on terrorism developed in the 1990s recognized the same dangers and used many of the same tropes as Bush's rhetoric in the wake of 9/11, yet there was no crisis. What solidified the crisis was the scale of 9/11, yes, but also the subsequent decision to respond with the War on Terror. Nine days after the attacks, President Bush declared the War on Terror and foreshadowed its expansive reach: "Our war on terror begins with Al Qaeda, but it does not end there. It will not end until every terrorist group of global reach has been found, stopped, and defeated."[78] As Krebs opines, the War on Terror "not only placed that day's horrific events in a meaningful context, but also set the terms of national security debate in the United States for the next decade."[79] There are three parts of this proclamation worth discussing here: the use of the term "war," the expansiveness of the enterprise, and the secrecy of its conduct.

By casting counterterrorism as part of a war, terrorism was identified as the defining national security issue of the twenty-first century. Tenet sent out a memo five days after the attacks, entitled "We're at War," in which he proclaimed that the CIA "must give people the authority to do things they might not ordinarily be able to do.... If there is some bureaucratic hurdle, leap it."[80] Similarly, John Poindexter, the new head of the Office of Information Awareness at the Defense Advanced Research Projects Agency (DARPA), remarked in its aftermath that "this is not business as usual, we must put introduction of new technology on a wartime basis."[81] This use of the term "war" reflects the seriousness of the crisis and places it alongside the other cases explored in this study.

Buoyed by the rhetoric of a whole new world, the expansiveness of the War on Terror was a choice that would have far-reaching consequences.[82] The War on Terror[83] broadened the fight from al-Qaeda to all terror, terrorism, and terrorists.[84] One year after the attacks, the 2002 NSS proclaimed the War on Terror "a global enterprise of uncertain duration."[85] One critic, calling it a "grossly manipulative piece of salesmanship," argued that "it would be impossible to define any way of there being an end."[86] It included not just the United States and its traditional allies, but even potential rivals such as Russia and China. It has changed the calculus of local struggles, such as in the Philippines.[87] As much as the "coalition of the willing" and talk of "new" and "old" Europe amongst Bush administration officials are highlighted, the War on Terror has proven to be a multilateral undertaking,[88] signifying the seriousness of the threat and the role of collusion in state transformation.

Finally, these two trends combined to throw a veil of secrecy over everything remotely related to national security. Essentially, "Calling the reaction to al Qaeda's 9/11 attack a 'war' ensured that the government could justify classifying everything associated with running it."[89] Privacy advocate Lee Tien concurs: "It is as if in order to mobilize for the War on Terror you have to spread this shroud of secrecy over more and more of the government."[90] The major impact of secrecy for our purposes is that it belies the creation of a crisis. If, as Mathew Levitt put it, "we won't be successful in today's world if we don't keep secrets,"[91] then the United States and its allies believe that al-Qaeda was so important that it had to keep its information hidden from the public.

FAILED STRATEGIES IN THE WAR ON TERROR

Not only did contemporary boundaries mask the threat that al-Qaeda posed and the attempts to make sense of it, leading to the War on Terror narrative, but it also shaped and ultimately limited early attempts to defeat it. Like the campaigns against the golden-age pirates and the anarchist terrorists, the early stages of the War on Terror were marked by ineffective and counterproductive strategies tied to previous boundaries: closing down borders, detaining and torturing suspects in black sites, and regime-change wars. First, however, it is worth briefly considering calling the effort a "war." The war frame certainly led to the ill-advised policies listed above, and its breadth unnecessarily stretched U.S. capabilities to the limit while taking the focus off al-Qaeda. Secrecy reduced trust in the government and was a major reason for the backlash following Edward Snowden's revelations.[92] It has been rightly criticized as morally and democratically problematic. Obama administration veterans I interviewed reminded me that the administration never used the term.[93] Yet, for as much of a mistake as it was, the War on Terror also created space for the successful policies outlined in the next section.

Border exclusion was enhanced through stricter airline security checks undertaken by the Transportation Security Administration (TSA) and by increasing random inspections of shipping containers. Both may (or may not) have proven useful in the wider War on Terror, but they were attempts to reinforce the boundaries that made al-Qaeda impossible to combat. Consequently, they made little impact on attempts to make sense of and defeat al-Qaeda. The enactment of the Patriot Act had a similar immediate effect, though its ultimate significance lies with future interpretations of surveillance powers in the bill.[94] These measures were more ineffective than counterproductive.

More counterproductive were the decisions to detain suspects in black sites run by the Joint Special Operations Command (JSOC) and CIA that regularly tortured prisoners.[95] This not only violated domestic norms but harmed the United States' international standing in ways still not repaired. Additionally, torture has a long history of ineffectiveness. This echoes attempts to territorially bound threats, with one of the biggest challenges being finding sites and keeping them secret in the digital age. Black sites could also be seen as a misguided attempt at creating a boundless empire. Interestingly, both the CIA and the Obama administration political team decided to move to targeted killing and signature strikes, because killing suspects was cleaner and less controversial than detaining them.[96] Failure led to creative action.

The most visible early response came from the belief that terrorism was caused by bad governments, an extension of the idea that threats emanate from local struggles.[97] This is the logic that brought the United States into wars in Iraq and Afghanistan. There was a clear tactical reason, and possible revenge motive, for going into Afghanistan: Taliban leader Muhammad Omar was providing shelter to bin Laden, al Zawahiri, and other core al-Qaeda figures. The war lasted two decades as the United States pulled out in August 2021. The conflict led to over 4,902 coalition fatalities[98] and many more local ones and still no stable Afghan government. However, while the invasion of Afghanistan could be interpreted as a necessary undertaking[99] that opened space for drone operations,[100] bin Laden's death, the crippling of the core of al-Qaeda, and the invasion of Iraq cannot. Even as the war ended up costing almost 4,500 American and over 100,000 Iraqi lives,[101] few links with al-Qaeda have been found. In fact, al-Qaeda became more active in the country after the invasion.

My interviewees differed in their opinions on the importance of 9/11 to the Iraq War. Some saw the two as unconnected. Pillar said that it was "something they [the administration] wanted to do anyway."[102] Talk of a reinvasion of Iraq was common in certain Republican national security circles during the 1990s.[103] One administration official remarked that internal debates on Iraq were "about not whether but when."[104] Zelikow argued that the narrative of Iraq was "substantially different from the narrative of the War on Terror."[105] However, others saw them as connected. John Poindexter told me that "it was part of the bigger picture in the War on Terror," and that "Saddam Hussein was supporting terrorists."[106] Still others were skeptical of a connection but saw causation. Benjamin argued that "the attacks of 9/11 spawned a kind of vacuum in national security thinking about what to do next that led to . . . the invasion of Iraq."[107] Zelikow pointed out that the "political climates [for Iraq and the War on Terror] are insoluble."[108]

Administration rhetoric tied the Iraq War into the War on Terror. Defense Secretary Donald Rumsfeld testified before the U.S. Senate in 2002 on Iraq: "Last week we commemorated the one-year anniversary of the most devastating attack our nation has ever experienced, more than 3,000 people killed in a single day. And today I want to discuss the task of preventing even more devastating attacks, attacks that could kill not thousands but potentially tens of thousands of our fellow citizens."[109]

Wolfowitz listed the reasons for the war as follows: "One is weapons of mass destruction, the second is support for terrorism, the third is the criminal treatment of the Iraqi people. Actually I guess you could say there's a fourth overriding one which is the connection between the first two."[110] Privately, he complained that the reason many were not tying Saddam to al-Qaeda was a "failure of imagination."[111] The war became part of a larger counterterrorism strategy built around a "community of democracies." As stated in the 2006 NSS, "Free governments are accountable to their people, govern their territory effectively, and pursue economic and political policies that benefit their citizens. Free governments do not oppress their people or attack other free nations. Peace and international stability are most reliably built on a foundation of freedom."[112] Even if the real reason for the war had little to do with al-Qaeda,[113] Iraq was justified through the War on Terror, sold as part of a larger "solution" to the crisis whereby bad states made terrorists. The dominant narrative became al-Qaeda vs. democracy and freedom; freedom came from states, and the only way to make the world safe for American ideals was to spread those ideals, with force if necessary.

REINSCRIBING: "THE ROBOT IS OUR ANSWER TO THE SUICIDE BOMBER"

It was with the failure of black sites, border checks, and regime-change wars that the shattering was completed and new ideas could take hold at the highest levels. The rest of this chapter will look at two of those new ideas: targeted killings and bulk data collection. I will provide some background on them, assess their "usefulness" in an attempt to argue that they are here to stay, and make some conjectures about the boundaries that targeted killings and bulk data collection are drawing around citizenship and state authority. We start with targeted killing and the technology that has been most associated with it: UAVs, or drones.

DRONE ATTACKS

The United States runs three drone programs.[114] The first is run by the U.S. Air Force and was in battle theatres in Iraq, Afghanistan, and Libya.[115] The second is run by the JSOC[116] and is more irregular, given freedom to "find, fix, and finish" those the United States deems terrorists. The third is the more regular program run by the CIA. There are two types of attacks under discussion. Targeted killings are attacks on specifically identified leaders and other important persons. Signature strikes are attacks based on patterns of behavior—frequent contacts, locations, buying patterns, and so on. The two terms bring with them different problems, though most of the problems of targeted killings are also present in signature strikes. For the rest of this chapter, I will refer to them as drone attacks when speaking globally but be more specific when warranted.

Drone attacks began under the Bush administration as CIA programs started in Yemen in 2002 and Pakistan in 2004. But the Obama administration took on "the more targeted, more kinetic operations, especially with drones . . . focusing on decapitation of terrorist groups."[117] The Bush administration oversaw 48 drone attacks in Pakistan between 2005 and 2009, while the Obama administration oversaw 52 strikes in 2009, followed by 122, 73, and 48 in 2010, 2011, and 2012, respectively.[118] That means that in each of his first four years in office, Barack Obama saw more drone attacks in Pakistan than his predecessor did in his last four years combined.[119] While the drone campaigns in Pakistan and Afghanistan have tailed off since 2012, those in Yemen and Somalia have picked up. There have been forty strikes in Somalia through 2016 targeting the al-Qaeda–affiliated al-Shabaab. In addition, there have been 169 drone strikes targeting al-Qaeda in the Arabian Peninsula. The Obama administration oversaw another 80 drone and 15 traditional air strikes in Yemen through 2015.[120] Drone strikes have killed 35 known al-Qaeda leaders in Yemen and 58 in Pakistan as of 2013, and, according to the New American Foundation, anywhere from 3,200 to 4,700 militants through

June 2017.¹²¹ Targeted killings have also occurred in Iraq and Syria, though these can be hard to detach from traditional theaters of war. Drone bases have proliferated over this period, though placements have been fluid. ¹²² There have been public outcries against drone bases, but these bases are more popular amongst local leaders. For instance, Pakistani general Ashfaq Kayani asked the United States for "continuous predator coverage" of the federally administrated tribal areas, even as he publicly assailed the program as "unjustified and intolerable."¹²³

While Predator and Reaper drones have become synonymous with the War on Terror, the history of drones predates 9/11. Budgeting and research for them in the United States started in the 1970s, and in 1986 drone attacks were envisioned as part of the Eagle program by Reagan administration officials. In the 1990s, GNAT 750 drones and early versions of the Predator drone were used to survey al-Qaeda in Afghanistan. Drones were also used for surveillance in the 1999 Kosovo air raids.¹²⁴ Richard Clarke pushed for the installation of a program using Predator drones armed with Hellfire missiles in counterterror operations prior to 9/11.¹²⁵ Of course, there was resistance. CIA director George Tenet thought it would be a "terrible mistake if the CIA fired the weapon."¹²⁶ James Pavitt, deputy director of operations at the CIA, asked, "Why would I want to do this?"¹²⁷ In July of 2001, Martin Indyk, the U.S. ambassador to Israel, publicly called his host country out for the targeted killings of Hamas officials, saying, "They are extrajudicial killings, we do not support that."¹²⁸ As Rob Finkelstein, president of Robotic Technology, Inc., complained, the lack of implementation over the past twenty years was due to "friggin brain dead bureaucrats who have no vision.... The sad thing is that many useful systems could have been fielded years ago [saving many lives]"¹²⁹ Following 9/11, this turned quickly. It was the "war" in the War on Terror that undergirded legal arguments about targeted killings.¹³⁰ As one U.S. researcher put it, "The robot is our answer to the suicide bomber."¹³¹

DATA SURVEILLANCE

The NSA bulk data-collection program is built on metadata. This is data about location, time, contact, etc., but not content. While for telephony data these distinctions are meant to protect users, for most internet data said distinction is meaningless. Knowing what sites have been visited when is more revealing than sites' public content. The NSA has worked in conjunction with tech companies to collect data in two different ways. First, there are "upstream" collections, where the NSA gains access to private fiber optic cables. This is done through a series of partnerships, such as FAIRVIEW and STORMBREW, where the NSA partners with a particular company.[132] Second, there is the PRISM program, where the NSA gains access to the servers of these companies.[133] There is evidence that the NSA has paid companies for compliance costs,[134] while Microsoft is alleged to have provided the NSA with access to new versions of Microsoft Outlook.[135] In the UK, GCHQ has been working with companies such as BT and Vodafone.[136] Other companies have begun to report such requests,[137] though some, like Apple, deny compliance despite evidence to the contrary.[138]

The NSA uses four legal tools for collection. The Foreign Intelligence Surveillance Act (FISA) 702—passed in 2008—allows for the collection of information of non-U.S. persons outside the United States. It must use the FISA Court established in 1978 to deal with matters of time-sensitive intelligence. Section 215 of the 2001 Patriot Act allows for bulk data collection in connection with a FISA court ruling.[139] Executive Order (EO) 12333, signed in 1981, allows for the collection, retention, and distribution of intelligence gathered in international spying and domestic law breaking. It has been bolstered by EOs 13355 (2004) and 13470 (2008). Finally, the Supreme Court ruled in *Smith v. Maryland* in 1979 (and antecedent cases) that the collection of phone-company data belongs to the company, not the individual.[140] Thus, corporate data collection has been instrumental in NSA programs.[141]

There are still legal obstacles to collection and use. Telephony data can be collected and stored only so long as one end of a conversation is outside the United States. Warrants are necessary to investigate internet searches and communications within the United States.[142] The U.S. Congress passed a law in 2015 that restricted the telephony program,[143] and there have been many court challenges. It should be noted, however, that section 215 was reupped in 2015 until 2019. To get around some of these constraints, the NSA has pushed boundaries. One example is the "three-hops" rule. The NSA starts with a number and can then look at the number of anyone connected to it within three degrees of separation.[144] When using internet data, analysts are given discretion and are warned not to "ask about or speculate on sources or methods."[145] If there is reason to think that the data is domestic, after capture the analyst is allowed to look to confirm. In addition, FISA rulings allow the NSA to keep such data for as long as it keeps international data.[146] Another potential end run is cooperation with allies.[147] The United States has given GCHQ $100 million for unknown "deliverables,"[148] since there are fewer restrictions for data collection in the UK.[149] France has a comparable program.[150] The NSA claims that it has worked in partnership with 30+ countries but maintains that it does not ask for "what the NSA is itself prohibited by law from doing."[151] In former CIA and NSA head Michael Hayden's words, "I will play in fair territory. But there will be chalk dust on my cleats."[152]

Much like the drone programs, data-collection systems have existed for some time. H. G. Wells introduced the idea in his 1938 book *World Brain*.[153] Former U.S. secretary of defense Robert McNamara attempted to design a data-collection system called IRIS in the early 1980s.[154] Poindexter started to develop basic systems as a response to the 1983 bombing of U.S. barracks in Lebanon by Hezbollah.[155] However, he "could not get the defense department interested."[156] In addition to project Able Danger, the United States also had a data system named Carnivore prior to 9/11.[157] Multiple sources confirmed that data collection had begun in the late 1990s,[158] but, as Kleinsmith and his colleagues discovered, it never got the full funding or attention its adherents thought necessary.

These barriers melted away after 9/11. The attack "obviously provided the rationale for the ramping up of increased surveillance. . . . It becomes easier to sell that we are doing that after 9/11."[159] It also made it easier to ask for assistance from telecommunications companies: "In 2002 or 2003 . . . it was easier for the NSA to go to the companies here in the States and say, 'This is a high national priority, we strongly want you to cooperate.' You get the cooperation."[160] It wasn't just public or corporate willingness. Government attitudes changed as a result of 9/11 and the War on Terror. Shoshana Zuboff argues that "in the course of a few days [after 9/11] the concern shifted from 'How do we regulate these companies that are violating privacy norms and rights' to 'How do we nurture and protect these companies so they can collect data for us?'"[161] Wertheimer recalls thinking, "I did not fight harder for that [data]. . . . I resolved then that I would not allow my conscience to be dictated by experts, if I thought something was wrong, I would fight for it."[162] It is entirely possible that large-scale data collection was something that would have happened without al-Qaeda, but the reason it did happen was al-Qaeda, and the fight against terrorism drove innovation.

This can be seen in the development of the Total Information Awareness (TIA) programs under John Poindexter.[163] In 1996, Poindexter was at DARPA, developing a program called Genoa meant to model terrorist activity using open-source data. He heard of the 9/11 attacks on his way to work and immediately called DARPA director Tony Tether to pitch "a Manhattan Project to combat terrorism." The TIA program moved Genoa out of the laboratory and worked with real data. The idea was to use red teams—a simulated competitor that provides security feedback from the competitor's perspective—to find patterns and then trace them in the real world. Calling 9/11 "significant" in the development of TIA, Poindexter explained, "When they realized that with technology we could begin to inverse that curve [to a bell curve], they began to see the value of it."[164] Genoa received $60 million from DARPA between 1996 and 2001, but TIA received $150 million in 2002 alone. In 2001, President Bush decided that the collection of metadata was constitutional.[165] This allowed NSA director Hayden to collect correspondence with at least one foreign person to create the BAG, or the "Big-Ass Graph." The BAG was a large network-analysis chart that demonstrated linkages between persons of interest (widely understood). This system was eventually merged with TIA to create the programs leaked by Edward Snowden in the summer of 2013.[166] Similar programs have been developed by other agencies, such as the Terrorist Finance Tracking Program (TFTP), which sorts through bank records and transactions passing through the Belgium-based company SWIFT—for which the Treasury Department has a subpoena. It reportedly led to the capture of at least one important Southeast Asian al-Qaeda leader in 2006.[167]

The War on Terror has been widely cited as justification for the collection of bulk metadata. Hayden changed his pitches to telecom from cyberattacks to terrorism immediately after 9/11, with success.[168] Decryption programs are justified as helping the United States defeat "terrorists, dissidents, and other targets,"[169] while the NSA uses the failure to "connect the dots" prior to 9/11 as a justification for its data-collection methods.[170] President Obama has justified the program with a specific example: "One of the 9/11 hijackers, Khalid al-Mihdhar, made a phone call from San Diego to a known al-Qaida safe house in Yemen."[171] Then FBI director Robert Mueller corroborated this in a House judiciary meeting: "If we had had this program in place at the time, we would have been able to identify that particular telephone number in San Diego."[172] The NSA claimed that three hundred terrorists were captured using the search tool XKeyScore,[173] and that signals intelligence—contrasted with human intelligence or intelligence gained by human means—alerted them to Najibullah Zazi, who was planning to attack the New York subway system.[174] The MI5 chief justified GCHQ's collection efforts with the fact that there are "several thousand Islamist extremists [in the UK]."[175] However, the Privacy and Civil Liberties Oversight Board (PCLOB) claimed that al-Mihdhar's call had been intercepted by the NSA, and the CIA had knowledge that he was in the country. To them, "This was a failure to connect the dots, not a failure to connect enough dots."[176]

"SUCCESS" IN THE WAR ON TERROR

Unlike the other two cases, jihadist violence is still narrated as a threat at the time of writing, making it necessary to evaluate the "success" of drones and data collection in the War on Terror. Some level of success in counterterrorism and/or the War on Terror needs to be perceived by those undertaking it. If operations were going badly, tools like targeted killing and data surveillance would be less likely to become practices. Additionally, targeted killing and data surveillance need to be narrated as key parts of that success. Perception is just as important as tangible success.

My interviewees were almost unanimous that the War on Terror has played a role in the limited number of attacks on U.S. soil and interests. As John Poindexter told me, "We have not had a major attack and we probably don't know of all of those that have been preempted."[177] Michael Wertheimer told me that "the intelligence community... has done remarkably well in finding these guys."[178] Others touted the decimation of the core of al-Qaeda[179] and its infrastructure and linked them to new funding streams.[180] Disagreements arose on two issues: whether success has been tactical or strategic,[181] and whether the final goal is the elimination of a "viable Islamic state"[182] or "managing terrorism."[183] Others were skeptical that the threat will dissipate anytime soon.[184]

The nature of the threat has also changed, becoming more localized. Many of those I interviewed mentioned this, with one stating, "I do think there has been a re-localization of the jihad."[185] Chris Kojm told me that "terrorism [is increasingly] internal to countries now, not cross-border."[186] The starkest example of this is the Islamic State (IS).[187] IS broke from al-Qaeda and rose to prominence by claiming territory in war-torn countries and declaring itself a caliphate. Unlike with al-Qaeda, territory is important to IS and its claims to a caliphate. This is why its early rhetoric was about pulling international sympathizers to IS as opposed to inspiring attacks,[188] what is called *hijrah*, or an obligatory duty to travel to the land of Islam.[189] This transnational aspect of ISIS circa 2014 is interesting in its own right, something best left to other spaces, except to say that, even with a transnational element, IS was still an organization or polity with a localized focus similar to many pre-9/11 transnational threats.[190] While rejecting much of the current architecture, IS also claimed to be a state as a way of gaining legitimacy.[191] It drew boundaries—the question was what their boundaries would be and whether they would play by current rules. Additionally, many of al-Qaeda's most active affiliates in Yemen, Somalia, and the Maghreb are embroiled in local struggles. This is despite al-Zawahiri's rhetoric still focusing on the United States and the West.[192] Some of my interviewees viewed this as a challenge for the United States—to keep up with a flexible enemy.[193] However, one could read it as a success. If the jihadist movement is now a series of franchisees focused on territory, then much of the battle has already been won, even if they threaten U.S. interests. They are functioning within a state system.[194] A transnational jihad has been disciplined into states.

Have drones and data been a part of this success? Much like the inconclusive academic literature,[195] the policy makers I interviewed characterized targeted killing as a tactical success but expressed skepticism on its strategic merits. Daniel Benjamin claimed that "if we had drone technology back then [the late 1990s], it would have been a whole different story but ... many see targeted killing as a tactic that has been elevated to a strategy with little purpose other than killing terrorists."[196] One former

Defense Department official mused, "So-and-so got schwacked, so-and-so is up to get schwacked, but where is the assessment of what this did to the network?"[197]

Many fear that attacks create more radicals by killing civilians,[198] such as sixteen-year-old American citizen Abdulrahman al-Awlaki, and causing psychological damage.[199] For instance, the 2012 Benghazi attack was retribution for a drone strike that killed al-Qaeda leader Abu Yahya al-Libi.[200] While the technology is more precise, this often leads to misuse.[201] One 2013 attack in Yemen is estimated to have killed eleven–fifteen civilians at a wedding attended by a supposed militant.[202] Targeting practices linked to signature strikes are also problematic. The United States targeted antiradical Yemeni cleric Salem Ahmed Ali Jaber because of a meeting he had with al-Qaeda operatives discussing his opposition.[203] Similarly, the fact that "military-aged males" are counted as combatants leads operators to find more acceptable targets than otherwise.[204] It becomes a "'we got a hammer, we start seeing more nails' kind of phenomenon."[205] This affects the image of the United States, even beyond active theaters. Michael Wertheimer claimed that "the way they portray drones in Asia is that we are cowards."[206] Additionally, the Pentagon has also started planning for the inevitable technological diffusion.[207] However, there are reports that bin Laden worried about the effects of drone attacks on his organization.[208] The Trump administration has increased drone usage even over the levels of Barack Obama's first term.[209] Drone attacks are seen as successful and have become a normal part of U.S. counterterror and defense strategy.

While there is a consensus that drone attacks have been tactically effective, there is more disagreement on bulk data collection. Most policy makers I spoke with were adamant that the programs were useful but were unable to point to specific successes. While one interviewee pointed to the capture of Zazi, others, like Kojm, who supports the 215 and 702 programs, opined that "you can't point to anything we have learned."[210] The PCLOB report refutes the numbers of thwarted attacks claimed by the NSA, and the presidential task force was unable to claim a single specific attack was thwarted.[211] Many blamed the uncertainties natural to signals intelligence: "It is very difficult ... to actually separate which particular intelligence programs ... contribute to various finished intelligence reports."[212] However, privacy advocate David Husband was skeptical of the inability to do a cost-benefit analysis.[213] Wertheimer pointed out that the mission that got bin Laden "was old fashioned. They found a courier and followed him there."[214]

Despite the skepticism, there are two narratives of success developing around drones and data. First, these programs make it harder for al-Qaeda to exist without territory. While goods, people, money, and ideas still flow across borders, it is harder to conceal those movements. This explains the re-localization of the jihad. Second, drones and data are becoming the go-to techniques of counterterrorism. If "robots are our answer to the suicide bomber," it is because they help state agents make al-Qaeda legible so it can be defeated. It may not help policy makers understand al-Qaeda and its political claims, but the group can be tracked and attacked. Similarly, these two "creative solutions" have become intertwined, with targeted killings based on tracked SIM cards and other information from bulk data collection.[215] As one National Counterterrorism Center (NCTC) official opined, "The CT [counterterrorism] effort is largely an intelligence game . . . the finish piece [drones] is the easy part."[216] Finally, it is unclear if these actions can be rolled back. Tien told me, "Even if you roll the law back, you have not made the Patriot Act vanish today as the effects of all of that would continue to add to surveillance technology."[217] Wertheimer claims that "the intelligence community sees every threat as if it is a terrorism threat. So now we have cyber security and we are taking the counterterrorism playbook and we are laying it on cybersecurity."[218]

THE WAR ON TERROR AND STATE TRANSFORMATION

The drone and data surveillance programs are new innovations developed for and justified by the War on Terror. They have met some success and have the potential to result in the redrawing of the boundaries of political authority. Where these new boundaries may be drawn is still unknown as the process of reforming and institutionalizing relevant practices is still developing.[219] Therefore what I discuss below is projection: an attempt to think through the consequences of each new development in one or more theoretically informed avenues.[220] I will focus on three major consequences and how they might result in redrawn boundaries: (1) the drawing of new cyberspace boundaries that have moved borders from sites of exclusion to sites of collection, (2) the extension of national security into new territorial realms, and (3) new boundaries of citizenship that split the person into discrete data streams.

The surveillance of the twentieth century, described in its nascent form in the previous chapter, was territorial and depended upon a state directly collecting data and/or spying on civilians. It is epitomized by Big Brother in George Orwell's *1984*. However, the surveillance of the twenty-first century is increasingly decentralized and de-territorialized and relies on "an array of state and non-state institutions, technologies, and forms of information that become temporarily and loosely stitched together."[221] PRISM depends upon data first collected from private entities such as Google and Verizon. Police work is often outsourced to private entities in the form of CCTV cameras at gas stations, malls, etc. The War on Terror has forced state agents to reinsert the state into this process. As David Lyon puts it, "The responses of September 11 are a stark reminder that for all its changing shape since World War II the nation state is still a formidable force."[222] The scope of state data collection is still undetermined,[223] but the state is the only entity that can make claims of national security, which open space for the bulk collection of metadata.

One new boundary deals with the meaning of borders. Targeted killing and data surveillance have institutionalized surveillance across borders. In response to the transboundary nature of al-Qaeda, the United States and others have begun to develop tools that adjust to these flows by drawing a new boundary that keeps track of them. Un- or pre-collected data is on one side of this boundary, collected data is on the other. Gilles Deleuze argues that what matters about borders in the twenty-first century "is not the barrier but the computer that tracks each person's position."[224] Security has changed from logics of exclusion, where borders are meant to keep people out, to logics of collection, where state agents can control flows.[225] Controlling flows does not mean that flows stop crossing borders but instead that state agents are aware of them, track them, and have the opportunity to funnel them into the spaces, territorial and conceptual, the state desires. Sovereignty is extended into the realm of cyberspace. This, not attempts to halt flows, is what has been dangerous to al-Qaeda.

As I demonstrated in the last chapter, borders as sites of exclusion are not natural to the state system. And the volume of transnational flows means that in the future borders will be associated more with checkpoints than with claimed territory. As Vukov and Sheller argue, "These securitized corridors reach further out into transnational space (i.e. US border checks on foreign territory) and deeper into domestic interior space (i.e. Mexican border checkpoints move hundreds of miles into US territory)."[226] However, more likely is a two-tiered system where the collection stations will be located irrespective of traditional borders (or in conceptual spaces like cyberspace), but those borders will still demarcate what is to be governed and protected, a new layering of sovereignty. As Shaw argues, the use of drones is meant to "immunize the U.S. homeland";[227] the original territory is still important but now as an object to be protected, not a limiting factor on force. Further necessitating this shift are cloud-based data storage and computing, which challenge claims to territorial jurisdiction.[228] This conception of borders is already making its way into the U.S. national security establishment. The 2014 Quadrennial Security Review states that one of the United States' highest priorities is "securing and managing flows of people and goods into and out of the United States."[229] Securing and managing flows has set the stage for the growing nationalization of the internet, notably manifest in weaponized interdependence[230] and China's centralized system.[231] This is something to watch going forward as a further consequence of the War on Terror.

As surveillance begins to travel across borders, it is inevitable that we will see claims of a breach in the sovereignty of other states. While programs like Boundless Informant allow for the collection and searching of data from the developing countries that make up the world's "hotspots," the NSA has been spying on allies as well.[232] However, it is the drone program that really presses this issue. The United States is implicitly claiming a unilateral right to kill the citizens of other countries that pose a threat to it. Of course, territorial borders and jurisdictions of weaker states have been breached by stronger states for centuries. However, in the second half of the twentieth century, a juridical norm of state independence formed as a part of decolonization. Even as borders are breached in the name of humanitarian (or other) intervention, the state as a juridical ideal is not challenged. This dynamic is front and center in the "failed" or "quasi-" state literature so prevalent since the end of the Cold War.[233] It became a part of the conceptual map of political elites to think that the world's problems are best "solved"—or the goods of a liberal system are best achieved—in a world completely delineated by sovereign entities. This may be unraveling.

There are two possibilities here. First, we could see the rise of what Hardt and Negri call "imperial sovereignty"—where space is always open and frontiers predominate over borders.[234] Ian Shaw describes Donald Rumsfeld's attempts to create a single global battlefield through the JSOC.[235] Drones kill foreign nationals in foreign countries without their explicit consent, creating a "permanent" exception that allows for imperium with "constant martial activity in the homeland and abroad."[236] As Lauren Wilcox argues, drone attacks create a "frontier zone outside of a state's territory for the exercise of the sovereign power to kill."[237] Additionally, drones allow for "pattern of life" analyses tracking the "space-time trajectories" of foreign populations. Power is no longer about projection but instead contraction.[238] Second, while some see an end to territory and sovereignty as part of an American "nonterritorial empire,"[239] others see it as a reconfiguration. Territory here is a "political technology"[240] that can be ephemeral.[241] The recognized territorial sovereignty of weaker states need not be extended vertically[242] or "through" landed spaces, as evidenced by the legal justifications of U.S. drone attacks.[243]

In these scenarios, weaker states keep their sovereignty and may even gain some measure of national security but would lose some of the control or authority that they currently have. It is possible that attacks from IS and al-Qaeda, like the recent Easter bombings in Sri Lanka claimed by IS,[244] would not challenge this type of system despite carrying all the technical hallmarks of previous attacks because they took place outside those able to claim state sovereignty. Another example is the proliferation of drone bases throughout Africa. While AFRICOM, or United States Africa Command, is too controversial for any African state to host (Germany hosts), drone bases have proliferated in Mali, Niger, and Djibouti, among others.[245] Even civilian airports have been used to launch operations.[246] Boundaries are redrawn to reflect the reality of drone campaigns. States that cannot capture data will be more vulnerable, because they will not be able to control flows and stop possible attacks and therefore will be under surveillance from those who can. Weaker states may even ask for surveillance and targeted killing from powerful states in the name of their own sovereignty, as Niger, Yemen, and Pakistan have.[247]

The other big possible change in boundaries is the effect of the creeping expansion of domestic surveillance on boundaries separating public/private and citizen/alien. Many of those I interviewed see the line between domestic and international intelligence vanishing, with 9/11 Commission cochair Lee Hamilton remarking that "it's kind of an artificial distinction . . . [and] must not be an inhibitor to the sharing of information."[248] This trend could manifest itself in two ways. First, it changes the state's view of its own citizens by shifting how it makes them legible.[249] Previously, surveillance tracked bodies and their traces—for instance, fingerprints and DNA samples. Surveillance in the twenty-first century is primarily about data streams. As one border security officer stated, "We know there is a person who has been doing this and this and this—we just don't know their name yet and we can stop them before we know it."[250] This has been called "dataveillance," the fingerprints of the twenty-first century.[251] As Hall and Mendel argue, fingerprint and other bodily markers re-create past events while "dataveillance" attempts to predict future events via the connections and relations between data elements—as opposed to the elements themselves. Predicting the "rare event" of terrorism now means looking into ordinary transactions such as shopping records and travel itineraries. This creates a "threatprint" or a "future digital footprint of a threat not yet in existence," which extends a person into the future.[252]

So what does this do to the citizen? Wall and Monahan argue that what they call "'the drone stare' is a type of surveillance that abstracts people from contexts, thereby reducing variation, difference, and noise that may impede action or introduce moral ambiguity."[253] Drones turn "bodies into 'targets' for remote monitoring and destruction."[254] While this is true for both citizens and foreign nationals, it does change how state agents views people and bodies, with the potential to draw new boundaries around citizenship.[255] Feminist and critical security scholars have already hit upon the body as an important site for war and the War on Terror.[256] In addition, data-collection programs also pull people out of context, making them legible as "data doubles" that become virtual representations of the self.²⁵⁷ The person becomes their flows and daily transactions, producing the data from which the "rare event" of terrorism is, theoretically, thwarted.²⁵⁸ A particular person is dissembled into a collection of attributes so that they become different things to different collectors. Their parts are analyzed without the context of the whole or its environment. The indivisibility of the individual is challenged, while the lack of context prevents it from ever being achieved. This has profound implications as "our data doppelgangers mediate our interactions."²⁵⁹ It is not mistake free, of course. This technique of viewing bodies is what led to the "guilt of association" that killed Ali Jaber.

The second major change stems from this loss of "wholeness." Such a loss allows for elements of the "data double" to be coded as on the other side of the domestic/international boundary. The citizen/alien boundary could be redrawn so that parts of the "citizen" are placed into the "alien" category and therefore made eligible for surveillance. If domestic inhabitants or citizens are fair game for NSA surveillance, the difference between them and foreign nationals erodes. This is driven home by the militarization of police in the United States. U.S. citizens, or at least parts of them, are treated as threats similar to terrorists, disconnected from the homeland being protected. U.S. border security and the use of drones therein are another example.²⁶⁰ Of course, there has been pushback, but "citizen" and "international" are overlapping in ways heretofore unknown.

CONCLUSION

In response to the 9/11 attacks, previous certainties were smashed, previous ways of looking at the world were no longer valid, and previous ways of doing things became antiquated. New ideas and tools that had previously had trouble gaining audiences and advocates were implemented. The United States' government and its allies created the War on Terror with an undefined, expansive scope, which had the effect of elevating the threat. The violence of al-Qaeda shattered the conceptual maps of state agents, its actions illegible to states within existing boundaries. State agents' response, like in the early eighteenth century and the turn of the twentieth, was to draw new boundaries, to make sense of al-Qaeda and turn its actions into recognizable patterns that can be countered effectively.

Early efforts in the War on Terror met with mixed results, especially as regards the plan of defeating "terror" through regime change in the Middle East. Such actions reinforced old boundaries and practices. If threats come from local struggles abroad, solving those local struggles is a sensible policy option. New practices had to be formed. Drone attacks and data surveillance programs have become accepted as successful in crippling al-Qaeda and giving the United States and its allies the upper hand in the War on Terror. These new programs are currently in the process of becoming practices as they draw new boundaries of political authority. Borders move from barriers to points of collection in order to control flows, national security claims are extended beyond traditional jurisdictions in the name of targeted killing, and the role of the citizen is likely to change drastically due to the use of big data in national security. None of this means that boundaries, or even borders, are no longer important. The justification of "protecting the homeland," a concept defined by boundaries and borders, demonstrates their importance. The state has adapted and is undertaking the creative action of following the movement of people, goods, and ideas across borders in the form of data so that it can act when it perceives a threat.

CONCLUSION

The state has the ability to remake itself in order to deal with challenges to the boundaries that construct it. This is demonstrated through the mechanisms of "shattering" and "reinscribing." In this book, I demonstrated this in three case studies of transnational violence—the golden age of piracy, "propaganda of the deed," and global jihadism. In each case, violence was illegible to the state, causing a crisis, which led to the state attempting to reinforce old practices and boundaries. The failure of these strategies completes the shattering. In response, states come up with creative solutions to these problems, which draw new boundaries as they are habituated from action to practice. The state reinscribes itself. Change begets continuity: because the state transforms, it preserves.

In the early eighteenth century, a "wave" of pirates took advantage of the sympathetic colonial publics and ungoverned spaces created by the "line"—an imaginary boundary separating Europe from the colonial Atlantic. As a response, England and other states extended their judicial reach into the colonies, took greater control of colonial governance, and enacted a propaganda campaign that framed colonists as part of the "nation" and the pirates as outside of it. They effectively abolished the line. At the turn of the twentieth century, anarchists practicing propaganda of the deed killed seven heads of state and numerous public officials, bombed public cafés and landmarks, and nearly pulled off the assassinations of the German kaiser and the Belgian king, among others. European states used newly available technologies to track and identify anarchists and other criminals, which resulted in tightly regulated cross-border movement and the modern surveillance state. Simultaneously, anarchist ideas were increasingly tolerated in public discourse, which had the effect of funneling anarchists into a newly legitimated labor movement that pushed for reforms such as the eight-hour workday. A century later, al-Qaeda ran planes into the Pentagon and the World Trade Center. The also pulled off a string of deadly attacks in Nairobi, Dar es Salaam, New York, London, Madrid, and Bali, among others As a response to al-Qaeda, the United States has developed counterterror innovations such as targeted killing and bulk data collection, which have transformed borders from sites of exclusion designed to keep out undesirables to sites of collection where they are tracked and controlled.

In each case, the crisis was triggered by an act of violence illegible to the state. The illegibility was not rooted in the act itself, but in the conceptual maps that state actors used to make sense of and govern their domains. Notice that the acts—sea raiding, assassinations, suicide attacks, etc.—tend to vary. Any single act can pose a multitude of different threats. In each case, the response was not just new policy but a remaking of the state and, by extension, global order. Thus, the state is not the static entity we often assume it to be but instead a dynamic one with myriad variations across space and time. This notion of the state as a project that is continually maintained and reinscribed through the redrawing of boundaries opens up avenues for transboundary processes to drive state transformation. While nothing is guaranteed and specifics will change from case to case, there is no reason that this cannot happen in other cases, allowing us to think about the nature of global order.

I conclude this book by discussing the major themes we can pull from this project and their implications. I will start by discussing the contributions of practice theory to state transformation outlined in chapter 2, considering my three cases. Then I will discuss the role of contention and contingency in drawing new boundaries using debates about privacy, the meaning of success using the rise and fall of IS, and the implications of this study for global order and, finally, for the future and possible end of the state in a globalized world.

CONCLUSION

TRANSNATIONAL VIOLENCE AND STATE TRANSFORMATION

The outcomes of my cases are contingent. The takeaway should not be that when threat *x* happens, outcome *y* occurs, i.e., *major terrorist attack surveillance*. I am not making claims about the relationship between violence and any particular part of the state over hundreds of years. The point is to focus on process and show how it can help us understand important aspects of international politics. Therefore, it is worth returning to the vision of state transformation derived from practice theories of the state. I outline four contributions to state formation: (1) it is continuous, (2) it comes from the margins, (3) it can happen via state collusion, and (4) it is configurational.

We often think of state transformation by looking at something to explain (democracy, bureaucracy, welfare) and finding the time and place in which that thing appears. This leads us to think about state transformation as periods of stability punctured by major events. This is not the situation. The cases in this book may seem ill-equipped to make this point. It would be better to have three cases chronologically adjacent to show how state formation is continuous. Yet, despite this "deficiency," it is still apparent that state formation is continuous. We can see many of the major state-transformation processes implicated. The development of the welfare state depended on the rise of the labor movement, and that was in partly due to the campaign against propaganda of the deed. Protections such as the eight-hour workday became major campaigns that anarchists fought for as they rejected bombings and assassinations. The open "Atlantic World" would not have developed as it did without piracy, which forced state actors to abandon controlling the oceans. Contemporary surveillance measures were developed in the War on Terror to defeat al-Qaeda and exported to other realms. In each case, we can see the continuation—how future crises built on previous ones to create what we see today.

The outcomes that I focus on did not happen entirely because of pirates, anarchists, and terrorists. They happened because future processes and crises built on what was learned from the ones under study. This has a number of implications. First, what was learned and built upon is contested and political, as will be demonstrated in the section on privacy below. Second, macro-processes are not freestanding entities but ideal typical constructions we devise to simplify and make sense of the world. Third, the end states are never final. Propaganda of the deed does not help us directly make sense of the welfare state of the 1970s or the surveillance state of the twenty-first century (though understanding its history is important) but the surveillance and welfare states of the 1920s and 1930s. The same thing goes for the Atlantic worlds of 1730 and 1800 and the surveillance state of 2020 and 2070. Thus, the things being explained in the traditional state-formation literature are themselves moving targets that require a practice approach.

Practice theories of the state direct us toward greater study of the importance of the "margins" in understanding the nature of the state. Highlighting boundaries refocuses our attentions away from the center and out into the places, conceptual and territorial, where contention is ongoing, allowing us to observe how the center is constructed. The justifications of the pirates, propagandists, and terrorists display worldviews illegible to the boundary-producing polities constructing global order. This is the reason why each episode threatens the state in ways that are unique to existing boundaries. Golden-age pirates took advantage of how practices of colonial rule clashed with the rise of mercantilist trade; propagandists took advantage of the tensions between mass media and conservative nationalism; al-Qaeda took advantage of the internet. These are men and women who lived in the margins of global order (the Atlantic colonies, the urban proletariat, and Central Asia), challenging the boundaries that constructed their respective orders by methods imperceptible to those not alert to their importance. The same is also true for the police chiefs, governors, merchants, and intelligence analysts (among others) who led and coordinated responses. A disaggregated state often means it is the margins of the state that act. In addition, it is only if we recognize that the threats that are produced from violence depend upon how violent action is situated—i.e., what narratives are built around it—that we can begin to study how violence plays a role in constructing the margins that produce the state.

Because the threat is to the state itself and not just a particular state, state collusion becomes a pathway for state formation. First, in none of the cases is there much competition in defeating the threat. This doesn't mean competition wasn't happening in general. There was a war just prior to the golden age of piracy and a short war in the middle of it. Propaganda of the deed happened while Europe was sliding into World War I. The U.S. War on Terror included the invasions of two countries, and drones and data are tools of state competition. However, in the process of defeating pirates, anarchists, and terrorists, there was no competition but instead diffusion and cooperation. In the pirate case, all states stopped using pardons eventually, as well as letters of marque during peacetime. In the anarchist case, passports and other ID documents diffused across the globe. Drones and data collection are not U.S. properties alone, even if they developed there.

The same goes for cooperation, even if this often happens at lower levels. English admiral Channeler Ogle cooperated with French anti-pirate efforts in the mission that killed Black Bart Roberts. The Treaty of Utrecht demonstrates how states were willing to work together to defeat piracy. While the Rome and St. Petersburg protocols themselves did not have much effect, they again show how states worked together to defeat propaganda of the deed even as they were themselves sliding into war. And cooperation at the level of police departments and intelligence services was vast if not also successful. In the War on Terror, the United States got cooperation from and lent a hand to other states willing to fight "terror," sometimes—like in the case of China and its Uyghur populations—with terrifying results. Thus, the state formation in each case depended on states working together and copying successful strategies.

One final note on my cases. It could be said that the transformations differ in scope. The pirate and al-Qaeda cases saw changes that mostly happened in one state, the anarchist case at the "system" level across many states. I think there are instructive reasons why it looks this way. The al-Qaeda case is probably too recent for many of the larger themes to be fully developed. Twenty years after Ravachol's attack in Paris, World War I had yet to start. It was still a decade or two further until passports and immigration restrictions really took hold. U.S. data surveillance may be seen as a cause for a nationalized internet (assuming this happens), which would be an important system-level change.

That leaves us with the pirate and anarchist cases. I think there are a few important points to make here. First, the transformations resulting from the golden age of piracy had important effects on international politics. Both Spain and France stopped peacetime privateering. The open Atlantic World is a major development. England was able to have an outsized effect on continental politics as a result the subsequent boom in trade. Second, England was dominant in the region in a way that no European state was at the turn of the twentieth century. Spain was able to keep its empire throughout the century but was not in a position to expand, having lost a lot of its continental power. At this point, it was relying pretty strongly on the effects of disease on offensive missions.[1] France's empire was never as strong as England's, was not quite in a position to take advantage of the new Atlantic World, and would lose large swathes of its empire within a few decades, in large part because of England's ability to take advantage of the new opportunities for trade.

This can tell us a few things. First, there is no reason that change must follow a single pathway up or down from the state. Second, that pathway is contingent. It depends on things like whether or not there was a single dominant power (as in the pirate and al-Qaeda cases) or multiple competing powers. Third, as part of this contingency, processes unfolding before and after shape the outcome. The Seven Years' War was not preordained by the golden age of piracy, nor was its outcome (though England's gains were important). That war caused France to make territorial concessions to England. In turn, this makes it more likely that we only see the transformations discussed in chapter 2 in the English Empire. All of this underlines my framework for state transformation.

CONTENTION, CHANGE, AND THE PRIVACY DEBATE

The solutions arrived at in my cases were not inevitable. Propaganda of the deed, for instance, had both vaguely liberal democratic (detailed in chapter 4) and totalitarian (Spain, Russia) "solutions" within Europe. Did the English have to deny rights to their North American colonists as they took more control of their colonies to fight piracy? No. Could they have developed a society that took care of the populations from which sailors and pirates came? Certainly. Were there solutions to propaganda of the deed that allowed for free movement? Quite possibly. Were there solutions to jihadist "terrorism" other than the United States claiming the right to kill anyone anywhere they suspected was a terrorist? Absolutely. This isn't a story of states finding the *right* solution but instead *a* solution that worked for them. I myself am deeply uncomfortable with many of these solutions, especially those used in the War on Terror. These solutions were the product of politics. I have tried to show how context has made certain options more likely than others when discussing the history of drones or surveillance. But even given this limitation, there was still room for contention, for other options to be chosen. While the cases are streamlined to fit the parameters of a single manuscript, each one involved actors fighting over these solutions and shaping them in unexpected ways. I will demonstrate this point by looking at the privacy debate that has surrounded the NSA's programs and Edward Snowden's revelations. I will argue that an inability to reimagine privacy threatens its existence and leads us down a darker path (from the War on Terror) than is otherwise necessary.

One of the insights of pragmatist social theory is that situations, not universal principles, determine the meaning and outcome of events. In *Reconstruction in Philosophy*, John Dewey argues there is no universal good; morality is situational: "The good of the situation has to be discovered, projected, and attained on the basis of the exact defect and trouble to be rectified."[2] Dewey has similar views of democracy; it only exists in particular formation in particular times and places, not as a universal ideal—it does not "perpetuate itself automatically."[3] Therefore, any universal principles, ranging from health to democracy to liberal education, only have meaning in particular situations. The same goes for privacy. Not only does the U.S. government have the capability to access large amounts of data, but this data is already being used by Google, Amazon, VISA, Verizon, Facebook, and others.[4] At this stage, this is unlikely to be undone; therefore, our conception of what privacy means and how it is protected must change.

This is something that many in the privacy advocacy community have been slow to adapt to. Much of the legal argument from the time was built around how bulk data collection violates the 1978 Foreign Intelligence Surveillance Act,[5] which was enacted prior to the rise of digital communication. The advocates I spoke to made it clear that privacy, while threatened, has not changed. One privacy advocate told me, "We had privacy, as a practical matter, in ways that we didn't think about for the longest time until the technology started exposing things in ways that they weren't in the past."[6] Another echoed this sentiment: "In many ways privacy doesn't really change, the threats to it change."[7] Another explained privacy this way: "I can hold this back from Congress, I can hold that back from my family and friends."[8] The ways in which privacy might change deal with the degree to which it is realized. As D.S. suggested to me, "maybe it changes because we change the balance of it."[9] Journalist Shane Harris opines that many activists are "clinging to . . . an outdated version or definition of privacy. And frankly, that is why they have not made more gains."[10] The problem here is not that privacy is "outdated" or no longer necessary, but that it was, still is, characterized as a universal ideal. Maybe privacy needs to adhere closer to what Lee Tien described: "less as a thing or a commodity that can be possessed but rather . . . an attitude."[11]

This has hampered attempts to rein in government surveillance. A few years after 9/11, the public got wind of DARPA's creation of the TIA system developed by John Poindexter.[12] Congress convened hearings amid the controversy, and Poindexter's operation was shut down. However, through a loophole in the legislation, much of what Poindexter and his team were working on was repackaged and sent to the NSA.[13] At this point, Bob Popp, Poindexter's second-in-command, sorted through the myriad features of the program with an eye toward cutting those that could not pass the "*Washington Post* smell test." Privacy was one of those programs. What was the NSA doing that required it to conduct privacy research?[14] The privacy protections originally imagined for TIA were written out of the program by the time it was operational because of the constraints placed by those focused on privacy as withholding information.[15]

Many argue that instead of focusing on withholding information, we should instead focus on the control of information.[16] Withholding is a particular manifestation of that ideal, one that does not fit all times and places. One example of controlling information is the radical transparency advocated by Bangladeshi activist and artist Hasan Elahi. The FBI detained Elahi in 2002, following an erroneous suspicion that he had left explosives in a storage facility in Florida. After a few days' detainment and another six months of FBI questioning, Elahi decided to completely open up his life.[17] He posts every time he changes his location or has opened up his bank accounts. This way the FBI cannot suspect him as a terrorist. In his words, "The best way to protect your privacy is to give it away.... You can monitor yourself much more effectively."[18] The strategy is that if everyone has the information, it is, in his words, "useless.... What is important is analyzing the information—what is the information telling you?" With suspicious pieces of data, "you cannot delete, but you can bury" them with a lot of other information.[19] By releasing data you provide the context: "Who do you want in control over that data? With us being proactive about it and deciding what that data is, and who that is, and how that represents you is much more direct than if it had been some random person who decided, 'Well this is good enough, I think that describes you.'"[20] Elahi does not think that past conceptions of privacy are useful in a digital world: "What we think is privacy today is definitely not what it was . . . the concept of it has changed." He echoes what some of the policy makers I talked to mentioned about the dangers to privacy: that what seems to be important is what is done with the data, not its collection.[21]

In addition to releasing information, Elahi argues that "we too can hold up a mirror," to demand data from corporations and governments. This can mean transparency in the processes of drone attacks and data surveillance. This would build public trust while, ironically, cementing drone attacks and data collection as legitimate pursuits (or not—the public can reject them!). A more conservative version of this might be what Michael Hayden has called translucency: an opaque process that details data collected but withholds what is done with it for a set period.[22] Transparency and control can also mean capturing the actions of public figures. For instance, when journalist Scott Olson was arrested as part of the Ferguson, Missouri, protests in 2014, pictures of the arrest made it out because it was so easy to capture the arrest and post photos online. This also drove sentiment in the Black Lives Matter protests of 2020, giving gravitas to the "defund the police" sentiment. The government is not the only entity able to do surveillance; people and other institutions can as well.

One hurdle faced by activists is that of public perception. The past eighteen years demonstrate that security from terrorism, even if overstated, is important to U.S. citizens. However, the data-collection question is still open. Most policy makers I talked to are of the belief that it is not important; one summed up the stance by saying, "Relatively few people care about this one way or another."[23] Ethan Zuckerman, who helped pioneer pop-up ads, argues that "users now accept that this sort of manipulation is an integral part of the online experience. . . . Even when widespread, clandestine government surveillance was revealed by a whistleblower, there has been little organized, public demand for reform and change."[24] Privacy advocates countered that people do not care only because they do not know enough about what is going on. As D.S. argued, "It will become more and more important as people begin to understand just how much information is being collected about them, what is being used, and how many different entities end up using that information."[25] This does not seem to be playing out in polling of U.S. citizens. If polling does not change, then transparency would seem to be a necessity.

THE ISLAMIC STATE AND THE MEANING OF "SUCCESS"

In chapter 4, I argued that the re-localization of the jihad counts as success in the War on Terror. I wanted to briefly return to this point and discuss IS in this context, as it is an important one in understanding state formation. George W. Bush's measure of success, ridding the world of terror and terrorists, did not and will never happen. It was probably the stated goal to allow space for a wide-ranging effort. But it was not just the War on Terror that "failed" such a test. Neither piracy nor sea raiding more broadly disappeared in the 1730s, but there was a system in place for dealing with pirates as common criminals. Sea raiding during wartime was standard practice into the nineteenth century. Anarchism and anarchist violence did not go away. Assassinations actually increased. They were shunted into legitimate (labor movement) or legible (anticolonial) pursuits. The same goes for the War on Terror. The important point here is that the threat is lessened, yes, but also normalized as standard procedures are built to detect and combat it. The transformed state is not one without pirates, anarchists, or terrorists but one in which the state can more easily combat these threats using newly developed practices so that boundaries are not threatened.

This bring us to the rise and fall of IS. As IS began to lose territory from its peak position in 2015, they also transnationalized with attacks in Paris and Brussels. As their position fell further, attacks in Nice, Hamburg, London, Manchester, and San Bernardino (among others) became more decentralized, following a "lone wolf" model not dissimilar to propaganda of the deed a century prior. Coming years after many of al-Qaeda's most deadly attacks, these actions were certainly threats but they also dissipated within a few years. The rise of IS (and its downfall) is largely tied to U.S. actions. The Iraq War led to the creation of al-Qaeda in Iraq and provided the environment for it to morph into IS. The transnationalization of the War on Terror may have also forced some local groups to transnationalize for support.[26] But drones and data have crippled al-Qaeda to the degree that IS was able to break out of its shadow and move in a territorial direction. U.S. actions against the caliphate, including drone attacks both on its territory and against its affiliates,[27] have led it to transnationalize,[28] which led to, or at least presaged, its downfall.[29]

And IS has suffered serious defeats in recent years. Then U.S. president Donald Trump declared victory over IS in 2018, and, as of early 2021, IS controls little, if any, territory. In 2019, Caliph Abu Bakr al-Baghdadi killed himself during a U.S. raid on his compound. Attacks are way down in the last few years. Where things go from here we cannot know.[30] There is evidence that al-Qaeda, forging a different path from IS,[31] have used coalition building and soft power to gain the ascendency.[32] There is evidence of cracks within IS,[33] but also of IS followers not rejecting the group even after losing its caliphate.[34] There are also warnings of U.S. strategy, in particular its withdraw from Northeast Syria, allowing IS to re-emerge in some form.[35] Others point to the need to be flexible in dealing with future terrorist threats.[36]

Is this success? A threat to U.S. interests brought about by an expansion of surveillance activities and U.S. claims to kill anyone it deems an enemy anywhere in the world? I argue yes, but I should be clear that it is a really narrow definition of "success." It means the state has reinscribed itself to manage a threat; it means that al-Qaeda, IS, and whatever group may come next are no longer threats to the practices that draw boundaries around political authority. Nor should we necessarily celebrate it—this was not the only outcome and it is not necessarily a good one.

GLOBAL ORDER

One major fault line of contention over global order is over an open vs. closed order. This is especially poignant since the current international order purports to be an open one. On its face, a closed order—something advocated for by a transnational right-wing populist movement often characterized by Donald Trump in the United States and myriad movements across Europe—would mean "harder" boundaries and a roll back of globalization. But this is not necessarily the case. First, populism, or at least right-wing populism, depends on transnational linkages and sympathies, such as those between much of the American Right and Russia. These linkages are not nationalist in a traditionalist sense, where two different nations are squaring off against each other—they are more opposed to something they call "globalism." If anything, this nationalism is more geared around certain racial conceptions of Western society against those of other societies. If this remains the case, and it is possible these are linkages of convenience right now, certain aspects of globalization would be preserved should right-wing populism win—especially when we consider that many parts of this movement could not have coalesced without social media, global capital flows, and other "globalizing" technologies (that also aided al-Qaeda and its offshoots). The only concrete way in which Trump proposed to slow down globalization was by rolling back "free" trade. This harkens back to a golden age—presumably the 1950s and 1960s, at least in the United States—before free trade, to when industries such as manufacturing and coal were thriving across the West. Of course, even this has as much to do with race and gender politics as economics.

An open global order, or even "globalization," may not go away but may become more open in some ways and less open in others. Remember, global order is a series of practices, thus it is disaggregated and can move in multiple directions simultaneously. The anarchist case is a good example—more open in allowing anarchists into the public sphere, more closed through passports and immigration restrictions. Moreover, "globalized" does not mean "liberal." That said, this "closed"—or maybe more accurately "populist"—system would affect the types of boundaries drawn in relation to certain threats. Remember that *how* and *which* boundaries are drawn in response to threats, and even the definition of what threats create crises, depends upon how actors view them, their prior worldviews, and their future goals. Populist authoritarianism is going to produce different boundaries, and even perceive different threats, than a more open, liberal context. Again, contention matters. Boundaries, and practices that draw them, do not naturally appear from events. And, of course, populism may lose.

Two final notes on the open- vs. closed-order debate. First, the rise of right-wing populism in the West is a reaction to 9/11 and jihadist terrorism *and* a consequence of the construction of the War on Terror. Most of these movements across the West focus on the danger of Muslim refugees and immigrants. In the United States, actions such as the "Muslim travel ban" and the border wall between the United States and Mexico show that the movement has roots in 9/11. Framing the response to 9/11 as a war has provided the language and fear necessary for such a movement across the West.[37] Of course, other factors such as media environment, economic dislocation, and long-dormant racial attitudes are also causes. However, right-wing populism and its desire for a relatively closed order are a consequence of one of the cases outlined in this project.

Second, drones and data are important parts of the new boundaries right-wing populism wants to draw. While most of the depictions of those boundaries in chapter 4 are more in line with the type of open order rejected by right-wing populists, populists are not rejecting these tools and may even repurpose boundaries. The Trump administration in the United States has even loosened restrictions on when and where drone attacks can occur. Again, the difference here may not be the presence of new boundaries but instead what these boundaries look like and how they are used. If anything, right-wing populism may accelerate the development of expansive international boundaries for powerful states and other developments many activists and analysts fear. But again, this depends on their "winning," which is questionable.

Finally, I want to speak briefly about the supposed liberal international order. As mentioned in the introduction, there has been a recent spate of scholarship and policy-related thought on the future of global order with a declining United States and the rise of right-wing populism. This project does not directly address the content of the current order, its future under Trump, whether China can/should be incorporated, or even whether it is worth saving. However, there is one point to be made here. This study demonstrates one of the problems with the type of global order that the liberal international order represents: it is built on shifting sand. This is a generally underappreciated challenge in this literature. As problems arise and boundaries are redrawn, the underlying structure of the world being ordered changes. Eventually, this means that old practices do not fit. If states practice sovereignty in new ways and interact with each other (and other actors) in new ways as a result, practices developed to deal with the world twenty, forty, sixty years ago will have to change as well. This can trigger or exacerbate power transitions, the most commonly discussed type of change. Often a declining power is more attached to the previous practices it helped to institute. It can also be the drive behind a reinvigoration, though time may be running short on that. Should a global order built on liberal principles be desirable, the question is not about saving it or reimposing it but instead reimagining it to fit with the new boundaries that are being drawn today. Liberal order is a Deweyan universal principle, much like privacy. Its manifestations depend upon context. One takeaway from this project is that boundaries have always been shattered and reinscribed; change is a constant, and the state is a project, a process. Whatever liberal goals are desired need to be reinterpreted at a practical level to fit any new order.

GLOBALIZATION AND THE FUTURE OF THE STATE

I write this amidst a third nationwide lockdown in the United Kingdom in less than a year, designed to slow the spread of the novel coronavirus. However, putting aside ongoing debates about its effects on global order[38] or what it will do to international politics,[39] it is worth pointing out that COVID-19 shares similarities with my three cases. All are transboundary and all have demonstrated weaknesses in contemporary boundary-drawing practices. The idea that travel bans from specific countries could halt the disease, and the fact that previous pandemic contenders such as Ebola, SARS, and MERS were regionally contained, have led most of the world to be underprepared, just as the confidence in its ability to exclude threats led the United States to overlook those planning the 9/11 attacks on its territory. This complacency, I would argue, is derived from a belief that the system set up perpetuates itself, and that the problems of the first half of the twentieth century were solved. This means thinking of the state (or any order) as stable, leading to the "big bang" of the coronavirus. However, recognizing that order takes constant work to maintain means continually doing that work and being cognizant of when it needs to change. Thus, the big bang is actually something caused by an end to the work being done perpetuating and stabilizing the order.

The obvious differences between a highly contagious respiratory disease and an episode of transnational violence also highlight the similarities. It reminds us that many of the challenges of the twenty-first century (and yes, previous centuries as well) come from processes that state actors cannot make sense of. And those processes may be proliferating. The idea that the state is receding in the face of globalization or that it is no longer as important as it once was is a straw man. The state was founded upon unbounded flows and processes and has been bounding them for centuries. But also misguided are claims that the state is unchanging in the face of globalization and will continue to dominate politics. Instead, I argue that the continuity of the state depends upon its ability to change, and shattering and reinscribing can help us to understand these dynamics.

The state faces episodes of violence that produce similar threats to boundaries as increased migration, trade, capital flows, pandemics, social networking, and environmental pressures do. Its response has been to redraw boundaries so that these episodes of violence can be made sense of, so that they can be normalized, and so that ultimately, even if they continue, they no longer pose the same type of threat. In the case of surveillance and the War on Terror, the state serves as the only actor realistically positioned to combine the data streams collected by private entities and has the only accepted, though certainly contested, justification for doing so: national security. This gives it an advantage over private conductors of surveillance and allows it to privatize or decentralize surveillance and collection without being threatened. The state is a practice so habitual that those with political power cannot imagine exercising their power without it. For these reasons, it is unlikely to fade away.

Of course, reinscription is by no means guaranteed. There are three ways that I can see this process unraveling, though I should point out that each reason merely creates space for a different conception of politics, a different sort of polity to emerge. Without such a development, they are unlikely to mean the end of the state. First, it is possible for a threat to arise that, for whatever reason, state agents never make sense of. It would depend not on the threat itself but the agents trying to make sense of it. This would create a crisis of legitimacy severe enough to begin unraveling the state and would create space for polities constructed through alternative logics of rule. This echoes Daniel Nexon's argument that the linkages between pro-Reformation groups were illegible to the imperial structures of early modern Europe, creating space for the rise of the modern state.[40] It is even more likely if for some reason there is a true competitor to the state.

Another possibility is that threats begin to evolve quicker than the state. The ever-changing nature of twenty-first-century threats is something that many of the people I interviewed for chapter 4 articulated to me. Matthew Levitt explained that the biggest concern in counterterrorism is "keeping up with things as they evolve. . . . It is a rapidly changing world and change is much, much faster."[41] Lee Hamilton described the terrorism threat as an "evolving threat that contains a number of elements"; he focuses specifically on cyberattacks, which ten years ago "we weren't focused on . . . at all."[42] The danger to the state in this scenario is not the transgression of boundaries, but the constantly changing nature of those transgressions, which makes it impossible to habituate the practices that draw new boundaries.

Finally, one thing that separates the globalization of the twenty-first century from the transboundary processes of previous centuries is not the qualitative differences between the respective processes or even the dynamics involved, but the quantity of processes. This produces a different set of threats and challenges to the state. It may be that states can deal with a few such challenges simultaneously but cannot deal with fifteen, twenty, twenty-five (or more). If boundaries are being redrawn concurrently on so many fronts that no new boundaries can be habituated, then we may be into the territory of some other, as yet unimagined, polity. If boundaries are constantly changing and being redrawn, the resulting world would no longer be adequately understood as a world of states. Two things could result. First, the idea of conceptual maps is challenged, and we have a world of boundaries that are ever shifting, wherein power and rule are clear only for short periods of time. This is, in part, the argument of postmodernism.[43] It may also be that the world gets so complex that we enter the realm of the singularity—where only artificial intelligence can cope with the complexity. Second, such a state of affairs may lead to the abandonment of rule through boundaries. Boundaries would no longer serve the purpose of demarcating rule or of separating territory, conceptual spaces, or people into ruled and not ruled. What, in such circumstances, would boundaries provide? This would be a shattering on a much higher scale; the result would not be the drawing of new boundaries but rather the finding of new ways of governance.

In order to get to this point, we need to understand the state as a series of practices that draw boundaries around political authority. Which practices those are and for what purposes will determine much about politics for the remainder of the twenty-first century. This means using shattering and reinscribing in other cases similar to those in chapters 2–4. And to take a step further back, it is important that scholars think about how politics and state transformation happen when we take practices, boundaries, transnational flows, and disaggregation seriously. Mine are certainly not the only processes of state transformation following these priors, and I welcome others. Figuring out how different processes of state (and global-order) transformation concatenate is paramount as we head deeper into a century currently defined by global flows and their backlash.

NOTES

INTRODUCTION

1. Rana Dasgupta, "The Demise of the Nation-State," *Guardian*, April 5, 2018.
2. Stephen J. Kobrin, "Back to the Future: Neomedievalism and the Postmodern Digital World Economy," *Journal of International Affairs* 51, no. 2 (1998): 364.
3. John Perry Barlow, "A Declaration of the Independence of Cyberspace," Electronic Frontier Foundation, January 20, 2016, https://www.eff.org/cyberspace-independence.
4. Martti Koskenniemi, "What Use for Sovereignty Today?," *Asian Journal of International Law* 1, no. 1 (2011): 61.
5. Susan Strange, *The Retreat of the State: The Diffusion of Power in the World Economy* (Cambridge: Cambridge University Press, 1996), 4.
6. Max G. Manwaring, "A Contemporary Challenge to State Sovereignty: Gangs and Other Illicit Criminal Organizations in Central America, El Salvador, Mexico, Jamaica, and Brazil" (Carlisle, PA: Strategic Studies Institute, 2007).
7. Willem Schinkel, "Dignitas Non-Moritur? The State of the State in an Age of Social Hypochondria," in *Globalization and the State: Sociological Perspectives on the State of the State*, ed. Willem Schinkel (New York: Palgrave Macmillan, 2009), 10.
8. Jan Klabbers, "Setting the Scene," in *The Constitutionalization of International Law*, ed. Jan Klabbers, Anne Peters, and Geir Ulfstein (Oxford: Oxford University Press, 2009), 12.
9. Cynthia E. Ayers, *Rethinking Sovereignty in the Concept of Cyberspace*, Cyber Sovereignty Workshop Series (Carlisle, PA: U.S. Army War College, 2016).
10. Emily Crawford and Rosemary Rayfuse, "Climate Change, Sovereignty, and Statehood," in *International Law in the Era of Climate Change*, ed. Rosemary Rayfuse and Shirley Scott (Cheltenham, UK: Edward Elgar, 2012), 243.

11. John S. Dryzek, Richard B. Norgaard, and David Schlosberg, "Climate Change and Society: Approaches and Responses," in *The Oxford Handbook of Climate Change and Society*, ed. Dryzek, Norgaard, and Schlosberg (Oxford: Oxford University Press, 2011), 14.
12. Jost Delbrück, "Global Migration—Immigration—Multiethnicity: Challenges to the Concept of the Nation-State," *Indiana Journal of Global Legal Studies* 2, no. 1 (1994): 46.
13. James N. Rosenau, *Turbulence in World Politics: A Theory of Change and Continuity* (Princeton, NJ: Princeton University Press, 1990), 5.
14. Philip G. Cerny, "Globalization and the Erosion of Democracy," *European Journal of Political Research* 36, no. 1 (1999): 1.
15. Molly Roberts, "Facebook Has Declared Sovereignty," *Washington Post*, January 31, 2019.
16. Kobrin, "Back to the Future," 364.
17. Flora Lewis, "The End of Sovereignty," *New York Times*, May 23, 1992.
18. Robert Gilpin, "The Politics of Transnational Economic Relations," in *Transnational Relations and World Politics*, ed. Robert O. Keohane and Joseph S. Nye (Cambridge, MA: Harvard University Press, 1972), 48–69; Stephen D. Krasner, "Abiding Sovereignty," *International Political Science Review* 22, no. 3 (2001): 229–51; Vivien A. Schmidt, "Putting the Political Back into Political Economy by Bringing the State Back in Yet Again," *World Politics* 61, no. 3 (2009): 516–46.
19. Arthur Borriello and Nathalie Brack, "'I Want My Sovereignty Back!' A Comparative Analysis of the Populist Discourses of Podemos, the 5 Star Movement, the FN and UKIP During the Economic and Migration Crises," *Journal of European Integration* 41, no. 7 (2019): 833–53; Cathrine Thorleifsson, "In Pursuit of Purity: Populist Nationalism and the Racialization of Difference," *Identities* 28, no. 2 (2021): 186–202.
20. Tanisha M. Fazal, "Health Diplomacy in Pandemical Times," *International Organization* 74, no. S1 (2020): E78–E97.
21. Michael R. Kenwick and Beth A. Simmons, "Pandemic Response as Border Politics," *International Organization* 74, no. S1 (December 2020): 36–58.
22. Henry Farrell and Abraham L. Newman, "Weaponized Interdependence: How Global Economic Networks Shape State Coercion," *International Security* 44, no. 1 (2019): 42–79.
23. Strange, *The Retreat of the State*; Rosenau, *Turbulence in World Politics*; Saskia Sassen, *Losing Control? Sovereignty in the Age of Globalization* (New York: Columbia University Press, 1996); Rodney Bruce Hall and Thomas J. Biersteker, eds., *The Emergence of Private Authority in Global Governance* (Cambridge: Cambridge University Press, 2002), 4; A. Claire Cutler, Virginia Haufler, and Tony Porter, eds., *Private Authority and International Affairs* (Albany: State University of New York Press, 1999); Patrick Thaddeus Jackson and Daniel Nexon, "Globalization, the Comparative Method, and Comparing Constructions," in *Constructivism and Comparative Politics*, ed. Daniel M. Green (Armonk, NY: M. E. Sharpe, 2002), 88–120; Roland Robertson, *Globalization: Social Theory and Global Culture* (London: Sage, 1992); David Harvey, *The*

Condition of Postmodernity: An Enquiry into the Origins of Cultural Change (Oxford: Wiley-Blackwell, 1991); Robert O. Keohane and Helen V. Milner, *Internationalization and Domestic Politics* (Cambridge: Cambridge University Press, 1996).

24. Joseph S. Nye and Robert O. Keohane, "Transnational Relations and World Politics: An Introduction," *International Organization* 25, no. 3 (1971): 329–49.

25. Eugene Staley, *World Economy in Transition: Technology vs. Politics, Laissez Faire vs. Planning, Power vs. Welfare* (New York: Council on Foreign Relations, 1939).

26. H. G. Wells, *Anticipations of the Reactions of Mechanical and Scientific Progress Upon Human Life and Thought* (Mineola, NY: Dover Publications, 1999). See also Duncan Bell, "Founding the World State: H. G. Wells on Empire and the English-Speaking Peoples," *International Studies Quarterly* 62, no. 4 (2018): 867–79; John S. Partington, "H. G. Wells and the World State: A Liberal Cosmopolitan in a Totalitarian Age," *International Relations* 17, no. 2 (2003): 233–46.

27. Shahar Hameiri and Lee Jones, *Governing Borderless Threats: Non-Traditional Security and the Politics of State Transformation* (Cambridge: Cambridge University Press, 2015). Saskia Sassen, *Territory, Authority, Rights: From Medieval to Global Assemblages* (Princeton, NJ: Princeton University Press, 2006).

28. Luke Glanville, "The Myth of 'Traditional' Sovereignty," *International Studies Quarterly* 57, no. 1 (March 2013): 79–90; Martha Finnemore, *The Purpose of Intervention: Changing Beliefs About the Use of Force* (Ithaca, NY: Cornell University Press, 2003).

29. James C. Scott, *Seeing Like a State: How Certain Schemes to Improve the Human Condition Have Failed* (New Haven, CT: Yale University Press, 1998). "Legibility" here is referring to the state and rule, but this is not its only use. See Jane Caplan, "Illegibility: Reading and Insecurity in History, Law and Government," *History Workshop Journal* 68, no. 1 (2009): 99–121.

30. Jim Mann, *The Great Rift: Dick Cheney, Colin Powell, and the Broken Friendship That Defined an Era* (New York: Henry Holt, 2020).

31. Robert M. Gates, *Duty: Memoirs of a Secretary at War* (New York: Knopf, 2014).

32. This argument is made in much more detail using firsthand accounts and interviews of national security officials in chapter 4.

33. Ronald R. Krebs and Jennifer K. Lobasz, "Fixing the Meaning of 9/11: Hegemony, Coercion and the Road to War in Iraq," *Security Studies* 16, no. 3 (2007): 409–51.

34. Charles Tilly, "Mechanisms in Political Processes," *Annual Review of Political Science* 4 (2001): 21–41.

35. Quoted in Richard Bach Jensen, "Daggers, Rifles and Dynamite: Anarchist Terrorism in 19th Century Europe," *Terrorism and Political Violence* 16, no. 1 (2004): 138.

36. Mark Shirk, "How Does Violence Threaten the State? Four Narratives on Piracy," *Terrorism and Political Violence* 29, no. 4 (2017): 656–73.

37. Jef Huysmans, "Security! What Do You Mean? From Concept to Thick Signifier," *European Journal of International Relations* 4, no. 2 (1998): 226–55; Jennifer Mitzen, "Ontological Security in World Politics: State Identity and the Security Dilemma," *European Journal of International Relations* 12, no. 3 (2006): 341–70; Brent J. Steele, *Ontological*

38. William J. Brenner, *Confounding Powers: Anarchy and International Society from the Assassins to Al Qaeda* (Cambridge: Cambridge: University Press, 2016); Stacie E. Goddard and Ronald R. Krebs, "Rhetoric, Legitimation, and Grand Strategy," *Security Studies* 24, no. 1 (2015): 5–36; Stacie E. Goddard, *When Might Makes Right: Rising Powers and World Order* (Ithaca, NY: Cornell University Press, 2018).

39. State formation should be state transformation. Late in his career, Charles Tilly—an early user of the term "state formation"—argued, "In order to avoid [...] teleology, let us speak of state *transformation*, recognizing it as a bundle of processes that produce multiple varieties of states, and continue indefinitely." Charles Tilly, "States, State Transformation, and War," in *Oxford Handbook of World History*, ed. Jerry H. Bentley (Oxford: Oxford University Press, 2011), 179.

40. Daniel H. Nexon, *The Struggle for Power in Early Modern Europe: Religious Conflict, Dynastic Empires, and International Change* (Princeton, NJ: Princeton University Press, 2009); Jordan Branch, *The Cartographic State: Maps, Territory, and the Origins of Sovereignty* (Cambridge: Cambridge University Press, 2014); Hendrik Spruyt, *The Sovereign State and Its Competitors: An Analysis of Systems Change* (Princeton, NJ: Princeton University Press, 1994); Daniel Philpott, *Revolutions in Sovereignty: How Ideas Shaped Modern International Relations* (Princeton, NJ: Princeton University Press, 2001); Rodney Bruce Hall, *National Collective Identity: Social Constructs and International Systems* (New York: Columbia University Press, 1999); Edgar Kiser and April Linton, "Determinants of the Growth of the State: War and Taxation in Early Modern Europe," *Social Forces* 80, no. 2 (2001): 411–48; John Gerard Ruggie, "Continuity and Transformation in the World Polity: Toward a Neorealist Synthesis," *World Politics* 35, no. 2 (1983): 261–85.

41. Barry Buzan and George Lawson, *The Global Transformation: History, Modernity and the Making of International Relations* (Cambridge: Cambridge University Press, 2015); Jennifer Mitzen, *Power in Concert* (Chicago: University of Chicago Press, 2013); Andreas Osiander, "Sovereignty, International Relations, and the Westphalian Myth," *International Organization* 55, no. 2 (2001): 251–87; Mlada Bukovansky, *Legitimacy and Power Politics: The American and French Revolutions in International Political Culture* (Princeton, NJ: Princeton University Press, 2002).

42. Philpott, *Revolutions in Sovereignty*.

43. Hall, *National Collective Identity*; Philpott, *Revolutions in Sovereignty*.

44. Bukovansky, *Legitimacy and Power Politics*.

45. J. Samuel Barkin and Bruce Cronin, "The State and the Nation: Changing Norms and the Rules of Sovereignty in International Relations," *International Organization* 48, no. 1 (1994): 107–30.

46. Spruyt, *The Sovereign State*.

47. Nexon, *The Struggle for Power*; Philip S. Gorski, *The Disciplinary Revolution: Calvinism and the Rise of the State in Early Modern Europe* (Chicago: University of Chicago Press, 2003).

48. Barrington Moore, *Social Origins of Dictatorship and Democracy: Lord and Peasant in the Making of the Modern World* (Boston: Beacon Press, 2003).
49. Philpott, *Revolutions in Sovereignty*.
50. Barkin and Cronin, "The State and the Nation"; Hall, *National Collective Identity*; Christian Reus-Smit, *The Moral Purpose of the State: Culture, Social Identity, and Institutional Rationality in International Relations* (Princeton, NJ: Princeton University Press, 1999); Philpott, *Revolutions in Sovereignty*; Bukovansky, *Legitimacy and Power Politics*; Branch, *The Cartographic State*.
51. William J. Brenner, *Confounding Powers*; Barak Mendelsohn, *Combating Jihadism: American Hegemony and Interstate Cooperation in the War on Terrorism* (University of Chicago Press, 2009); Andrew Phillips, *War, Religion and Empire: The Transformation of International Orders* (Cambridge: Cambridge University Press, 2011).
52. Matthew Kroenig and Jay Stowsky, "War Makes the State, but Not as It Pleases: Homeland Security and American Anti-Statism," *Security Studies* 15, no. 2 (2006): 225–70.
53. Hall, *National Collective Identity*.
54. Whether the treaties of Westphalia had any lasting impact at all is also debated. See Osiander, "Sovereignty, International Relations, and the Westphalian Myth"; Benno Teschke, *The Myth of 1648: Class, Geopolitics, and the Making of Modern International Relations* (London: Verso, 2003); Benjamin de Carvalho, Halvard Leira, and John M. Hobson, "The Big Bangs of IR: The Myths That Your Teachers Still Tell You About 1648 and 1919," *Millennium—Journal of International Studies* 39, no. 3 (2011): 735–58.
55. Richard Bean, "War and the Birth of the Nation State," *Journal of Economic History* 33, no. 1 (1973): 203–21; Charles Tilly, "Reflections on the History of European State-Making," in *The Formation of National States in Western Europe*, ed. Charles Tilly (Princeton, NJ: Princeton University Press, 1975), 3–84; Charles Tilly, *Coercion, Capital, and European States, AD 990–1990* (Oxford: Blackwell, 1990); Brian M. Downing, *The Military Revolution and Political Change: Origins of Democracy and Autocracy in Early Modern Europe* (Princeton, NJ: Princeton University Press, 1992); Kiser and Linton, "Determinants of the Growth of the State"; Jan Glete, *War and the State in Early Modern Europe: Spain, the Dutch Republic, and Sweden as Fiscal-Military States, 1500–1600* (London: Routledge, 2002); Meyer Kestnbaum, "Mars Revealed: The Entry of Ordinary People Into War Among States," in *Remaking Modernity: Politics, History, and Sociology*, ed. Julia Adams, Elisabeth S. Clemens, and Ann Shola Orloff (Durham, NC: Duke University Press, 2005), 249–85.
56. Robert Brenner, "Agrarian Class Structure and Economic Development in Pre-Industrial Europe," *Past and Present* 70, no. 1 (1976): 30–75; Perry Anderson, *Lineages of the Absolutist State* (London: Verso, 1979); Philip Corrigan, *Capitalism, State Formation, and Marxist Theory: Historical Investigations* (London: Quartet Books, 1980); Michael Hechter and William Brustein, "Regional Modes of Production and Patterns of State Formation in Western Europe," *American Journal of Sociology* 85, no. 5 (1980): 1061–94; Gordon L. Clark and Michael Dear, *State Apparatus: Structures and Language of Legitimacy* (Boston: Allen and Unwin, 1984); Douglass C. North, *Institutions,*

Institutional Change and Economic Performance, 2nd ed. (Cambridge: Cambridge University Press, 1990).

57. Gorski, *The Disciplinary Revolution*; George Steinmetz, ed., *State/Culture: State-Formation After the Cultural Turn* (Ithaca, NY: Cornell University Press, 1999); Reus-Smit, *The Moral Purpose of the State*; Bukovansi, *Legitimacy and Power Politics*; Hall, *National Collective Identity*; Philpott, *Revolutions in Sovereignty*.
58. For an overview, see Daniel H. Nexon, "Zeitgeist? The New Idealism in the Study of International Change," *Review of International Political Economy* 12, no. 4 (2005): 700–719.
59. B. H. Liddell Hart, *A History of the Second World War* (London: Pan, 2014).
60. Charles Tilly, "War Making and State Making as Organized Crime," in *Bringing the State Back In*, ed. Peter B. Evans, Dietrich Rueschemeyer, and Theda Skocpol (Cambridge: Cambridge University Press, 1985), 169–91.
61. One exception is Paul Musgrave, "Bringing the State Police In: The Diffusion of U.S. Statewide Policing Agencies, 1905–1941," *Studies in American Political Development* 34, no. 1 (2020): 3–23.
62. Emanuel Adler and Vincent Pouliot, "International Practices," *International Theory* 3, no. 1 (2011): 1–36; Hans Joas, *The Creativity of Action* (Chicago: University of Chicago Press, 1996).
63. Mustafa Emirbayer, "Manifesto for a Relational Sociology," *American Journal of Sociology* 103, no. 2 (1997): 281–317; Patrick Thaddeus Jackson and Daniel H. Nexon, "Relations Before States: Substance, Process, and the Study of World Politics," *European Journal of International Relations* 5, no. 3 (1999): 291–332; David M. McCourt, "Practice Theory and Relationalism as the New Constructivism," *International Studies Quarterly* 60, no. 3 (2016): 475–85.
64. Barry Buzan and Richard Little, *The Logic of Anarchy: Neorealism to Structural Realism* (New York: Columbia University Press, 1993).
65. David A. Lake, *Hierarchy in International Relations* (Ithaca, NY: Cornell University Press, 2009); Tarak Barkawi and Mark Laffey, "Retrieving the Imperial: Empire and International Relations," *Millennium—Journal of International Studies* 31, no. 1 (2002): 109–27; Ayşe Zarakol, ed., *Hierarchies in World Politics* (Cambridge: Cambridge University Press, 2017).
66. Hall, *National Collective Identity*; Bukovansky, *Legitimacy and Power Politics*; Reus-Smit, *The Moral Purpose of the State*; Spruyt, *The Sovereign State*; Nexon, *The Struggle for Power*; Branch, *The Cartographic State*.
67. Hedley Bull, *The Anarchical Society: A Study of Order in World Politics* (New York: Columbia University Press, 2002); Andrew Hurrell, *On Global Order: Power, Values, and the Constitution of International Society* (Oxford: Oxford University Press, 2007).
68. Naeem Inayatullah, "Beyond the Sovereignty Dilemma: Quasi-States as Social Construct," in *State Sovereignty as Social Construct*, ed. Thomas J. Bierstecker and Cynthia Weber (Cambridge: Cambridge University Press, 1996), 50–77; Margaret E. Keck and Kathryn Sikkink, *Activists Beyond Borders: Advocacy Networks in International Politics* (Ithaca, NY: Cornell University Press, 1998); Jordan Branch, "'Colonial Reflection'

and Territoriality: The Peripheral Origins of Sovereign Statehood," *European Journal of International Relations* 18, no. 2 (2012): 277–97; Andrew Phillips and J. C. Sharman, *International Order in Diversity: War, Trade and Rule in the Indian Ocean* (Cambridge: Cambridge University Press, 2015); Amitav Acharya, *Constructing Global Order: Agency and Change in World Politics* (Cambridge: Cambridge University Press, 2018).

69. G. John Ikenberry, *Liberal Leviathan: The Origins, Crisis, and Transformation of the American World Order* (Princeton, NJ: Princeton University Press, 2012); Robert Jervis et al., eds., *Chaos in the Liberal Order: The Trump Presidency and International Politics in the Twenty-First Century* (New York: Columbia University Press, 2018); Kyle M. Lascurettes, *Orders of Exclusion: Great Powers and the Strategic Sources of Foundational Rules in International Relations* (Oxford: Oxford University Press, 2020); Thomas J. Wright, *All Measures Short of War: The Contest for the Twenty-First Century and the Future of American Power* (New Haven, CT: Yale University Press, 2018); Amitav Acharya, *The End of American World Order* (Cambridge: Polity, 2018); Jean-François Drolet and Michael C. Williams, "Radical Conservatism and Global Order: International Theory and the New Right," *International Theory* 10, no. 3 (2018): 285–313.

70. Buzan and Lawson, *The Global Transformation*; Daniel M. Green, ed., *Bifurcated Century: The Two Worlds of Nineteenth Century International Relations* (London: Routledge, 2018); Andrew Phillips, "Contesting the Confucian Peace: Civilization, Barbarism and International Hierarchy in East Asia," *European Journal of International Relations* 24, no. 2 (2018): 740–64; Erik Ringmar, "Performing International Systems: Two East-Asian Alternatives to the Westphalian Order," *International Organization* 66, no. 1 (2012): 1–25; L. H. M. Ling, "Worlds Beyond Westphalia: Daoist Dialectics and the 'China Threat,'" *Review of International Studies* 39, no. 3 (2013): 549–68.

71. Alexander Cooley and Daniel Nexon, *Exit from Hegemony: The Unraveling of American Global Order* (Oxford: Oxford University Press, 2020); Stacie E. Goddard and Daniel H. Nexon, "The Dynamics of Global Power Politics: A Framework for Analysis," *Journal of Global Security Studies* 1, no. 1 (2016): 4–18; Stacie E. Goddard, "Embedded Revisionism: Networks, Institutions, and Challenges to World Order," *International Organization* 72, no. 4 (2018): 763–97; Daniel H. Nexon and Iver B. Neumann, "Hegemonic-Order Theory: A Field-Theoretic Account," *European Journal of International Relations* 24, no. 3 (2018): 662–86; Stacie E. Goddard, Paul K. MacDonald, and Daniel H. Nexon, "Repertoires of Statecraft: Instruments and Logics of Power Politics," *International Relations* 33, no. 2 (2019): 304–21; G. John Ikenberry and Daniel H. Nexon, "Hegemony Studies 3.0: The Dynamics of Hegemonic Orders," *Security Studies* 28, no. 3 (2019): 395–421; Farrell and Newman, "Weaponized Interdependence."

72. Christian Bueger and Frank Gadinger, "The Play of International Practice," *International Studies Quarterly* 59, no. 3 (2015): 449–60.

73. Goddard and Nexon, "The Dynamics of Global Power Politics."

74. Nexon and Neumann, "Hegemonic-Order Theory."

75. Goddard, "Embedded Revisionism"; Alexander Cooley, Daniel Nexon, and Stephen Ward, "Revising Order or Changing the Balance of Military Power? An Alternative Typology of Revisionist and Status Quo States," *Review of International Studies* 45, no. 4 (2019): 689–708.

1. CHANGE AND CONTINUITY IN POLITICAL ORDER

1. Karl Marx and Friedrich Engels, *The Marx-Engels Reader*, ed. Richard Tucker (New York: Norton, 1978).
2. Bob Jessop, *State Power: A Strategic-Relational Approach* (Malden, MA: Polity, 2007); Bob Jessop, *State Theory: Putting the Capitalist State in Its Place* (State College: Pennsylvania State University Press, 1990); Nicos Poulantzas, *State, Power, Socialism* (London: Verso, 2014).
3. Max Weber, *The Vocation Lectures*, trans. Rodney Livingstone (Indianapolis, IN: Hackett, 2004).
4. Peter B. Evans, Dietrich Rueschemeyer, and Theda Skocpol, eds., *Bringing the State Back In* (Cambridge: Cambridge University Press, 1985).
5. Pierre Bourdieu, "Some Properties of Fields," in *Sociology in Question*, ed. Pierre Bourdieu (London: Sage, 1993), 72–77; Pierre Bourdieu, "The Field of Cultural Production, or the Economic World Reversed," *Poetics* 12 (1983): 311–56.
6. Michel Foucault, *The Birth of Biopolitics*, trans. Graham Burchell (New York: Palgrave Macmillan, 2008); Michel Foucault, *Security, Territory, Population: Lectures at the College de France* (New York: Picador, 2009).
7. Kimberly J. Morgan and Ann Shola Orloff, "Introduction: The Many Hands of the State," in *The Many Hands of the State: Theorizing Political Authority and Social Control*, ed. Morgan and Orloff (Cambridge: Cambridge University Press, 2017), 1–32.
8. Emanuel Adler and Vincent Pouliot, "International Practices," *International Theory* 3, no. 1 (2011): 1–36; Hans Joas, *The Creativity of Action* (Chicago: University of Chicago Press, 1996).
9. Christian Bueger and Frank Gadinger, "The Play of International Practice," *International Studies Quarterly* 59, no. 3 (2015): 453.
10. Joas, *The Creativity of Action*, 128.
11. John Dewey, *The Public and Its Problems* (Athens: Ohio University Press, 1954), 61.
12. John Dewey, *Reconstruction in Philosophy* (New York: Cosimo, 2008), 77; Patrick Thaddeus Jackson, *The Conduct of Inquiry in International Relations: Philosophy of Science and Its Implications for the Study of World Politics* (London: Routledge, 2010).
13. Bueger and Gadinger, "The Play of International Practice," 453.
14. Philip Abrams, "Notes on the Difficulty of Studying the State," *Journal of Historical Sociology* 1, no. 1 (March 1988): 58–89; Patrick Thaddeus Jackson and Daniel H. Nexon, "Relations Before States: Substance, Process, and the Study of World Politics," *European Journal of International Relations* 5, no. 3 (1999): 291–332; Pierre Bourdieu, *On the*

1. CHANGE AND CONTINUITY IN POLITICAL ORDER   159

State: Lectures at the College de France, 1989–1992 (London: Polity, 2015); Andrew Abbott, *Processual Sociology* (Chicago: University of Chicago Press, 2016).

15. Niccolò Machiavelli, *The Prince and the Discourses*, ed. Max Lerner (New York: McGraw Hill, 1950).
16. David Hume, *Treatise of Human Nature* (Amherst, NY: Prometheus Books, 1992).
17. Daniel Levine, *Recovering International Relations: The Promise of Sustainable Critique* (Oxford: Oxford University Press, 2012).
18. Iza Hussin, "Making Legibility Between Colony and Empire: Translation, Conflation, and the Making of the Muslim State," in Morgan and Orloff, *The Many Hands of the State*, 349–68.
19. Graham T. Allison, "Conceptual Models and the Cuban Missile Crisis," *American Political Science Review* 63, no. 3 (1969): 689–718.
20. Morgan and Orloff, "Introduction," 3.
21. Matthew Norton, "Real Mythic Histories: Circulatory Networks and State-Centrism," in *Global Historical Sociology*, ed. Julian Go and George Lawson (Cambridge: Cambridge University Press, 2017), 42.
22. Bounded political authority is reflected in the modern tendency to categorize experience and make knowledge a "quest for certainty, understood as the correct modelling of an 'external reality' in the internal exhibit of the mind." Timothy Mitchell, *Colonising Egypt* (Cambridge: Cambridge University Press, 1988), 177. See also René Descartes's mind/world or mind/body distinction: René Descartes, *Discourse on Method and Meditations on First Philosophy*, trans. Donald A. Cress (Indianapolis, IN: Hackett, 1980). If Jens Bartelson is correct that "sovereignty and knowledge implicated each other logically and produce each other historically," then a world in which the reasoning individual, separated from the world, is the sole arbiter of the known is likely to be governed by bounded polities. Jens Bartelson, *A Genealogy of Sovereignty* (Cambridge: Cambridge University Press, 1995), 5.
23. Michele Lamont and Virag Molnar, "The Study of Boundaries in the Social Sciences," *Annual Review of Sociology* 28 (2002): 167–95; Charles Tilly, "Social Boundary Mechanisms," *Philosophy of the Social Sciences* 34, no. 2 (2004): 211–36; Mark A. Pachuki, Sabrina Pendergrass, and Michele Lamont, "Boundary Processes: Recent Developments and New Theoretical Contributions," *Poetics* 35, no. 6 (2007): 331–51. For the state, see Paul Starr, "Social Categories and Claims in the Liberal State," *Social Research* 59, no. 2 (1992): 263; Aradhana Sharma and Akhil Gupta, eds., *The Anthropology of the State: A Reader* (Oxford: Blackwell, 2006); Bourdieu, *On the State*; Damon Mayrl and Sarah Quinn, "Defining the State from Within: Boundaries, Schemas, and Associational Policymaking," *Sociological Theory* 34, no. 1 (2016): 1–26.
24. Janice E. Thomson, "State Sovereignty in International Relations," *International Studies Quarterly* 39, no. 2 (1995): 217.
25. Robert H. Jackson, *Quasi-States: Sovereignty, International Relations, and the Third World* (Cambridge: Cambridge University Press, 1990).
26. Robert D. Putnam, "Diplomacy and Domestic Politics: The Logic of Two-Level Games," *International Organization* 42, no. 3 (1988): 428–60; Andrew Moravscik,

"Taking Preferences Seriously: A Liberal Theory of International Politics," *International Organization* 51, no. 4 (1997): 513–53; Jeffrey Legro, *Rethinking the World: Great Power Strategies and International Order* (Ithaca, NY: Cornell University Press, 2005).

27. John Dewey and Arthur Fisher Bentley, *Knowing and the Known* (Boston: Beacon Press, 1949).
28. Jackson and Nexon, "Relations Before States."
29. R. B. J. Walker, "Genealogy, Geopolitics and Political Community: Richard K. Ashley and the Critical Social Theory of International Politics," *Alternatives* 13 (1988): 85.
30. Yale H. Ferguson and Richard W. Mansbach, "Polities Past and Present," *Millennium* 37, no. 2 (2008): 365–79.
31. Alexander Wendt, *Social Theory of International Politics* (Cambridge: Cambridge University Press, 1999).
32. Johan Galtung, "A Structural Theory of Imperialism," *Journal of Peace Research* 8, no. 2 (1971): 81–117; Alexander Motyl, *Imperial Ends: The Decay, Collapse, and Revival of Empires* (New York: Columbia University Press, 2001); Alexander Motyl, *Revolutions, Nations, Empires: Conceptual Limits and Theoretical Possibilities* (New York: Columbia University Press, 1999); Daniel H. Nexon and Thomas Wright, "What's at Stake in the American Empire Debate," *American Political Science Review* 101, no. 2 (2007): 253–71.
33. Hendrik Spruyt, *The Sovereign State and Its Competitors: An Analysis of Systems Change* (Princeton, NJ: Princeton University Press, 1994).
34. Winichakul Thongchai, *Siam Mapped: A History of the Geo-Body of a Nation* (Honolulu: University of Hawai'i Press, 1994); James C. Scott, *The Art of Not Being Governed: An Anarchist History of Upland Southeast Asia* (New Haven, CT: Yale University Press, 2009).
35. Spruyt, *The Sovereign State.*
36. Hedley Bull, *The Anarchical Society: A Study of Order in World Politics* (New York: Columbia University Press, 2002); Stephen J. Kobrin, "Back to the Future: Neomedievalism and the Postmodern Digital World Economy," *Journal of International Affairs* 51, no. 2 (1998): 361–86.
37. Mark Shirk, "'Bringing the State Back In' to the Empire Turn: Piracy and the Layered Sovereignty of the Eighteenth Century Atlantic," *International Studies Review* 19, no. 2 (2017): 143–65. See also chapter 2.
38. For the rest of this book, I use "border" for this type of boundary.
39. As an example, see Nexon and Wright's argument about how empires tend to collapse the international/domestic distinction. Nexon and Wright, "What's at Stake in the American Empire Debate."
40. See work on social identity theory: Rupert Brown, "Social Identity Theory: Past Achievements, Current Problems and Future Challenges," *European Journal of Social Psychology* 30, no. 6 (2000): 745–78; Michael A. Hogg, "Social Identity Theory," in *Contemporary Social Psychological Theories*, ed. Peter J. Burke (Stanford, CA: Stanford Social Sciences, 2006).

41. Timothy Mitchell, "The Limits of the State: Beyond Statist Approaches and Their Critics," *American Political Science Review* 85, no. 1 (1991): 77–96.
42. Mitchell, *Colonising Egypt*.
43. Jordan Branch, *The Cartographic State: Maps, Territory, and the Origins of Sovereignty* (Cambridge: Cambridge University Press, 2014).
44. Kerry Goettlich, "The Rise of Linear Borders in World Politics," *European Journal of International Relations* 25, no. 1 (2019): 203–28.
45. Garrett Mattingly, "No Peace Beyond What Line?," *Transactions of the Royal Historical Society* 5, no. 13 (1963): 145–62; Lauren Benton, *A Search for Sovereignty: Law and Geography in European Empires 1400–1900* (Cambridge: Cambridge University Press, 2010).
46. Shirk, "'Bringing the State Back In' to the Empire Turn."
47. Mark Shirk, "Boundaries in the Sea," in *International Relations and the Sea*, ed. Halvard Leira and Benjamin de Carvalho (Manchester: Manchester University Press, forthcoming).
48. C. A. Bayly et al., "AHR Conversation: On Transnational History," *American Historical Review* 111, no. 5 (2006): 1441–64; Akira Iriye, *Global and Transnational History: The Past, Present, and Future* (New York: Springer, 2012); Go and Lawson, *Global Historical Sociology*.
49. John Agnew, *Globalization and Sovereignty: Beyond the Territorial Trap* (London: Rowman and Littlefield, 2017); John Agnew and Luca Muscarà, *Making Political Geography* (London: Rowman and Littlefield, 2012). In IR, see Branch, *The Cartographic State*; Goettlich, "The Rise of Linear Borders in World Politics."
50. "Above" and "below" are directional only because of the existence of the state and do not reflect the flows themselves. "Around," "about," and "through" would probably be more accurate.
51. Motyl, *Imperial Ends*; Tarak Barkawi and Mark Laffey, "Retrieving the Imperial: Empire and International Relations," *Millennium—Journal of International Studies* 31, no. 1 (2002): 109–27; Nexon and Wright, "What's at Stake in the American Empire Debate"; David A. Lake, *Hierarchy in International Relations* (Ithaca, NY: Cornell University Press, 2009); Jane Burbank and Frederick Cooper, *Empires in World History: Power and the Politics of Difference* (Princeton, NJ: Princeton University Press, 2011); Julian Go, *Patterns of Empire: The British and American Empires, 1688 to the Present* (Cambridge: Cambridge University Press, 2011).
52. Shirk, "'Bringing the State Back In' to the Empire Turn."
53. Andrew Phillips and J. C. Sharman, *International Order in Diversity: War, Trade and Rule in the Indian Ocean* (Cambridge: Cambridge University Press, 2015).
54. Pierre Bourdieu, *Outline of a Theory of Practice* (Cambridge: Cambridge University Press, 1977); Pierre Bourdieu, *The Logic of Practice* (Stanford, CA: Stanford University Press, 1990); Ted Hopf, "The Logic of Habit in International Relations," *European Journal of International Relations* 16, no. 4 (2010): 539–61.
55. George Steinmetz, ed., *State/Culture: State-Formation After the Cultural Turn* (Ithaca, NY: Cornell University Press, 1999), 9.

56. Mark Shirk, "The Universal Eye: Anarchist 'Propaganda of the Deed' and Development of the Modern Surveillance State," *International Studies Quarterly* 63, no. 2 (2019): 334–45.
57. Robert M. Axelrod, *The Evolution of Cooperation* (New York: Basic Books, 1984); Kenneth A. Oye, "Explaining Cooperation Under Anarchy: Hypotheses and Strategies," *World Politics* 38, no. 1 (1985): 1–24; Helen V. Milner, "International Theories of Cooperation Among Nations," *World Politics* 44, no. 3 (1992): 466–96.
58. Turan Kayaoglu, "The Extension of Westphalian Sovereignty: State Building and the Abolition of Extra-Territoriality," *International Studies Quarterly* 51, no. 3 (2007): 649–75; John M. Hobson, "Provincializing Westphalia: The Eastern Origins of Sovereignty," *International Politics* 46, no. 6 (2009): 671–90; Jordan Branch, "'Colonial Reflection' and Territoriality: The Peripheral Origins of Sovereign Statehood," *European Journal of International Relations* 18, no. 2 (2012): 277–97; L. H. M. Ling, "Worlds Beyond Westphalia: Daoist Dialectics and the 'China Threat,'" *Review of International Studies* 39, no. 3 (2013): 549–68.
59. Thongchai, *Siam Mapped*.
60. Martin J. Bayly, *Taming the Imperial Imagination: Colonial Knowledge, International Relations, and the Anglo-Afghan Encounter, 1808–1878* (Cambridge: Cambridge University Press, 2016).
61. Gunnar Cederlof, *Founding an Empire on India's North-Eastern Frontiers, 1790–1840: Climate, Commerce, Polity* (Oxford: Oxford University Press, 2014).
62. Friedrich Nietzsche, *On the Genealogy of Morality*, ed. Keith Ansell-Pearson, trans. Carol Diethe (Cambridge: Cambridge University Press, 2007), 53; See also Bartelson, *A Genealogy of Sovereignty*.
63. Friedrich V. Kratochwil, "Sovereignty, Property, and Propriety," in *The Puzzles of Politics: Inquiries Into the Genesis and Transformation of International Relations* (London: Routledge, 2011), 76; Erik Ringmar, "On the Ontological Status of the State," *European Journal of International Relations* 2, no. 4 (1996): 439.
64. Joseph R. Strayer, *On the Medieval Origins of the Modern State* (Princeton, NJ: Princeton University Press, 1970).
65. Jackson, *Quasi-States*.
66. James Mayall, *Nationalism and International Society* (Cambridge: Cambridge University Press, 1990).
67. Gianfranco Poggi, *The Development of the Modern State: A Sociological Introduction* (Stanford, CA: Stanford University Press, 1978); Spruyt, *The Sovereign State*.
68. Charles Tilly, "War Making and State Making as Organized Crime," in *Bringing the State Back In*, ed. Peter B. Evans, Dietrich Rueschemeyer, and Theda Skocpol (Cambridge: Cambridge University Press, 1985), 169–91.
69. Dewey, *The Public and Its Problems*, 33.
70. For similar, see Tilly, "Social Boundary Mechanisms"; Mayrl and Quinn, "Defining the State from Within," 6–9.
71. Max Weber, *Max Weber on the Methodology of the Social Sciences*, trans. Edward Shils (Glencoe, IL: Free Press, 1949). In IR, see Jackson, *The Conduct of Inquiry*.

72. Harry Bauer and Elisabetta Brighi, eds., *Pragmatism in International Relations* (London: Routledge, 2011); Jorg Friedrichs and Friedrich Kratochwil, "On Acting and Knowing: How Pragmatism Can Advance International Relations Research and Methodology," *International Organization* 63, no. 4 (2009): 701–31; Molly Cochran, "Pragmatism and International Relations: A Story of Closure and Opening," *European Journal of Pragmatism and American Philosophy* 4, no. 1 (2012): 1–22; Bueger and Gadinger, "The Play of International Practice"; Simon Frankel Pratt and Sebastian Schmidt, "Pragmatism in IR: The Prospects for Substantive Theorizing," *International Studies Review* (May 2021), https://doi.org/10.1093/isr/viab019.

73. Similarly, Rebecca Adler-Nissen distinguishes between "ordering" and "disordering" practices. Rebecca Adler-Nissen, "Towards a Practice Turn in EU Studies: The Everyday of European Integration," *Journal of Common Market Studies* 54, no. 1 (2016): 87–103.

74. Joas, *The Creativity of Action*, 127–44. Joas draws heavily on the work of John Dewey; see John Dewey, *Democracy and Education* (New York: Free Press, 1997); John Dewey, *Experience and Nature* (McCutchen Press, 2013). This is also prominent in Simon Frankel Pratt, "Pragmatism as Ontology, Not (Just) Epistemology: Exploring the Full Horizon of Pragmatism as an Approach to IR Theory," *International Studies Review* 18, no. 3 (2016): 508–27.

75. Joas, *The Creativity of Action*, 128.

76. Joas, *The Creativity of Action*, 131.

77. Ole Waever, "Securitization and Desecuritization," in *On Security*, ed. Ronnie D. Lipschutz (New York: Columbia University Press, 1995), 46–86; Thierry Balzacq, *Understanding Securitisation Theory: How Security Problems Emerge and Dissolve* (London: Routledge, 2010); Scott D. Watson, "'Framing' the Copenhagen School: Integrating the Literature on Threat Construction," *Millennium—Journal of International Studies* 40, no. 2 (2012): 279–301.

78. For more on legitimacy, see Stacie E. Goddard and Ronald R. Krebs, "Rhetoric, Legitimation, and Grand Strategy," *Security Studies* 24, no. 1 (2015): 5–36.

79. James C. Scott, *Seeing Like a State: How Certain Schemes to Improve the Human Condition Have Failed* (New Haven, CT: Yale University Press, 1998), 3.

80. Pamela Engel, "Watertown Resident Describes Finding Boston Bombing Suspect Dzhokhar Tsarnaev in His Boat," *Business Insider*, October 16, 2013.

81. Hans Joas, *Pragmatism and Social Theory* (Chicago: University of Chicago Press, 1993), 4.

82. Joas, *Creativity of Action*, 55–121.

83. Matthew Festenstein, "Pragmatism's Boundaries," *Millennium—Journal of International Studies* 31, no. 3 (2002): 549–71; Nicholas Greenwood Onuf, *World of Our Making: Rules and Rule in Social Theory and International Relations* (Columbia: University of South Carolina Press, 1989), 258–62.

84. Joas, *Pragmatism and Social Theory*, 4.

85. Bueger and Gadinger, "The Play of International Practice," 453; Michael Lynch, "Ehtnomethodology and the Logic of Practice," in *The Practice Turn in Contemporary*

Theory, ed. Theodore R. Schatzki, Karin Knorr Cetina, and Eike von Savigny (London: Routledge, 2001), 131.
86. Joas, *The Creativity of Action*, 154.
87. For more on this aspect of Dewey's thought, see Dewey, *Democracy and Education*; Dewey, *Experience and Nature*. See also William James, *Pragmatism and Other Writings* (New York: Penguin Books, 2000).
88. Allan Sekula, "The Body and the Archive," *October* 39 (1986): 3–64.
89. Onuf, *World of Our Making*, 258–89; Friedrich V. Kratochwil, *Rules, Norms, and Decisions: On the Conditions of Practical and Legal Reasoning in International Relations and Domestic Affairs* (Cambridge: Cambridge University Press, 1991), 21–44; Max Weber, "Prefatory Remarks to Collected Essays in the Sociology of Religion," in *Protestant Ethic and the Spirit of Capitalism*, trans. Stephen Kalberg (London: Roxbury, 2002), 149–64.

2. THE GOLDEN AGE OF PIRACY AND THE CREATION OF AN ATLANTIC WORLD

1. Mlada Bukovansky, *Legitimacy and Power Politics: The American and French Revolutions in International Political Culture* (Princeton, NJ: Princeton University Press, 2002); Don Higginbotham, "War and State Formation in the Revolutionary Atlantic," in *Empire and Nation: The American Revolution in the Atlantic World*, ed. Peter S. Onuf and Eliga H. Gould (Baltimore, MD: Johns Hopkins University Press, 2005), 54–71; Jeremy Adelman, *Sovereignty and Revolution in the Iberian Atlantic* (Princeton, NJ: Princeton University Press, 2009).
2. Janice E. Thomson, *Mercenaries, Pirates, and Sovereigns: State-Building and Extraterritorial Violence in Early Modern Europe* (Princeton, NJ: Princeton University Press, 1994).
3. For historical critiques of Thomson, see Tarak Barkawi, "Democratic States and Societies at War: The Global Context," *Comparative Social Research* 20 (2002): 361–76.
4. Daniel H. Nexon and Thomas Wright, "What's at Stake in the American Empire Debate," *American Political Science Review* 101, no. 2 (2007): 253–71; Daniel H. Nexon, *The Struggle for Power in Early Modern Europe: Religious Conflict, Dynastic Empires, and International Change* (Princeton, NJ: Princeton University Press, 2009); Alexander Motyl, *Imperial Ends: The Decay, Collapse, and Revival of Empires* (New York: Columbia University Press, 2001); Jeppe Mulich, "Microregionalism and Intercolonial Relations: The Case of the Danish West Indies, 1730–1830," *Journal of Global History* 8, no. 1 (2013): 72–94.
5. Philip J. Stern, *The Company-State: Corporate Sovereignty and the Early Modern Foundations of the British Empire in India* (Oxford: Oxford University Press, 2012).
6. Morten Skumsrud Andersen, "Semi-Cores in Imperial Relations: The Cases of Scotland and Norway," *Review of International Studies* 42, no. 1 (2016): 1–26.
7. John Darwin, *The End of the British Empire: The Historical Debate* (Oxford: Wiley-Blackwell, 2006), 4.

8. Motyl, *Imperial Ends*; Nexon, *The Struggle for Power*.
9. Jane Burbank and Frederick Cooper. *Empires in World History: Power and the Politics of Difference* (Princeton, NJ: Princeton University Press, 2011).
10. Mark Shirk, "'Bringing the State Back In' to the Empire Turn: Piracy and the Layered Sovereignty of the Eighteenth Century Atlantic," *International Studies Review* 19, no. 2 (2017): 143–65.
11. Lauren Benton, *A Search for Sovereignty: Law and Geography in European Empires 1400–1900* (Cambridge: Cambridge University Press, 2010).
12. The placement of West Africa vis-à-vis the line is unclear. It was certainly not Europe, and there were colonies, even if they had fewer settlers. It also played a role in piracy, with attacks on slave ships and pirates using its coast to rest and retool. However, West Africa was not the West Indies or North America, where "beyond the line" originated. There is also little evidence that it was included in many of the effects of erasing the line.
13. Garrett Mattingly, "No Peace Beyond What Line?," *Transactions of the Royal Historical Society* 5, no. 13 (1963): 145–62.
14. Mattingly, "No Peace Beyond What Line?," 145.
15. Ian Kenneth Steele argues that the line became the equator, with an exception for North America. He also points to the fiftieth meridian west, the supposed line drawn up in the papal bull *Inter Caetara*, signed by Pope Alexander VI in 1493. Ian Kenneth Steele, *The English Atlantic, 1675–1740: An Exploration of Communication and Community* (Oxford: Oxford University Press, 1986); Benton, *A Search for Sovereignty*, 114n20.
16. Mark Shirk, "Boundaries in the Sea," in *International Relations and the Sea*, ed. Halvard Leira and Benjamin de Carvalho (Manchester: Manchester University Press, forthcoming).
17. Steele, *The English Atlantic*, 191.
18. Frances Gardiner Davenport, *European Treaties Bearing on the History of the United States and Its Dependencies* (Clark, NJ: Lawbook Exchange, 2012), 42.
19. Philip J. Stern, "Companies: Monopoly, Sovereignty, and the East Indies," in *Mercantilism Reimagined: Political Economy in Early Modern Britain and Its Empire*, ed. Philip J. Stern and Carl Wennerlind (Oxford: Oxford University Press, 2014), 183.
20. Colonialism of this period was also characterized by religious zeal and/or freedom from religious persecution. These are other reasons why colonies were still "international" during this period.
21. Spain would dominate the Caribbean until the nineteenth century despite declining as a continental power due to timing and disease vectors. John Robert McNeill, *Mosquito Empires: Ecology and War in the Greater Caribbean, 1620–1914* (Cambridge: Cambridge University Press, 2010).
22. Burbank and Cooper, *Empires in World History*, 162–70.
23. Philip E. Steinberg, *The Social Construction of the Ocean* (Cambridge: Cambridge University Press, 2001).
24. Hugo Grotius, *The Law of War and Peace. De Jure Belli Ac Pacis, Libri Tres* (Indianapolis, IN: Bobbs-Merrill, 1962), 466.

25. See Benton, *A Search for Sovereignty*, 131–37; Stern, "Companies."
26. Jan Glete, *Warfare at Sea, 1500–1650: Maritime Conflicts and the Transformation of Europe* (London: Routledge, 2000).
27. The term "buccaneer," derived from the French *boucanier* or the Carib *Bukan*, refers to a method of preserving meat by smoking. It reflects early seventeenth-century pirate origins as coming from a group of "French political and religious refugees . . . [who] eked out a living providing hides, tallow, and dried meat . . . in exchange for guns and ammunition." Thomson, *Mercenaries, Pirates, and Sovereigns*, 46.
28. Joel H. Baer, "Bold Captain Avery in the Privy Council: Early Variants of a Broadside Ballad from the Pepys Collection," *Folk Music Journal* 7, no. 1 (1995): 4–26; Douglas R. Burgess Jr., "Piracy in the Public Sphere: The Henry Every Trials and the Battle for Meaning in Seventeenth-Century Print Culture," *Journal of British Studies* 48, no. 4 (2009): 887–913.
29. The National Archives, Kew, London, UK (hereafter NA), Colonial Office Papers (hereafter CO), 1/25, f. 160.
30. "A Copy of Verses Composed by Captain Henry Every," University of California–Santa Barbara, English Broadside Ballad Archive, 22206, http://ebba.english.ucsb.edu/ballad/22206/xml.
31. "Pirate" here meant privateer from a rival state. Alexander O. Exquemelin, *The Buccaneers of America*, trans. Alexis Brown (Mineola, NY: Dover Publications, 1969), 125.
32. Bryan Mabee, "Pirates, Privateers, and the Political Economy of Private Violence," *Global Change, Peace, and Security* 21, no. 2 (2009): 139–52.
33. Benton, *A Search for Sovereignty*, 113.
34. Exquemelin, *The Buccaneers of America*, 200–201. For the whole saga, see 186–208.
35. Matthew Norton, "Classification and Coercion: The Destruction of Piracy in the English Maritime System," *American Journal of Sociology* 119, no. 6 (2014): 1537–75; Jeremy Black, *Eighteenth-Century Europe* (New York: St. Martin's Press, 1999); Philip J. Stern, "British Asia and British Atlantic: Comparisons and Connections," *William and Mary Quarterly* 63, no. 4 (2006): 693–712.
36. McNeill, *Mosquito Empires*.
37. Leonard Woods Labaree, ed., *Royal Instructions to British Colonial Governors* (New York: Octagon Books, 1967), doc. 43.
38. October 19, 1698, NA, CO, 5/1116, f. 2.
39. Lionel Wafer, *A New Voyage & Description of the Isthmus of America*, ed. Lillian Elwyn Elliot Joyce (London: Hakluyt Society, 1934); John Taylor, *Jamaica in 1687: The Taylor Manuscripts at the National Library of Jamaica*, ed. David Buisseret (Kingston: University of the West Indies Press, 2008).
40. "Letter from Captain John Balcher," May 13, 1716, NA, Admiralty Papers (hereafter ADM), 1/1471, f. 14; "A List of Vessels Commissioned by His Excellency, the Lord Archibald Hamilton," May 19, 1716, NA, CO, 137/11, f. 94.
41. J. Franklin Jameson, ed. *Privateering and Piracy in the Colonial Period, Illustrative Documents*, Kindle Edition, 2012, doc. 127; Jan Martin Lemnitzer, "'That Moral

42. League of Nations Against the United States': The Origins of the 1856 Declaration of Paris," *International History Review* 35, no. 5 (2013): 1068–88; Thomson, *Mercenaries, Pirates, and Sovereigns*, 69–76.
42. "Governor Codrington to Lords of Trade and Plantations," March 1, 1690, Calendar of State Papers Colonial Series, America and the West Indies (hereafter CSPCS), 13/789, https://www.british-history.ac.uk/search/series/cal-state-papers--colonial--america-west-indies.
43. For a copy of the letter of marque, see "Copy of Commission for Captain William Kidd," 1695, NA, High Court of the Admiralty (hereafter HCA), 25/12. For a copy of the ship's registration, see "Registration of the Adventure Galley," December 11, 1695, NA, HCA, 26/13, f. 59.
44. *Documents Related to the Colonial History of New York: Procured in England, Holland, and France* (*New York Colonial Documents*), vol. 4, trans. and ed. E. B. O'Callaghan (Albany, NY: Weed Parsons, 1854) (hereafter *NYCD*), June 18, 1697.
45. "Letter from Lord Bellomont to William Kidd," June 19, 1699, NA, CO, 5/860, f. 165.
46. *NYCD*, December 6, 1700.
47. Jameson, *Privateering and Piracy*, doc. 82.
48. Robert C. Ritchie, *Captain Kidd and the War Against the Pirates* (Cambridge, MA: Harvard University Press, 1986), 209.
49. For more, see Daniel DeFoe, *A General History of the Robberies and Murders of the Most Notorious Pyrates*, ed. Manuel Schonhorn (Mineola, NY: Dover Publications, 1999), 440–51.
50. Kevin P. McDonald, "'A Man of Courage and Activity': Thomas Tew and Pirate Settlements of the Indo-Atlantic Trade World, 1645–1730" (working paper, University of California–Berkeley, 2005), http://escholarship.org/uc/item/7tmo78mp; DeFoe, *A General History*, 419–39.
51. Mark G. Hanna, *Pirate Nests and the Rise of the British Empire, 1570–1740* (Chapel Hill: University of North Carolina Press, 2015), 329–50.
52. Burgess, "Piracy in the Public Sphere"; DeFoe, *A General History*, 49–62.
53. Marcus Rediker, *Villains of All Nations: Atlantic Pirates in the Golden Age* (Boston: Beacon Press, 2004), 24.
54. Michael J. Jarvis, *In the Eye of All Trade: Bermuda, Bermudians, and the Maritime Atlantic World, 1680–1783* (Chapel Hill: University of North Carolina Press, 2012), 84–85.
55. "Mr. Gale to Colonel Thomas Pitt," November 4, 1718, NA, CO, 23/1, f. 47.
56. Jameson, *Privateering and Piracy*, doc. 108.
57. Alejandro Colas and Bryan Mabee, "The Flow and Ebb of Private Seaborne Violence in Global Politics," in *Mercenaries, Pirates, Bandits, and Empires: Private Violence in Historical Context*, ed. Colas and Mabee (New York: Columbia University Press, 2011), 83–106; Thomson, *Mercenaries, Pirates, and Sovereigns*.
58. To go "upon the account" means to become a pirate. Rediker, *Villains of All Nations*, 29–30.

59. Roberts was a third mate on a ship attacked by pirates. He decided to go "upon the account" and eventually became the ship's captain; see Jameson, *Privateering and Piracy*, doc. 117.
60. "Their design, as they said themselves, was upon the wrecks. They went to sea, and in a shorter time than could be expected, return'd again with a considerable sum of money." "Letter from Captain John Belcher," May 13, 1716, NA, ADM, 1/1471, f. 14.
61. Arne Bialuschewski, "Pirates, Markets and Imperial Authority: Economic Aspects of Maritime Depredations in the Atlantic World, 1716–1726," *Global Crime* 9, no. 1/2 (2008): 54–56.
62. Max Savelle, *Empires to Nations: Expansion in America, 1713–1824* (Minneapolis: University of Minnesota Press, 1974), 122.
63. Bialuschewski, "Pirates, Markets and Imperial Authority," 55.
64. Rediker, *Villains of All Nations*.
65. Lawrence H. Officer and Samuel H. Williamson, "Five Ways to Compute the Relative Value of the UK Pound Amount, 1270 to Present," Measuring Worth, 2015. https://www.measuringworth.com/calculators/ukcompare/.
66. "Governor and Council of South Carolina to the Council on Trade and Plantations," October 21, 1718, CSPCS, 30/730.
67. Bialuschewski, "Pirates, Markets and Imperial Authority"; Rediker, *Villains of All Nations*.
68. James S. Pritchard, *In Search of Empire: The French in the Americas, 1670–1730* (Cambridge: Cambridge University Press, 2004).
69. "Memorat of Merchants Trading to Virginia and Maryland About the Pyrats," 1717, NA, State Papers (hereafter SP), 42/123.
70. Niklas Frykman, "Pirates and Smugglers: Political Economy in the Red Atlantic," in Stern and Wennerlind, *Mercantilism Reimagined*, 224.
71. Rediker, *Villains of All Nations*, 35.
72. "Deposition of Captain William South," May 27, 1719, NA, CO, 23/13, f. 53; "Letter of John Balcher," May 17, 1716, NA, ADM, 1/1471, f. 14.
73. "Governor Alexander Spottswood to Harry Beverley," June 15, 1716, NA, CO, 5/1317, f. 249.
74. "Representation of the Merchants Against Lord Archibald Hamilton," May 19, 1716, NA, CO, 137/11, f. 105; see ff. 92–109 for correspondence on this issue.
75. "Governor Alexander Spottswood to Lords," July 3, 1716, NA, CO, 5/1317, ff. 245–46; "Governor Archibald Hamilton to Secretary Stanhope," November 14, 1715, NA, CO, 137/11, f. 47.
76. This war led to the commissioning of privateers and probably damaged early progress in the fight against piracy. "Instructions Accompanying a Letter of Marque," January 1, 1719, NA, SP, 42/123. Many English pirates also took Spanish commissions to spite the king. Peter Earle, *The Pirate Wars* (New York: St. Martin's Press, 2003), 206.
77. "Deposition of Captain William South," May 27, 1719, NA, CO, 23/13, f. 53.
78. Mark Shirk, "How Does Violence Threaten the State? Four Narratives on Piracy," *Terrorism and Political Violence* 29, no. 4 (2017): 656–73.

79. Of course the Barbary powers were not recognized states given that they were often part of the Ottoman Empire, but in many ways they functioned similarly to seventeenth-century privateers. See Adrian Tinniswood, *Pirates of Barbary: Corsairs, Conquests, and Captivity in the Seventeenth-Century Mediterranean* (New York: Riverhead Books, 2010); William J. Brenner, *Confounding Powers: Anarchy and International Society from the Assassins to Al Qaeda* (Cambridge: Cambridge University Press, 2016), 151–98.
80. David J. Starkey, "Pirates and Markets," in *Bandits at Sea: A Pirates Reader*, ed. C. R Pennell (New York: New York University Press, 2001), 69–81.
81. Earle, *The Pirate Wars*, 209–28; Jeppe Mulich, "Republican Privateering: Local Networks and Political Order in the Western Atlantic," in *The Two World of Nineteenth Century International Relations: The Bifurcated Century*, ed. Daniel M. Green (London: Routledge, 2018), 43–59; David Head, "New Nations, New Connections: Spanish American Privateering from the United States and the Development of Atlantic Relations," *Early American Studies* 11, no. 1 (2013): 161–75; Matthew McCarthy, "'A Delicate Question of a Political Nature': The Corso Insurgente and British Commercial Policy During the Spanish-American War of Independence, 1810–1824," *International Journal of Maritime History* 23, no. 1 (2011): 277–92.
82. Apostolos Delis, "A Hub of Piracy in the Aegean: Syros During the Greek War of Independence," in *Corsairs and Pirates in the Eastern Mediterranean, Fifteenth–Nineteenth Centuries*, ed. Gelina Harlaftis, Dimitris Dimitropolous, and David J. Starkey (Athens: Sylvia Ioannou Foundation, 2016), 41–54; Leonidas Mylonakis, *Piracy in the Eastern Mediterranean* (London: Bloomsbury, 2021).
83. Mark Shirk, "An Evil of Ancient Date: Piracy and the Two Pax Britannicas in Nineteenth-Century Southeast Asia," in *The Two Worlds of Nineteenth Century International Relations: The Bifurcated Century*, ed. Dan Green (London: Routledge, 2019), 177–95; Stefan Ekloff Amirell, *Pirates of Empire: Colonisation and Maritime Violence in Southeast Asia* (Cambridge: Cambridge University Press, 2019).
84. Joseph MacKay, "Pirate Nations: Maritime Pirates as Escape Societies in Late Imperial China," *Social Science History* 37, no. 4 (2013): 551–73; Robert J. Antony, *Like Froth Floating on the Sea: The World of Pirates and Seafarers in Late Imperial South China* (Berkeley, CA: Institute of East Asian Studies, 2003); Dian Murray, "Living and Working Conditions in Chinese Pirates Communities 1750–1850," in *Pirates and Privateers: New Perspectives on the War on Trade in the Eighteenth and Nineteenth Centuries*, ed. David J. Starkey, E. S. Van Eych van Heslinga, and J. A. de Moor (Exeter, UK: University of Exeter Press, 1997), 47–68.
85. Jon Vagg, "Rough Seas? Contemporary Piracy in South East Asia," *British Journal of Criminology* 35, no. 1 (1995): 63–80; Robert Farley and Yoav Gortzak, "Fighting Piracy: Experiences in Southeast Asia and Off the Horn of Africa," *Journal of Strategic Security* 2, no. 1 (2009): 1–24; Ryan S. Jablonski and Steven Oliver, "The Political Economy of Plunder: Economic Opportunity and Modern Piracy," *Journal of Conflict Resolution* 57, no. 4 (2013): 682–70; Judith Burdin Asumi, "Understanding the Armed Groups of the Niger Delta" (working paper, Council on Foreign Relations, 2009).

86. Rommel C. Banlaoi, "The Abu Sayyaf Group: Threat of Maritime Piracy and Terrorism," in *Violence at Sea: Piracy in the Age of Global Terrorism*, ed. Peter Lehr (New York: Routledge, 2007), 121–23; Soliman M. Santos Jr. and Octavio A. Dinampo, "Abu Sayyaf Reloaded: Rebels, Agents, Bandits, Terrorists (Case Study)," in Soliman M. Santos Jr. and Paz Verdades M. Santos, *Primed and Purposeful: Armed Groups and Human Security Efforts in the Philippines* (Geneva: Small Arms Survey, Graduate Institute of International and Development Studies, 2010), 115–38.
87. Mark Shirk, "Busting Blackbeard's Ghost: Somali Piracy in Historical Context," *Global Change, Peace, and Security* 28, no. 1 (2016): 17–34; Christian Bueger, "Practice, Pirates and Coast Guards: The Grand Narrative of Somali Piracy," *Third World Quarterly* 34, no. 10 (December 2013): 1811–27.
88. Chijioke J. Nwalozie, "Exploring Contemporary Sea Piracy in Nigeria, the Niger Delta and the Gulf of Guinea," *Journal of Transportation Security* 13, no. 3 (2020): 159–78; Maurice Ogbonnaya, "From Nationalist Movements to Organised Crime Groups," *ENACT Research Papers*, no. 22 (2020): 1–22.
89. For characterizations of pirates—including those of the golden age—as chiefly concerned with economic gains, see Bialuschewski, "Pirates, Markets and Imperial Authority"; James G. Lydon, *Pirates, Privateers, and Profits* (Upper Saddle River, NJ: Gregg Press, 1970); Hugh F. Rankin, *The Golden Age of Piracy* (Williamsburg, VA: Holt, Rinehart and Winston, 1969).
90. "The Tryals of the Pyrates Begun at Cabo Corso East on the Coast of Africa, Joseph Mansfield," March 20, 1722, NA, HCA, 1/99, f. 116.
91. Bellamy is quoted by a man who reached Boston following a period as a prisoner upon his ship. Given that the quote was made aboard Bellamy's ship and a number of interlocutors were between Bellamy and DeFoe, it is likely that it was embellished. However, it does do a good job of capturing the mood of the pirates of this era. DeFoe, *A General History*, 587.
92. "The Trials of Eights Persons Indited for Piracy, etc.," October 18, 1717 (Boston: B. Green, 1718), NA, CO, 5/867, f. 16. This expression was apparently a common one. One report from a survivor of a pirate attack said that the pirates "pretended to be Robbin Hood's Men"; see Jameson, *Privateering and Piracy*, doc. 111.
93. Rediker, *Villains of All Nations*, 10.
94. DeFoe, *A General History*, 606.
95. "Deposition of Edward North," May 22, 1718, NA, CO, 37/10, f. 37.
96. Rediker, *Villains of All Nations*, 8.
97. Hornigold was allowed to leave on a small ship with twenty-six loyalists, eventually becoming an anti-pirate privateer. Jameson, *Privateering and Piracy*, doc. 108.
98. Jameson, *Privateering and Piracy*, doc. 117.
99. Jameson, *Privateering and Piracy*, doc. 117.
100. Rediker, *Villains of All Nations*, 80–81.
101. Chris Land, "Flying the Black Flag: Revolt, Revolution and the Social Organization of Piracy in the 'Golden Age,'" *Management and Organizational History* 2, no. 2 (2007): 169–92.

102. DeFoe, *A General History*; Marcus Rediker, "Hydrarchy and Libertalia: The Utopian Dimensions of Atlantic Piracy in the Early Eighteenth Century," in Starkey, van Heslinga, and de Moor, *Pirates and Privateers*, 29–46.
103. Jameson, *Privateering and Piracy*, doc. 108.
104. Colin Woodward, *The Republic of Pirates: Being the True and Surprising Story of the Caribbean Pirates and the Man Who Brought Them Down* (New York: Harcourt, 2007), 208.
105. "Gale to Pitt," November 4, 1718, NA, CO, 23/1, ff. 47–48.
106. "Deposition of John Le Bois," December 19, 1718, NA, CO, 152/12/4, f. 136ii.
107. B. R. Burg, *Sodomy and the Pirate Tradition: English Sea Rovers in the Seventeenth-Century Caribbean* (New York: New York University Press, 1995); "Pirate Utopias: Under the Banner of King Death," *Dum De Dum De Dum* (blog), http://dumdedumdedum.wordpress.com/pirate-utopias/.
108. Marcus Rediker, "Liberty Beneath the Jolly Roger: The Lives of Anne Bonny and Mary Read, Pirates," in *Bandits at Sea: A Pirates Reader*, ed. C. R. Pennell (New York: New York University Press, 2001), 299–310.
109. E. T. Fox, "Jacobitism and the 'Golden Age' of Piracy, 1715–1725," *International Journal of Maritime History* 22, no. 2 (2010): 277–303.
110. Philip Bobbitt, *Terror and Consent: The Wars for the Twenty-First Century* (New York: Knopf, 2008), 32.
111. Gabriel Kuhn, *Life Under the Jolly Roger: Reflections on Golden Age Piracy* (Oakland, CA: PM Press, 2010); Rediker, *Villains of All Nations*.
112. "Letter of Ellis Brand," January 26, 1720, NA, ADM, 1/1472.
113. Rediker, *Villains of All Nations*, 42.
114. Quoted in Peter Linebaugh and Marcus Rediker, *The Many-Headed Hydra: Sailors, Slaves, Commoners, and the Hidden History of the Revolutionary Atlantic* (Boston: Beacon Press, 2000), 160.
115. "Tryals of 100 Pyrates, John Phillips," March 20, 1722, NA, HCA, 1/99, f. 102.
116. "Mr. James Craggs to Council of Trade and Plantations," January 29, 1718, NA, CO, 23/1, f. 76.
117. DeFoe, *A General History*, 244.
118. "Tryals of 100 Pyrates, Edward Watts," March 20, 1722, NA, HCA, 1/99, f. 138.
119. Pirates were quite honest about who was and was not forced; see "Governor Walter Hamilton to Council of Trade and Plantations," March 25, 1724, NA, CO, 152/14, f. 283; "Trial at High Court of Admiralty of St. Christopher's," March 7, 1724, NA, CO, f. 292.
120. "Tryals of 100 Pyrates, John Johnson," March 20, 1722, NA, HCA, 1/99, f. 28.
121. Jameson, *Privateering and Piracy*, doc. 113.
122. Quoted in Rediker, *Villains of All Nations*, 152–53.
123. Jameson, *Privateering and Piracy*, doc. 117.
124. Rediker, *Villains of All Nations*, 151.
125. Jameson, *Privateering and Piracy*, doc. 117.
126. Quoted in Rediker, *Villains of All Nations*, 11–12, 148–69.

127. For a "transcript" of a mock trial by the crew of Thomas Antsis, see DeFoe, *A General History*, 292–94.
128. "Letter from Colonel Alexander Spottswood to the Board," May 31, 1717, NA, CO, 5/1364, f. 483.
129. "Gale to Pitt," November 4, 1718, NA, CO, 23/1, f. 47.
130. Rediker, *Villains of All Nations*, 14.
131. "Letter of Captain Ellis Brand," May 22, 1718, NA, ADM, 1/1472.
132. For examples, see Kuhn, *Life Under the Jolly Roger*; Rediker, *Villains of All Nations*.
133. "The Tryals of Sixteen Persons for Piracy, etc.," July 4, 1726 (Boston: Printed for Joseph Edwards, 1726), NA, CO, 5/869, f. 401.
134. "Reports of New York," October 19, 1698, NA, CO, 5/1116, f. 2.
135. "Colonel Hope to the Board," January 17, 1724, NA, CO, 37/11, f. 37.
136. Rediker, *Villains of All Nations*, 13, 15.
137. Jameson, *Privateering and Piracy*, doc. 117.
138. Rediker, *Villains of All Nations*, 7.
139. The term dates to Cicero's condemnation of Mithradates II's privateers in a war against the Romans but was often used as a synonym for "tyrant" until the seventeenth century. See Harry Gould, "Cicero's Ghost: Rethinking the Social Construction of Piracy," in *Maritime Piracy and the Construction of Global Governance*, ed. Jon D. Carlson, Mark T. Nance, and Michael J. Struett (London: Routledge, 2012), 23–46; Alfred P. Rubin, *The Law of Piracy* (Newport, RI: Naval War College Press, 1988).
140. Australian Capital Territory Government, "ACT Legislation Register—Offences at Sea Act 1536 28 Hen 8 c 15," http://www.legislation.act.gov.au/a/db_1803//.
141. There is evidence that the term was used in connection to piracy in the Caribbean as early as 1676 as privateering was becoming a problem, but it was not coded into law until 1699. "Reports of Jamaica," July 20, 1676, NA, CO, 138/3, ff. 81–83.
142. Shirk, "Busting Blackbeard's Ghost."
143. Earle, *The Pirate Wars*; Lydon, *Pirates, Privateers, and Profits*; Rankin, *The Golden Age of Piracy*; Frykman, "Pirates and Smugglers."
144. Daniel A. Baugh, "Maritime Strength and Atlantic Commerce: The Uses of a Grand Marine Empire," in *An Imperial State at War: Britain from 1689 to 1815*, ed. Lawrence Stone (London: Routledge, 1994), 185–223.
145. Pritchard, *In Search of Empire*.
146. "Earl of Bellomont to Council of Trade," July 8, 1699, NA, CO, 5/860, ff. 149–51; "Lt. Governor Alexander Spottswood to Council of Trade," July 3, 1716, NA, CO, 23/12, f. 104; "Letter from Planters," December 6, 1716, NA, CO, 23/12, f. 107; "Letter from Woodes Rogers," June 1718, NA, CO, 23/13, f. 30; "Letter from J. Addison," September 3, 1717, NA, CO, 152/12/1, f. 34; "Captain Warren to Plantations General," July 22, 1698, NA, CO, 323/2, f. 343; "A Scheme for Stationary Men of War in the West Indies for Better Securing the Trade There from Pirates," October 23, 1723, NA, CO, 323/8, f. 137; "Letter to Lords of the Admiralty," April 1, 1717, NA, SP, 42/14; "Governor Hamilton to the Council of Trade and Plantations," March 1, 1717, CSPCS, 29/484; "Governor Sir N. Lawes to the Council of Trade and Plantations," June 21, 1718, CSPCS, 30/566; "Governor Rodgers to Council of Trade and Plantations," May 29, 1719, CSPCS, 31/209.

147. "Letter from Addison," September 3, 1717, NA, CO, 152/12/1, f. 34.
148. "Orders to Captain Ogle of the Swallow," November 24, 1720, NA, ADM, 2/50, ff. 290–93; "Ships Logs, Swallow," February 5, 1722, NA, ADM, 51/954.
149. For complaints along these lines, see "Anonymous Paper Relating to the Sugar and Tobacco Trades," July 22, 1724, NA, CO, 388/24, f. 186.
150. Hanna, *Pirate Nests*, 371–72.
151. "Resolved That His Majesty's Proclamations Promising Pardon to Such Pyrates Who Will Surrender," September 24, 1717, NA, ADM, 3/31.
152. Woodward, *The Republic of Pirates*, 257–58.
153. "Letter of Vincent Pearse," January 21, 1721, NA, ADM, 1/2282.
154. Rediker, *Villains of All Nations*.
155. Jameson, *Privateering and Piracy*, doc. 117.
156. "Letter from Captain Rogers," October 31, 1718, NA, CO, 23/1, ff. 23–24; see also "Letter from Woodes Rogers," n.d., NA, CO, 23/13, ff. 20–24.
157. "Letter from Colonel Shute, Governor of New England," June 26, 1718, NA, CO, 5/867, f. 7; "Ship's Logs, *Phoenix*," February 6, March 14, March 18–19, March 22–24, 1717, NA, ADM, 51/690; "Letter from Woodes Rogers," January 30, 1719, NA, CO, 23/13, ff. 28–29; "Captain Vernon to Governor Marquis de Serel," August 29, 1720, CSPCS, 32/527xxiv(c).
158. "Governor Hunter to the Council of Trade and Plantations," November 3, 1718, CSPCS, 30/738.
159. "Governor Hamilton to the Council of Trade and Plantations," October 3, 1720, CSPCS, 32/251.
160. DeFoe, *A General History*; Rediker, *Villains of All Nations*; Woodward, *The Republic of Pirates*.
161. Norton, "Classification and Coercion," 1572.
162. E. D. Dickinson, "Is the Crime of Piracy Obsolete," *Harvard Law Review* 38, no. 3 (1925): 334–60; Joshua Michael Goodwin, "Universal Jurisdiction and the Pirate: Time for an Old Couple to Part," *Vanderbilt Journal of Transnational Law* 39, no. 3 (2006): 973–1011.
163. Frykman, "Pirates and Smugglers," 224; Rediker, *Villains of All Nations*, 26–28, 35; Ritchie, *Captain Kidd*, 142–44.
164. Benton, *A Search for Sovereignty*, 145–48.
165. That there is a difference here between crimes against the colonies and crimes against England demonstrates the effectiveness of the line.
166. "Letter from Woodes Rogers," January 30, 1719, NA, CO, 23/13, f. 28.
167. Ritchie, *Captain Kidd*, 144.
168. "Letter from Rich Lloyd," July 20, 1676, NA, CO, 138/3, ff. 81–83. However, there was still confusion over jurisdiction; see "Journal of the Lords of Trade and Plantation," July 6, 1676, CSPCS, 9/976.
169. "Letter from R. Sawyer, H. Finch, Tho. Stone, and Rich Lloyd," March 4, 1684, NA, CO, 1/54, f. 117.
170. "Draught of a Bill to Be Past Here in Parliament for the Tryal of Pirates in Any of His Majesty's Dominions," April 6, 1698, NA, CO, 323/2, f. 289; "Abstract of Several Papers Relating to Piracies in the East Indies," February 26, 1697, NA, CO, 323/2, ff. 271–76.

174   2. THE GOLDEN AGE OF PIRACY AND THE ATLANTIC WORLD

171. Jameson, *Privateering and Piracy*, doc. 76.
172. "Notes of the Plantations General," September 1, 1698, NA, CO, 324/6, f. 163.
173. "Letter of Francis Hume," July 9, 1718, NA, ADM, 1/1879.
174. "Report of Admiralty Jurisdiction for Piracies in Plantations," June 20, 1720, NA, CO, 323/8, f. 10.
175. Hanna, *Pirate Nests*, 330–51.
176. "Colonel Spottswood to Board," n.d., NA, CO, 5/1364, ff. 505–20. See also Ritchie, *Captain Kidd*.
177. Ritchie, *Captain Kidd*.
178. For more on Fletcher, see "Report on Piracy in New York," October 19, 1698, NA, CO, 5/1116, ff. 2–12; "Report on Piracy in New York," August 28 and September 14, 1695, NA, CO, 391/8, ff. 49–51, 54–56; "At a Meeting for His Majesty's Commissioners for Trade and Plantations," January 4 and January 7, 1698, NA, CO, 391/10, 195–96; *NYCD*, August 22, 1696; March 9, 1699.
179. Archibald Hamilton was deposed in part because he was offering commissions for privateers to procure Spanish gold. "Several Papers Received from Secretary Stanhope Containing Complaints and Accusations Against the Lord Archibald Hamilton, Governor of Jamaica," May 19, 1716, NA, CO, 137/11, ff. 92–109. See "The Lords of His Majesty's Most Honorable Privy Council," May 21, 1716, NA, CO, 137/12, f. 103, for his revocation.
180. "Letter from Ro. Molesworth, Jn. Cokburne, John Chetwynd, Cha. Cooke, P. Docminique," December 14, 1715, NA, CO, 23/12, f. 92.
181. For a firsthand account of the state of the Bahamas, see "Letter from Walker to Lords of the Admiralty," August 5, 1716, NA, SP, 42/16. For complaints by governors of other islands, see "Letter from A. Spottswood," n.d., NA, CO, 5/1317, ff. 245–46; "Spottswood to Board," August 6, 1717, NA, CO, 5/1364, ff. 483–87; "Spottswood to Council of Trade," July 3, 1716, NA, CO, 23/12, ff. 103–4; "Letter from Suffolk, Jacob Ashley, Jo. Cokburne, J. Chetwynde, Docminique, J. Addison, Molesworth," December 6, 1716, NA, CO, 23/12, f. 107; "Letter from Addison," September 3, 1717, NA, CO, 152/12/1, f. 34; "Captain Matthew Musson to Council of Trade and Plantations," July 5, 1717, CSPCS, 29/635; "Governor Johnson to the Council of Trade and Plantations," June 18, 1718, CSPCS, 30/556.
182. "Co-Partners for Settling Bahama Islands to the Council of Trade and Plantations," May 19, 1721, CSPCS, 32/498.
183. "Letter from Woodes Rogers," n.d., NA, CO, 23/13, f. 20.
184. "Ship's Logs, *Phoenix*," March 22, 1717, NA, ADM, 51/690.
185. Woodward, *The Republic of Pirates*.
186. "Letter from Ro. Molesworth, Jn. Cokburne, John Chetwynd, Cha. Cooke, P. Docminique," December 14, 1715, NA, CO, 23/12, f. 90.
187. Hanna, *Pirate Nests*, 372.
188. Hanna, *Pirate Nests*, 378.
189. Hanna, *Pirate Nests*, 373. For a deeper discussion, see pp. 365–415.
190. Bialuschewski, "Pirates, Markets and Imperial Authority."

191. Rediker, *Villains of All Nations*, 152.
192. Hanna, *Pirate Nests*, 371.
193. "Letter from Walter Hamilton to Council of Trade and Plantations," March 25, 1724, NA, CO, 152/14, f. 284.
194. Hanna, *Pirate Nests*, 373.
195. Rediker, *Villains of All Nations*, 11.
196. Hanna, *Pirate Nests*, 370.
197. For proceedings of a trial for piracy in 1740, see "Proceedings of the Court of Vice Admiralty," August 11, 1740, NA, HCA, 1/99.
198. This is where the revolutionary Atlantic plays a role. Mulich, "Republican Privateering"; Head, "New Nations, New Connections"; McCarthy, "'A Delicate Question.'"
199. George Chandler Scarlett, *The Treaty of Utrecht: Considered from the Viewpoints of the Past and Present State of Spain, the Slave Trade Monopoly That Set It Up, Christian Colonization, and the International Struggle* (New York: Cosmos Greek-American Printing, 1939).
200. Fox, "Jacobitism and the 'Golden Age' of Piracy," 292.
201. Arne Bialuschewski, "Between Newfoundland and the Malacca Strait: A Survey of the Golden Age of Piracy, 1695–1725," *Mariner's Mirror* 90, no. 2 (2004): 167–86.
202. Bialuschewski, "Between Newfoundland and the Malacca Strait," 178.
203. Rediker, *Villains of All Nations*; Mulich, "Microregionalism and Intercolonial Relations."
204. "Orders to Captain Ogle of the Swallow," November 24, 1720, NA, ADM, 2/50, ff. 290–93.
205. "Anonymous Relating to the Tobacco and Sugar Trades," July 22, 1724, NA, CO, 388/24, f. 184.
206. Steinberg, *The Social Construction of the Ocean*, 111.
207. Thomson, *Mercenaries, Pirates, and Sovereigns*, 108.
208. Kuhn, *Life Under the Jolly Roger*.
209. Michael Kempe, "'Even in the Remotest Corners of the World': Globalized Piracy and International Law, 1500–1900," *Journal of Global History* 5, no. 3 (2010): 353–72.
210. Mattingly, "No Peace Beyond What Line?"
211. Benton, *A Search for Sovereignty*.
212. Bernard Bailyn, "Idea of Atlantic History," *Itinerario* 20 (1996): 19–44; Jerry H. Bentley, "Sea and Ocean Basins as Frameworks of Historical Analysis," *Geographical Review* 89 (1999): 215–24; Paul Butel, *The Atlantic*, trans. Iain Hamilton Grant (London: Routledge, 1999); Peter A. Coclanis, ed., *The Atlantic Economy During the Seventeenth and Eighteenth Centuries: Organization, Operation, Practice, and Personnel* (Columbia: University of South Carolina Press, 2005); Felipe Fernandez-Armesto, "Origins of the European Atlantic," *Itinerario* 24 (2009): 111–23; Alison Games, "Introduction, Definitions, and Historiography: What Is Atlantic History?" *OAH Magazine of History* 18 (2004): 3–7. For a debate on the strengths and weaknesses of this turn, see Peter A. Coclanis, "Drang Nach Osten: Bernard Bailyn, the World-Island, and the Idea of Atlantic History," *Journal of World History* 13, no. 1 (2002): 169–82.

176   2. THE GOLDEN AGE OF PIRACY AND THE ATLANTIC WORLD

213. Robert S. DuPlessis, "Cloth and the Emergence of the Atlantic Economy," in Coclanis, *The Atlantic Economy During the Seventeenth and Eighteenth Centuries*, 72–94.
214. Mulich, "Microregionalism and Intercolonial Relations"; Matthew Norton, "Real Mythic Histories: Circulatory Networks and State-Centrism," in *Global Historical Sociology*, ed. Julian Go and George Lawson (Cambridge: Cambridge University Press, 2017), 37–57.
215. John Brewer, *The Sinews of Power: War, Money, and the English State* (New York: Knopf, 1989).
216. M. S. Anderson, *Europe in the Eighteenth Century, 1713–1783* (London: Longman, 1987); Raymond Birn, *Crisis, Absolutism, Revolution: Europe and the World, 1648–1789* (Ontario: Broadview Press, 2005); William Doyle, *The Old European Order: 1660–1800*, Short Oxford History of the Modern World (Oxford: Oxford University Press, 1978); Isser Woloch, *Eighteenth-Century Europe, Tradition and Progress, 1715–1789* (New York: Norton, 1982).
217. Rodney Bruce Hall, *National Collective Identity: Social Constructs and International Systems* (New York: Columbia University Press, 1999); K. J. Holsti, *Taming the Sovereigns: Institutional Change in International Politics* (Cambridge: Cambridge University Press, 2004); Richard N. Rosecrance, *Action and Reaction in World Politics; International Systems in Perspective* (Boston: Little, Brown, 1963).
218. The attack on Jenkins happened in 1731, and many believe that it was fear of losing the *asiento*—slave-trading rights in the Spanish Empire—that brought England into war. But Jenkins' Ear was the rhetorical device used—hard to fathom during the era of "no peace."
219. Glete, *Warfare at Sea*, 1.
220. Scarlett, *The Treaty of Utrecht*.
221. McNeill, *Mosquito Empires*.
222. Eliga H. Gould, "Zones of Law, Zones of Violence: The Legal Geography of the British Atlantic, Circa 1772," *William and Mary Quarterly* 60, no. 3 (2003): 471–510.
223. Burgess, "Piracy in the Public Sphere"; Linebaugh and Rediker, *The Many-Headed Hydra*.
224. Steele, *The English Atlantic*.
225. Benton, *A Search for Sovereignty*.

3. "PROPAGANDA OF THE DEED," SURVEILLANCE, AND THE LABOR MOVEMENT

1. Not all attacks were by anarchists, but they were attributed to anarchists. Nihilists, and even some nationalists, were popularly referred to as "anarchists." As an example, see the news report of a bomb explosion in San Francisco falsely attributed to anarchists in Ruth Kinna, ed., *Early Writings on Terrorism* (London: Routledge, 2006), 3:258–60.

2. The period in question lasted roughly from 1880 to 1930, with a concentration from 1892 to 1906.
3. Adam Bruno Ulam, *In the Name of the People: Prophets and Conspirators in Prerevolutionary Russia* (New York: Viking Press, 1977); Norman M. Naimark, "Terrorism and the Fall of Imperial Russia," *Terrorism and Political Violence* 2, no. 2 (1990): 171–92; Hugh Phillips, "The War Against Terrorism in Late Imperial and Early Soviet Russia," in *Enemies of Humanity*, ed. Isaac Land (New York: Palgrave Macmillan, 2008), 203–22.
4. Scott Miller, *The President and the Assassin: McKinley, Terror, and Empire at the Dawn of the American Century* (New York: Random House, 2011).
5. Richard Bach Jensen, "The Evolution of Anarchist Terrorism in Europe and the United States from the Nineteenth Century to World War I," in *Terror: From Tyrannicide to Terrorism*, ed. Brett Bowden and Michael T. Davis (Queensland: University of Queensland Press, 2008), 149.
6. Richard Bach Jensen, "Police Reform and Social Reform: Italy from the Crisis of the 1890s to the Giolittian Era," *Criminal Justice History: An International Annual* 10 (1989): 179–200; Richard Bach Jensen, "Criminal Anthropology and Anarchist Terrorism in Spain and Italy," *Mediterranean Historical Review* 16, no. 2 (2001): 31–44.
7. Richard D. Sonn, *Anarchism and Cultural Politics in Fin de Siècle France* (Lincoln: University of Nebraska Press, 1989); Alexander Varias, *Paris and the Anarchists: Aesthetes and Subversives During the Fin de Siècle* (New York: St. Martin's Press, 1996); John Merriman, *The Dynamite Club: How a Bombing in Fin-de-Siècle Paris Ignited the Age of Terror* (New York: Houghton Mifflin Harcourt, 2009).
8. Richard Bach Jensen, *The Battle Against Anarchist Terrorism: An International History, 1878–1934* (Cambridge: Cambridge University Press, 2014), 34–35.
9. I will use this term to denote violence adhering to "propaganda of the deed" in order to separate it from other types of violence used by anarchists. It is common to use the term "anarchist terrorism," but there are problems with this characterization. First, this was not a common contemporary moniker. Second, anarchists claimed the "terrorists" were the capitalists and the states that supported them. Third, since the term "terrorism" is as much political as descriptive, using it has the effect of leveling judgment. This is not the intent. Finally, the anarchist movement was not only larger than the propagandists during this period (see below) but also continued after they fell out of favor. In addition to nonviolent groups, syndicalists and sections of the Red Army Faction were anarchists that used violence after this period in ways that many would label "anarchist terrorism." Thus, the term confuses more than elucidates.
10. Benedict R. Anderson, *Under Three Flags: Anarchism and the Anti-Colonial Imagination* (London: Verso, 2005); Steven Hirsch and Lucien van der Walt, eds., *Anarchism and Syndicalism in the Colonial and Postcolonial World, 1870–1940: The Praxis of National Liberation, Internationalism, and Social Revolution* (Boston: Brill, 2010).
11. Jensen, *The Battle Against Anarchist Terrorism*, 36. This is not a complete list of attacks, but gives a good overview.

12. Robbie Robertson, *The Three Waves of Globalization: A History of a Developing Global Consciousness* (New York: Zed Books, 2002).
13. Duncan Bell, ed. *Victorian Visions of Global Order: Empire and International Relations in Nineteenth-Century Political Thought* (Cambridge: Cambridge University Press, 2007); David Long and Brian C. Schmidt, eds. *Imperialism and Internationalism in the Discipline of International Relations* (Albany: State University of New York Press, 2005); Robert Vitalis, *White World Order, Black Power Politics: The Birth of American International Relations* (Ithaca, NY: Cornell University Press, 2015).
14. "Extract from *Standard*," April 24, 1894, the National Archives, Kew, London, UK (hereafter NA), Home Office (hereafter HO), 144/259/A55860/2.
15. John Torpey, "The Great War and the Birth of the Modern Passport System," in *Documenting Individual Identity: The Development of State Practices in the Modern World*, ed. Jane Caplan and John Torpey (Princeton, NJ: Princeton University Press, 2001), 256–70.
16. Craig Robertson, *The Passport in America: The History of a Document* (Oxford: Oxford University Press, 2010); Jay Feldman, *Manufacturing Hysteria: A History of Scapegoating, Surveillance, and Secrecy in Modern America* (New York: Pantheon, 2011); David Vincent, *Privacy: A Short History* (Cambridge: Polity, 2016).
17. Murray Bookchin, *The Spanish Anarchists: The Heroic Years, 1868–1936* (Chico, CA: AK Press, 2001); James Joll, *The Anarchists* (Cambridge, MA: Harvard University Press, 1980); Peter Marshall, *Demanding the Impossible: A History of Anarchism* (London: HarperCollins, 1992); George Woodcock, *Anarchism: A History of Libertarian Ideas and Movements* (New York: New American Library, 1962).
18. Marie Fleming, "Propaganda by the Deed: Terrorism and Anarchist Theory in Late Nineteenth Century Europe," in *Terrorism in Europe*, ed. Yonah Alexander and Kenneth A. Myers (New York: St. Martin's Press, 1982), 8–28; Varias, *Paris and the Anarchists*, 84–89.
19. Constance Bantman, "Internationalism Without an International? Cross-Channel Anarchist Networks, 1880–1914," *Revue Belge de Philologie et d'histoire* 84, no. 4 (2006): 961–81; Sonn, *Anarchism and Cultural Politics*; Varias, *Paris and the Anarchists*.
20. Anderson, *Under Three Flags*; Ayşe Zarakol, "What Makes Terrorism Modern? Terrorism, Legitimacy, and the International System," *Review of International Studies* 37, no. 5 (2011): 2311–36.
21. Alex Butterworth, *The World That Never Was: A True Story of Dreamers, Schemers, Anarchists, and Secret Agents* (New York: Pantheon Books, 2010), 392–410.
22. Feldman, *Manufacturing Hysteria*.
23. Barbara Wertheim Tuchman, *The Guns of August and the Proud Tower* (New York: Library of America, 2012).
24. Butterworth, *The World That Never Was*, 392–410.
25. Carl Levy, "Anarchism, Internationalism, and Nationalism in Europe, 1860–1939," *Australian Journal of Politics and History* 50, no. 3 (2004): 330–42.

26. Martin Lloyd, *The Passport: The History of Man's Most Travelled Document* (Gloucestershire: Sutton Publishing, 2003); Mark Salter, *Rights of Passage: The Passport in International Relations* (Boulder, CO: Lynne Rienner Publishers, 2003); Jane Caplan and John Torpey, eds. *Documenting Individual Identity: The Development of State Practices in the Modern World* (Princeton, NJ: Princeton University Press, 2001).
27. Salter, *Rights of Passage*, 78.
28. Kathy E. Ferguson, "Anarchist Printers and Presses: Material Circuits of Politics," *Political Theory* 42, no. 4 (2014): 391–414.
29. Lucien van der Walt and Stephen Hirsch, "Rethinking Anarchism and Syndicalism: The Colonial and Postcolonial Experience, 1870–1940," in Hirsch and van der Walt, *Anarchism and Syndicalism*, xxxviii.
30. Temma Kaplan, *Anarchists of Andalusia, 1868–1903* (Princeton, NJ: Princeton University Press, 1977); Ferguson, "Anarchist Printers and Presses."
31. The famous London Congress of 1881 advocated a "study of the new technical and chemical sciences from the point of view of their revolutionary value." Fleming, "Propaganda by the Deed," 16.
32. Quoted in Tuchman, *The Guns of August and the Proud Tower*, 638. *Germinal* became something of a revolutionist favorite, so much so that Émile Henry quoted it at his trial. "Émile Henry's Statement, *Le Petits Temps*," April 29, 1894, Archive de Prefecture de Police, Paris, France (hereafter APP), Police Dossiers (hereafter BA), 1115. Documents from this archive have been translated from French by Annie Rehill.
33. Brian Morris, *Bakunin: The Philosophy of Freedom* (New York: Black Rose Books, 1993), 117–35.
34. "Émile Henry's Statement."
35. Levy, "Anarchism, Internationalism, and Nationalism in Europe."
36. Butterworth, *The World That Never Was*, 64.
37. Paul Avrich, *The Haymarket Tragedy* (Princeton, NJ: Princeton University Press, 1984).
38. Tuchman, *The Guns of August and the Proud Tower*, 640.
39. British Consul to Chicago: "The verdict has brought relief to every class of society, anarchists now know that they cannot push their liberty to abuse." "Dispatch from Her Majesty's Consul in Chicago," September 7, 1886, NA, HO, 45/9660/A42380F.
40. The name means "The People's Will." The group was led by a protégé of Bakunin named Sergei Nychaev. Norodnaya Volya, it should be noted, was notionally a nihilist organization. However, their actions were adopted by anarchists and the larger revolutionary movement.
41. An 1883 attempt on Kaiser Wilhelm failed when its leader, August Rheinsdorf, sprained his ankle and was unable to take part in the mission. The plan was to blow up a bridge during a public procession. The bomb was in place and the attack timed perfectly when the man taking Rheinhart's place managed to get the fuse wet. Richard Bach Jensen, "Daggers, Rifles and Dynamite: Anarchist Terrorism in 19th Century Europe," *Terrorism and Political Violence* 16, no. 1 (2004): 116–53.

42. Not all anarchists shunned organization. Many believed that small, decentralized communes would bring about the revolution and form the basis of revolutionary society. However, the strain of anarchism from which propaganda of the deed arose did shun organization. I thank Kirwin Ray Shaffer for bringing this to my attention.
43. Fleming, "Propaganda by the Deed," 14.
44. Kropotkin was a former Russian aristocrat turned exiled revolutionary and was seen as Bakunin's successor as chief intellectual of the movement. Emile Capouya and Keitha Tompkins, eds., *The Essential Kropotkin* (New York: Liveright, 1975); Caroline Cahm, *Kropotkin and the Rise of Revolutionary Anarchism, 1872-1886* (Cambridge: Cambridge University Press, 1989).
45. Carlo Cafiero, "Action," in *Anarchism: A Documentary History of Libertarian Ideas*, ed. Robert Graham (Tonawanda, NY: Black Rose Books, 2005), 152.
46. Fleming, "Propaganda by the Deed."
47. Joll, *The Anarchists*, 131.
48. John Rewald, "Extracts of an Unedited Journal by Paul Signac," *Gazzette Des Beaux-Arts* 6, no. 36 (1949): 113, author's translation.
49. Whitney Kassel, "Terrorism and the International Anarchist Movement of the Late Nineteenth and Early Twentieth Centuries," *Studies in Conflict and Terrorism* 32, no. 3 (2009): 246.
50. For more on human nature and rule during this period, see Philipp Blom, *The Vertigo Years: Europe, 1900-1914* (New York: Basic Books, 2008).
51. Isaac Land, ed., *Enemies of Humanity: The Nineteenth-Century War on Terrorism* (New York: Palgrave Macmillan, 2008).
52. Jensen, *The Battle Against Anarchist Terrorism*, 60.
53. Salter, *Rights of Passage*; Torpey, "The Great War and the Birth of the Modern Passport System."
54. Paul Knepper, *The Invention of International Crime: A Global Issue in the Making, 1881-1914* (New York: Palgrave, 2010), 94.
55. Gerard Chaliand and Arnaud Blin, "The 'Golden Age' of Terrorism," in *The History of Terrorism: From Antiquity to Al Qaeda*, ed. Gérard Chaliand and Arnaud Blin (Berkeley: University of California Press, 2007),183.
56. Philip Bobbitt, *The Shield of Achilles: War, Peace, and the Course of History* (New York: Knopf, 2002).
57. Quoted in Jensen, *The Battle Against Anarchist Terrorism*, 7.
58. Quoted in Jensen, *The Battle Against Anarchist Terrorism*, 11.
59. Quoted in Richard Bach Jensen, "The United States, International Policing and the War Against Anarchist Terrorism, 1900-1914," *Terrorism and Political Violence* 13, no. 1 (2001): 19.
60. George Bernard Shaw, *The Impossibilities of Anarchism* (Kypros Press, 2016).
61. *Anarchism and Outrage* (London: C. M. Wilson, 1893), 7.
62. Jensen, *The Battle Against Anarchist Terrorism*.
63. Hirsch and van der Walt, *Anarchism and Syndicalism*.
64. *Anarchism and Outrage*, 2.

3. "PROPAGANDA OF THE DEED," SURVEILLANCE, AND LABOR   181

65. Charles Malato, "Some Anarchist Portraits," *Fortnightly Review* 62 (1894), 331.
66. "Paris," January 31, 1894, APP, BA, 79.
67. Quoted in Kinna, *Early Writings on Terrorism*, 3:355.
68. Chaliand and Blin, "The 'Golden Age' of Terrorism," 175.
69. Arthur MacDonald, "Assassins of Rulers," *Journal of the American Institute of Criminal Law and Criminology* 2, no. 4 (1911): 505–20.
70. Franklin L. Ford, "Reflections on Political Murder: Europe in the Nineteenth and Twentieth Centuries," in *Social Protest, Violence, and Terror in Nineteenth and Twentieth Century Europe*, ed. Wolfgang J. Mommsen and Gerhard Hirschfeld (New York: St. Martin's Press, 1982), 1–12.
71. Knepper, *The Invention of International Crime*, 145–46.
72. Constance Bantman, *The French Anarchists in London, 1880–1914: Exile and Transnationalism in the First Globalisation* (Liverpool: Liverpool University Press, 2013).
73. Jensen, *The Battle Against Anarchist Terrorism*, 95.
74. Jensen, *The Battle Against Anarchist Terrorism*, 37.
75. "Letter from the German Correspondent," February 22 [no year], APP, BA, 1509.
76. Ruth Kinna, *Early Writings on Terrorism*, 2:147.
77. Of course anarchists of other nationalities were also active in London, but these numbers make an estimate of eight thousand in 1894 very unlikely. Bantman, *The French Anarchists in London*, 1–2.
78. "Report on Convict Who Has Completed 10 Years of Sentence: Giuseppe Fornara," May 3, 1904, NA, HO, 144/1711/A55860D/2.
79. "Letter Signed Off with 'Vive Anarchy, Which Will Regenerate Humanity,'" n.d., APP, BA, 1132.
80. "Telegram to the Anarchist Charles at Stafford," May 5, 1892, NA, HO, 144/242/A53582.
81. For similar overestimations of threat, usually by non-English states, see "Anarchists en Route to England," January 11, 1911, NA, HO, 144/258/A5568/3; "Copy of a Dispatch Relative to an Anarchist Plot," February 1, 1901, and "Anarchist Plots Formed in London for Simultaneous Outrages in Italy, Belgium, and Spain," April 24, 1902, NA, HO, 144/545/A55176; "Anarchist Plots," June 19 and 22, 1906, NA, Foreign Office (hereafter FO), 371/136, ff. 60–67; "Departure of Anarchist for England to Assassinate HM the King," December 31, 1910, NA, HO, 144/1112/202225; "Anarchists Contemplate United Action on the 15 Jan in Paris, Berlin, and London," January 23, 1893, NA, HO, 144/485/X37842B. The search for such a plot was common; see "Paris," January 31, 1894, APP, BA, 79.
82. Butterworth, *The World That Never Was*.
83. Bantman, *The French Anarchists in London*.
84. Kinna, *Early Writings on Terrorism*, 3:349.
85. Kinna, *Early Writings on Terrorism*, 3:360. See also "Extract from *Law Time*," June 16, 1894, NA, HO, 144/485/X37842/15.
86. "Giuseppe Fornara," May 3, 1904, NA, HO, 144/1711/A55860D/2.
87. Quoted in Jensen, "Daggers, Rifles and Dynamite," 138.
88. "Memo from M. de Bunson," June 19, 1906, NA, HO, 144/757/118516.
89. Kinna, *Early Writings on Terrorism*, 3:348.

90. "Indictment of Johann Most," March 19, 1881, NA, HO, 144/77/A3385.
91. "Letter from the German Correspondent," February 22 [no year], APP, BA, 1509.
92. See discussion on Cesare Lombroso and Alphonse Bertillon below.
93. The First International Congress of Eugenics had as vice presidents Winston Churchill and Alexander Graham Bell, among others, and its president was Major Leonard Darwin, son of Charles Darwin. Blom, *The Vertigo Years*, 334.
94. Anderson, *Under Three Flags*, 3.
95. "Extract from the 'Congressional Record,' no. 4," December 5, 1901, NA, FO, 412/67, no. 10.
96. There were also claims of sodomy by those tortured. "To Each of the 40 (?) Jury Members," April 24, 1892, APP, BA, 1132.
97. These crimes include the murder and burglary of an old man a few years earlier. There is some debate on whether not Ravachol was an anarchist/propagandist or a common criminal. However, many anarchists embraced Ravachol, and his trial transcript shows anarchist sympathies. Malato, "Some Anarchist Portraits."
98. Tuchman, *The Guns of August and the Proud Tower*, 653.
99. These songs had lines like "All the bourgeois will taste the bomb" and "Let's dance the Ravachole!" Merriman, *The Dynamite Club*, 84–85. One police document reports that his name was sung at a soup kitchen administered by anarchists in Paris. See "Big Commotion Last Night at the Salle Favie," n.d., APP, BA, 77.
100. Tuchman, *The Guns of August and the Proud Tower*, 654.
101. For more on the Meunier case, see NA, HO, 144/485/X37842. Meunier was sentenced to life in prison, where he died ten years later. "Ravachol's Avenger," *L'Eclair*, November 5, 1902, APP, BA, 1215.
102. For multiple documents relating to this explosion, see APP, BA, 140.
103. Vaillant was the first person executed in nineteenth-century France for crimes that did not include murder.
104. *Les Lois Scélérates de 1893–1894* (Paris: Revue Blanche, 1899).
105. "Excerpts Done (12), 'The Companions . . . ,'" January 29, 1894, APP, BA, 77; "Bouchon," January 30, 1894, APP, BA, 79.
106. For multiple documents relations to police searching for Pauwels, see APP, BA, 1215.
107. Interestingly, Henry had originally spoken out against Ravachol, claiming that "a real anarchist . . . goes and strikes his particular enemy down; he does not dynamite houses where there are women, children, workmen, and domestic servants." Malato, "Some Anarchist Portraits."
108. "Attitude of the Dynamiter," n.d., APP, BA, 141.
109. "Émile Henry Before the Jury," *Le Petits Temps*, April 29, 1894, APP, BA, 1115.
110. Malato, "Some Anarchist Portraits."
111. "Report on Fortune Henry," November 22, 1892, APP, BA, 1115.
112. Tuchman, *The Guns of August and the Proud Tower*, 669.
113. Tuchman, *The Guns of August and the Proud Tower*, 661.
114. That Spanish responses to anarchism were atrocious and counterproductive was readily apparent to the English authorities, who expressed shock at the Montjuic atrocities

and repeatedly treated Spanish anti-anarchist policies with contempt. See "Anarchists in Spain," June 3, 1897, NA, HO, 45/9743/A56151C/3.
115. Kaplan, *Anarchists of Andalusia*, 172–85.
116. Kinna, *Early Writings on Terrorism*, 3:347.
117. Feldman, *Manufacturing Hysteria*, 26–32.
118. The authorities were not oblivious to this dynamic. For instance, they attempted to survey Paris before and after Ravachol's execution to see if they were in danger for reprisal. "Surveillance of Various [???] of Paris, Concerning Ravachol," July 12, 1892, APP, BA, 1132. Similar steps were taken with Vaillant. "In Anarchist Circles," January 29, 1894, APP, BA, 77.
119. Jensen, *The Battle Against Anarchist Terrorism*, 349.
120. The English rejected this definition: "Every act having for its object the destruction by violent means of any social organization . . . will be considered an Anarchist anyone who commits an anarchical act according to the above definition." They also rejected a Russian proposal to make all opposition to social organizations "anarchism," as this would have included any political opposition. See "Sir P. Currie to the Marquess of Salisbury," November 30, 1898, and "The Marquess of Salisbury to Sir P. Currie," December 2, 1898, NA, FO, 881/7179, no. 8, 9.
121. "Foreign Office to Baron Eckardstein," November 3, 1900, NA, FO, 412/67, no. 3.
122. Woodcock, *Anarchism*, 279.
123. England claimed that l'Autonomie was more social than political. "Autonomie Club and Autonomie Newspaper," May 26, 1893, NA, HO, 45/9739/A54881/2.
124. For German requests for info on the Autonomie Club and the English response to it, see "The 'Autonomie' Club and the 'Autonomie' Newspaper in London," May 18, 1893, NA, HO, 45/9739/A54881. For French accusations, see "Les Anarchistes, La Cocarde," n.d., APP, BA, 141.
125. "Letter from the German Correspondent," February 22 [no year], APP, BA, 1509.
126. Kinna, *Early Writings on Terrorism*, 3:289.
127. Jensen, *Battle Against Anarchist Terrorism*, 77.
128. This point should not be overblown; most attacks were by propagandists. See Jensen, *The Battle Against Anarchist Terrorism*, 52.
129. Butterworth, *The World That Never Was*, 340–45.
130. "Memorandum from Commissioner of Police," May 24, 1902, NA, HO, 144/545/A55176.
131. See also Pietro Di Paola, "The Spies Who Came in from the Heat: The International Surveillance of the Anarchists in London," *European History Quarterly* 37, no. 2 (2007): 189–215.
132. "Memorandum from Commissioner of Police," May 24, 1902, NA, HO, 144/545/A55176.
133. For attempts by Russia, see "Forward Draft of Reply to Russian Ambassador," December 17, 1906, NA, HO, 144/757/118516/5; for attempts by Italy, see "Forward Memo from Italian Ambassador," May 15, 1902, NA, HO, 144/545/A55176; for German attempts, see "The 'Autonomie' Club and the 'Autonomie' Newspaper in London," May 18, 1893, NA, HO, 45/9739/A54881, and "Observations on Proposals of German Gov't," April 29, 1902, NA, HO, 45/10254/X3650/130; for repeated attempts by the Spanish, see "Anarchists

Spaniards," January 21, 1897, NA, HO, 144/545/A55176; "Visit of Spanish Detectives to London," August 16, 1906, NA, HO, 144/757/118516/36; "Earl of Rosebury to Sir H. Drummond Wolff," November 22, 1893, NA, FO, 881/6427, no. 2.
134. "Visit of Spanish Detectives to London," August 15, 1906, NA, HO, 144/757/118516.
135. "Memo from the Commissioner of Police," May 24, 1902, NA, HO, 144/545/A55176.
136. One such instance was the Spanish warning about a series of attacks and a supposed "anarchist police" meant to undermine the real police. The English replied that they found no reason to be alarmed. "Anarchist Plots," June 22, 1906, NA, FO, 371/136, ff. 64, 66.
137. Butterworth, *The World That Never Was*.
138. "Spanish Anarchists Coming to England," July 19, 1897, NA, HO, 144/587/B2840C/70.
139. "Letter from the German Correspondent," February 22 [no year], APP, BA, 1509.
140. "Commissioner of Metropolitan Police to Home Office," April 29, 1902, NA, FO, 412/68, no. 10.
141. "Memorandum from E. Henry," January 7, 1902, NA, HO, 45/10254/X3650/126.
142. "Dispatch from Constantine Phipps," December 10, 1902, NA, HO, 144/668/X84164/8. For troubles with the Spanish, see "Anarchists in Spain," June 3, 1897, NA, HO, 45/9743/A56151C/3.
143. Kinna, *Early Writings on Terrorism*, 2:181.
144. Jensen, "Police Reform and Social Reform"; Jensen, *The Battle Against Anarchist Terrorism*; Merriman, *The Dynamite Club*.
145. Bantman, "Internationalism Without an International?"
146. Bantman, *The French Anarchists in London*; Knepper, *The Invention of International Crime*; Jensen, *The Battle Against Anarchist Terrorism*.
147. Jensen, *The Battle Against Anarchist Terrorism*, 18–19.
148. For more on this trial, see Merriman, *The Dynamite Club*, 163–202.
149. For evidence of debates within the anarchist community on Ravachol's tactics, see "Anarchist Meeting of the Salle du Commerce, 94 rue du Faubourg," n.d., APP, BA, 1132.
150. Malato, "Some Anarchist Portraits."
151. Merriman, *The Dynamite Club*, 203.
152. Jensen, "The Evolution of Anarchist Terrorism," 145.
153. There is one exception: in 1905–1906, a gang of men performed a string of robberies in the French countryside. Claiming to be anarchists, they garnered attention. However, the anarchist community rejected these men without the debate the propagandists had sparked a decade prior.
154. "Letter from the German Correspondent," February 22 [no year], APP, BA, 1509.
155. "Anarchists Spaniards," January 21, 1897, NA, HO, 144/545/A55176.
156. However, these publications were often tracked. See "Anarchist Publications," September 19, 1894, NA, HO, 144/258/A55684/11, for British attempts to track Émile Pouget's *Il N'est Pas Mort*.
157. This law was used to sentence the inflammatory German anarchist Johann Most to sixteen months hard labor in 1881. "Indictment of Johann Most," March 19, 1881, NA,

HO, 144/77/A3385. Commonweal editor David Nicoll was arrested for "incitement to murder." Kinna, *Early Writings on Terrorism*, 3:282.
158. "Anarchist Newspapers," June 29, 1906, NA, HO, 144/834/144519/8.
159. For Meunier's extradition, see NA, HO, 144/485/X37842. He was conflicted, wanting to be free but also wanting to claim responsibility for the attack. "Regarding the Meunier Trial," July 24, 1894, APP, BA, 1509. For François, see NA, HO, 144/485/X37842A, as the possible cause of an attack. Dumont, "Since Last Evening the Principle Anarchist Centers," December 2, 1892, APP, BA, 77.
160. Kinna, *Early Writings on Terrorism*, 2:78.
161. Anarchists named Balotta, Charles, and Cails were arrest under the explosives act and sentenced to ten years in prison, with another accomplice sentenced to five. See the court proceedings, "Regina V. Charles and Others," March 23, 1892, NA, Court of the Assize (ASSI), 6/27/9; see also Kinna, *Early Writings on Terrorism*, 3:299; Hermia Oliver, *The International Anarchist Movement in Late Victorian London* (New York: St. Martin's Press, 1983).
162. Polti talked of avenging Vaillant and stoked conspiracy theories that anarchists were done on the continent and about to be active in London. He also identified Giuseppe Fornara as his accomplice. Fornara admitted to the crime and claimed that he "wanted to kill the capitalists." For more, see "Newspaper Extracts (*Chronicle* and *Standard*)," April 1894, NA, HO, 144/259/A55860/2.
163. Bourdin may only have set off the bomb upon tripping while wearing it on a trip to Paris. Due to concurrent attacks in Paris, the event created a media firestorm and brought pressure upon the police. One paper refuted police claims to be monitoring the anarchists, while others feared it was part of a larger plot gone awry. There is little evidence of any of this. Contemporary information on the attack can be found in NA, HO, 144/257/A55660; see also Kinna, *Early Writings on Terrorism*, 3:362. The attack was also the inspiration for Joseph Conrad's famous novel *The Secret Agent* (Champaign, IL: Project Gutenberg, 1999).
164. "Anarchists," December 1, 1893, NA, HO, 144/545/A55176/5.
165. Butterworth, *The World That Never Was*, 396–98.
166. Richard Bach Jensen, "The International Campaign Against Anarchist Terrorism, 1880–1930s," *Terrorism and Political Violence* 21, no. 1 (2009): 89–109.
167. See essays in Land, *Enemies of Humanity*.
168. This led some anarchists to write in non-anarchist papers to publicize their ideas. See "Extract *London Morning*," September 19, 1898, NA, HO, 144/545/A55176/32.
169. For a discussion of splits within the anarchist movement, see Kirwin Ray Shaffer, *Anarchism and Countercultural Politics in Early Twentieth Century Cuba* (Gainesville: University of Florida Press, 2005).
170. Jensen, "The International Campaign," 99.
171. Andrew R. Carlson, *Anarchism in Germany* (Metuchen: Scarecrow Press, 1972), 395.
172. Jensen, *The Battle Against Anarchist Terrorism*, 364.
173. Oliver, *The International Anarchist Movement*, 110.

174. Georges Sorel, *Sorel: Reflections on Violence*, ed. Jeremy Jennings (Cambridge: Cambridge University Press, 1999).
175. Bantman, "Internationalism Without an International," 964.
176. Merriman, *The Dynamite Club*, 211.
177. For an anarchist debate over syndicalism, see Pierre Monatte and Errico Malatesta, "Syndicalism—For and Against," in *Anarchism: A Documentary History of Libertarian Ideas*, ed. Robert Graham (London: Black Rose Books, 2005), 206–11.
178. David Lyon, *The Electronic Eye: The Rise of Surveillance Society* (Minneapolis: University of Minnesota Press, 1994); Kevin D. Haggarty and Richard V. Erickson, "The Surveillant Assemblage," *British Journal of Sociology* 51, no. 4 (2000): 605–22; Toni Weller, ed., *Information History in the Modern World: Histories of the Information Age* (Basingstoke: Palgrave, 2010); Blair Wilkinson and Randy Lippert, "Moving Images Through an Assemblage: Police, Visual Information, and Resistance," *Critical Criminology* 20, no. 3 (2012): 311–25; Tamara Vukov and Mimi Sheller, "Border Work: Surveillant Assemblages, Virtual Fences, and Tactical Counter-Media," *Social Semiotics* 23, no. 2 (2013): 225–41; Kirstie Ball and David Murakami Wood, "Political Economies of Surveillance," *Surveillance and Society* 11, no. 1/2 (2013): 1–3; Kees Boersma et al, eds., *History of State Surveillance in Europe and Beyond* (London: Routledge, 2014).
179. Edward Higgs, *The Information State in England: The Central Collection of Information on Citizens Since 1500* (London: Palgrave Macmillan, 2004); Rosamund Van Brakel and Xavier Van Kerckhoven, "The Emergence of the Identity Card in Belgium and Its Colonies," in Boersma et al., *History of State Surveillance in Europe and Beyond*, 170–185; Friso Roest et al., "Policy Windows for Surveillance: The Phased Introduction of the Identification Card in the Netherlands Since the Early Twentieth Century," in Boersma et al., *History of State Surveillance in Europe and Beyond*, 150–69.
180. Alfred W. McCoy, *Policing America's Empire: The United States, the Philippines, and the Rise of America's Surveillance State* (Madison: University of Wisconsin Press, 2009).
181. Daniel C. Turack, "Freedom of Movement and the International Regime of Passports," *Osgoode Hall Law Journal* 6, no. 2 (1968): 230–51; Lloyd, *The Passport*.
182. Jensen, *The Battle Against Anarchist Terrorism*, 124.
183. Jensen, *The Battle Against Anarchist Terrorism*, 76.
184. Paul Avrich, *Sacco and Vanzetti: The Anarchist Background* (Princeton, NJ: Princeton University Press, 1991); Stanley Coben, *A. Mitchell Palmer: Politician* (New York: Columbia University Press, 1963), 217–45.
185. Jensen, *The Battle Against Anarchist Terrorism*, 91.
186. Jensen, *The Battle Against Anarchist Terrorism*, 75–77.
187. Jensen, *The Battle Against Anarchist Terrorism*, 91.
188. Quoted in Knepper, *The Invention of International Crime*, 154.
189. Mathieu DeFlem, "Wild Beasts Without Nationality: The Uncertain Origins of Interpol, 1898–1910," in *Handbook of Transnational Crime and Justice*, ed. Philip Reichel (Thousand Oaks, CA: Sage Publications, 2005), 281.

190. Richard Bach Jensen, "The International Anti-Anarchist Conference of 1898 and the Origins of Interpol," *Journal of Contemporary History* 16, no. 2 (1981): 323–47.
191. Jensen, "The International Anti-Anarchist Conference," 342.
192. Cesare Lombroso, *Criminal Man*, trans. Mary Gibson and Nicole Hahn Rafter (Durham, NC: Duke University Press, 2006); Isaac Land, "Men with the Faces of Brutes: Physiognomy, Urban Anxieties, and Politics States," in *Enemies of Humanity: The Nineteenth Century War on Terrorism*, ed. Isaac Land (London: Palgrave Macmillan, 2008), 117–35; For more on the connection between Lombroso and eugenics, see Blom, *The Vertigo Years*, 346.
193. Knepper, *The Invention of International Crime*, 172.
194. Martine Kaluszynski, "Republican Identity: Bertillonage as Government Technique," in Caplan and Torpey, *Documenting Individual Identity*, 124–38; Knepper, *The Invention of International Crime*, 159–86; Peter Becker, "The Standardized Gaze: The Standardization of the Search Warrant in Nineteenth Century Germany," in Caplan and Torpey, *Documenting Individual Identity*, 139–63.
195. For correspondence between the British and the Americans on this topic, see NA, FO, 27/3102.
196. Robertson, *The Passport in America*, 64.
197. Allan Sekula, "The Body and the Archive," *October* 39 (1986): 3–64; Simon A. Cole, "The 'Opinionization' of Fingerprint Evidence," *BioSocieties* 3, no. 1 (2008): 105–13.
198. Robertson, *The Passport in America*, 241.
199. Alexandra Hall and Jonathan Mendel, "Threatprints, Threads and Triggers," *Journal of Cultural Economy* 5, no. 1 (2012), 17.
200. Arthur Conan Doyle, *Sherlock Holmes: The Complete Novels and Stories* (New York: Bantam Books, 1986).
201. Jensen, *The Battle Against Anarchist Terrorism*, 183.
202. Knepper, *The Invention of International Crime*, 159.
203. Jensen, "The International Anti-Anarchist Conference," 332.
204. Jensen, *The Battle Against Anarchist Terrorism*, 166.
205. Jensen, *The Battle Against Anarchist Terrorism*, 184.
206. William Preston Jr., *Aliens and Dissenters: Federal Suppression of Radicals, 1903–1933* (Cambridge, MA: Harvard University Press, 1963), 21–34.
207. Jensen, *The Battle Against Anarchist Terrorism*, 256.
208. Robert J. Goldstein, "The Anarchist Scare of 1908: A Sign of Tensions in the Progressive Era," *American Studies* 15, no. 2 (1974): 55–78.
209. Bantman, *The French Anarchists in London*, 131–56.
210. Knepper, *The Invention of International Crime*, 140.
211. United States Department of Commerce, *Historical Statistics of the United States, 1789–1945* (Washington, DC: U.S. Government Printing Office, 1949), 33.
212. Richard Bach Jensen, "Anarchist Terrorism and Global Diasporas, 1878–1914," *Terrorism and Political Violence* 27, no. 3 (2015): 441–53.
213. Avrich, *Sacco and Vanzetti*; Louis Joughin and Edmund M. Morgan, *The Legacy of Sacco and Vanzetti* (Princeton, NJ: Princeton University Press, 1976).

214. "Communication by the Italian Ambassador," April 23, 1902, and "Response," April 24, 1902; "Forward Memos from the Italian Ambassador and Memorandum as to the Proposal by the Commissioner of Police," May 15, 1902, NA, HO, 144/545/A55176/39&44; "Visit of Spanish Detectives to London," August 15, 1906, NA, HO, 144/757/118516/36.
215. Salter, *Rights of Passage*, 1.
216. Jensen, *The Battle Against Anarchist Terrorism*, 182.
217. Jensen, *The Battle Against Anarchist Terrorism*, 204.
218. For a recounting of the 1926 Geneva Conference, see "Actions Taken by Governments on the Recommendations Adopted by the Second Conference of the International Regime of Passports," 1929, NA, FO, 612/355; for more on British policy toward passports, see NA, FO, 612/265.
219. Torpey, "The Great War and the Birth of the Modern Passport System," 265; United States Department of Labor, *Annual Report of the Secretary of Labor* (Washington, DC: U.S. Government Printing Office, 1920), 65; Kinna, *Early Writings on Terrorism*, 3:343.
220. "Persons to Whom Egyptian Passports and Visas Are to Be Refused," n.d., NA, FO, 141/811/19. For lists of those denied passports and why, see "Particulars of Visas Granted," July-September 1920, NA, FO, 366/791, ff. 190–95. For how to use such lists, see instructions in "Index of Passport Warning Circulars," May 4, 1932, NA, FO, 612/265.
221. Knepper, *The Invention of International Crime*, 93–96.
222. Turack, "Freedom of Movement."
223. Osvaldo Bayer, *Anarchism and Violence: Severino Di Giovanni in Argentina, 1923–1931* (London: Elephant Editions, 1985).
224. Ronald R. Krebs and Patrick Thaddeus Jackson, "Twisting Tongues and Twisting Arms: The Power of Political Rhetoric," *European Journal of International Relations* 13, no. 1 (2007): 35–66; Ronald R. Krebs and Jennifer K. Lobasz, "Fixing the Meaning of 9/11: Hegemony, Coercion and the Road to War in Iraq," *Security Studies* 16, no. 3 (2007): 409–51.
225. Turack, "Freedom of Movement."
226. Steven Hirsch and Lucien van der Walt, "Final Reflections: The Vicissitudes of Anarchist and Syndicalist Trajectories, 1940 to the Present," in Hirsch and van der Walt, *Anarchism and Syndicalism*, 404–7.
227. Marcel van der Linden and Wayne Thorpe, *Revolutionary Syndicalism: An International Perspective* (Brookfield, VT: Scolar Press, 1990), 117–19.
228. Daniel James, *Resistance and Integration: Peronism and the Argentine Working Class, 1946–1976* (Cambridge: Cambridge University Press, 1988), 28–40; Hirsch and van der Walt, "Final Reflections," 406; Michael Forman, *Nationalism and the International Labor Movement: The Idea of the Nation in Socialist and Anarchist Theory* (State College: Pennsylvania State University Press, 1998).
229. Philip Bonner and Jonathan Hyslop, and Lucien van der Walt, "Worker's Movements," in *The Palgrave Dictionary of Transnational History*, ed. Akira Iriye and Pierre-Yves Saunier (London: Palgrave, 2009), 1121–28.

4. AL-QAEDA, THE WAR ON TERROR, AND THE BOUNDARIES OF THE TWENTY-FIRST CENTURY

1. Audrey Kurth Cronin, "How Al Qaeda Ends: The Decline and Demise of Terrorist Groups," *International Security* 31, no. 1 (2006): 7–48; Andrew Phillips, *War, Religion and Empire: The Transformation of International Orders* (Cambridge: Cambridge University Press, 2011); Monica Duffy Toft, Daniel Philpott, and Timothy Samuel Shah, *God's Century: Resurgent Religion and Global Politics* (New York: Norton, 2011).
2. Christina Hellmich "'Here Come the Salafis': The Framing of Al Qaeda's Ideology Within Terrorism Research," in *Knowing Al Qaeda: The Epistemology of Terrorism*, ed. Andreas Behnke and Christina Hellmich (Abingdon, UK: Ashgate Publishing, 2012), 12–27.
3. Ian G. R. Shaw, *Predator Empire: Drone Warfare and Full Spectrum Dominance* (Minneapolis: University of Minnesota Press, 2016).
4. Christopher J. Fuller, *See It/Shoot It: The Secret History of the CIA's Lethal Drone Program* (New Haven, CT: Yale University Press, 2017).
5. Bernard Lewis, *The Crisis of Islam: Holy War and Unholy Terror* (New York: Modern Library, 2003); Olivier Roy, *Globalized Islam: The Search for a New Ummah* (New York: Columbia University Press, 2006); Quintan Wiktorowicz, "Anatomy of the Salafi Movement," *Studies in Conflict and Terrorism* 29, no. 3 (2006): 207–39; Mark Juergensmeyer, *Global Rebellion: Religious Challenges to the Secular State, from Christian Militias to al Qaeda* (Berkeley: University of California Press, 2009).
6. Sayyid Qutb, *Milestones* (Islamic Book Service, 2006), 28–32.
7. Al-Qaeda still exists, but since the major events of this chapter happened over a decade ago, the past tense will be used to talk about them. Present tense will be used only when discussing al-Qaeda as presently constituted.
8. Lewis, *The Crisis of Islam*.
9. "[Al-Qaeda's (and ISIS's) goal] is to establish a caliphate that puts Islam as the major if not only religion of the world with the total control of Sharia law." John Poindexter, personal conversation with author, Maryland, February 9, 2015.
10. Daniel Benjamin and Steve Simon, *The Age of Sacred Terror* (New York: Random House, 2002); Fawaz A. Gerges, *The Far Enemy: Why Jihad Went Global* (Cambridge: Cambridge University Press, 2009).
11. See quotes from Clinton and Bush below.
12. Daniel Byman, personal conversation with author, Washington, DC, June 27, 2014; Paul Pillar, phone conversation with author, July 3, 2014; Samuel Brannen, personal conversation with author, Washington, DC, June 26, 2014; Lee Hamilton, phone conversation with author, July 24, 2014.
13. "They are sort of nihilist, they reject basically everything." Brannen, conversation with author.
14. Daniel Benjamin, Skype conversation with author, June 27, 2014; Brannen, conversation with author; Hamilton, conversation with author.
15. Byman, conversation with author.

16. Brannen, conversation with author. This was echoed by many interviewees. Even today, many have trouble comprehending al-Qaeda circa 2001.
17. Micah Zenko, phone conversation with author, July 8, 2014.
18. For similar arguments, see Thomas L. Friedman, *Longitudes and Attitudes: Exploring the World After September 11* (New York: Farrar, Strauss and Giroux, 2002); Lewis, *The Crisis of Islam*.
19. John Gray, *Al Qaeda and What It Means to Be Modern* (New York: The New Press, 2003); Jean Baudrillard, *The Spirit of Terrorism and Other Essays*, ed. Chris Turner (New York: Verso, 2012).
20. "The 9/11 Commission Report: Final Report of the National Commission on Terrorist Attacks Upon the United States" (Washington, DC: 2004), 340, http://www.9-11commission.gov/report/911Report.pdf.
21. Faisal Devji, *Landscapes of the Jihad: Militancy, Morality, Modernity* (Ithaca, NY: Cornell University Press, 2005).
22. Devji, *Landscapes of the Jihad*, 6–7.
23. Cian O'Driscoll, "From Versailles to 9/11: Non-State Actors and Just War in the Twentieth Century," in *Ethics, Authority, and War: Non-State Actors and the Just War Tradition*, ed. Eric Heinze and Brent J. Steele (New York: Palgrave, 2009), 38.
24. Devji, *Landscapes of the Jihad*, 8–9; "Investigation Into Alleged Misconduct by Senior DoD Officials Concerning the Able Danger Program and Lt. Col. Anthony A. Shaffer, U.S. Army Reserve (Case Number H05L97905217)"; Memorandum for Undersecretary of Defense (Arlington, VA: Department of Defense, Inspector General, September 18, 2006), 17, http://fas.org/irp/agency/dod/ig-abledanger.pdf.
25. Kathleen Hicks, personal conversation with author, Washington, DC, August 22, 2014.
26. Osama bin Laden, *Messages to the World: The Statements of Osama Bin Laden*, ed. Bruce Lawrence, trans. James Howarth (New York: Verso, 2005), 9.
27. Devji, *Landscapes of the Jihad*; Matthew Levitt, personal conversation with author, Washington, DC, July 23, 2014.
28. Laura Mansfield, *His Own Words: Translation and Analysis of the Writings of Dr. Ayman al Zawahiri* (Old Tappan, NJ: TLG Publications, 2006); see also Devji, *Landscapes of the Jihad*.
29. This is reflected in its strategy of attacking the "far enemy," the United States, instead of the "near enemy," apostate Arab regimes (à la Qutb). Bin Laden, *Messages to the World*; Benjamin and Simon, *The Age of Sacred Terror*; Gerges, *The Far Enemy*; Byman, conversation with author; Benjamin, conversation with author; Vanda Felbab-Brown, personal conversation with author, Washington, DC, July 23, 2014; Hicks, conversation with author; Pillar, conversation with author.
30. Devji, *Landscapes of the Jihad*, 3.
31. Devji, *Landscapes of the Jihad*, 76, 31. Al-Qaeda's mission was confusing to and rejected by many Islamic fundamentalists, who view their struggle in local terms.
32. Shane Harris, personal conversation with author, Washington, DC, June 24, 2014.
33. Devji, *Landscapes of the Jihad*, 30.

34. Ayse Zarakol, "What Makes Terrorism Modern? Terrorism, Legitimacy, and the International System," *Review of International Studies* 37, no. 5 (2011): 2316.
35. Ronald Krebs and Jennifer K. Lobasz, "Fixing the Meaning of 9/11: Hegemony, Coercion and the Road to War in Iraq," *Security Studies* 16, no. 3 (2007), 442.
36. Patrick Thaddeus Jackson, *Civilizing the Enemy: German Reconstruction and the Invention of the West* (Ann Arbor: University of Michigan Press, 2006).
37. Quoted in Shane Harris, *The Watchers: The Rise of America's Surveillance State* (New York: Penguin Press, 2011), 146.
38. Janine Davison, personal conversation with author, Washington, DC, September 24, 2014.
39. Byman, conversation with author.
40. Bill Clinton, "Remarks at the University of Connecticut in Storrs," October 15, 1995, Public Papers of President (hereafter PPP), National Archives online, https://www.govinfo.gov/app/collection/PPP/3.
41. Zarakol, "What Makes Terrorism Modern?"
42. "Interview: Richard A. Clarke," *Frontline*, March 20, 2002.
43. Benjamin, conversation with author.
44. Benjamin and Simon, *The Age of Sacred Terror*, 256.
45. Chris Kojm, personal conversation with author, Washington, DC, January 22, 2015.
46. Richard A. Clarke, "Presidential Policy Initiative/Review—The Al-Qida Network," NSC Memorandum, January 25, 2001, http://www2.gwu.edu/~nsarchiv/NSAEBB/NSAEBB147/clarke%20memo.pdf.
47. An expression notoriously used in *Wag the Dog*, a popular 1997 movie starring Dustin Hoffman and Robert De Niro, in which a president fabricates a war to distract from a sex scandal: http://www.imdb.com/title/tt0120885/.
48. Byman, conversation with author.
49. Benjamin, conversation with author; Hamilton, conversation with author; Kojm, conversation with author; Hamilton, conversation with author; Levitt, conversation with author; Pillar, conversation with author.
50. "The 9/11 Commission Report," 212.
51. Phillip Zelikow, phone conversation with author, July 22, 2014.
52. "The 9/11 Commission Report," 11.
53. For an official overview, see "Investigation Into Alleged Misconduct."
54. For more, see Harris, *The Watchers*, 115–35.
55. Michael Wertheimer, personal conversation with author, University of Maryland, May 15, 2015.
56. This is one of the major premises behind the 9/11 Commission report and the creation of the Department of Homeland Security. "The 9/11 Commission Report."
57. Hamilton, conversation with author.
58. Wertheimer, conversation with author.
59. Quoted in Harris, *The Watchers*, 155.
60. Wertheimer, conversation with author.

61. Brigitte Lebens Nacos, *Mass-Mediated Terrorism: The Central Role of the Media in Terrorism and Counterterrorism* (Basingstoke: Rowman and Littlefield, 2007).
62. Daniel Marcus, personal conversation with author, Washington, DC, July 9, 2014.
63. "Timeline: Al Qaeda's Global Context," *Frontline*, 2004, https://www.pbs.org/wgbh/frontline/article/timeline-al-qaedas-global-context/.
64. "Al-Qaida Timeline: Plots and Attacks," *MSNBC*, April 23, 2004, http://www.nbcnews.com/id/4677978/ns/world_news-hunt_for_al_qaida/t/al-qaida-timeline-plots-attacks/.
65. "Timeline: Al Qaeda's Global Context."
66. "Shoe Bomber: Tale of Another Failed Terrorist Attack," *CNN*, December 25, 2009.
67. "US 'Foils Underwear Bomb' Plot," *BBC*, May 8, 2012.
68. Krebs and Lobasz, "Fixing the Meaning of 9/11," 432n81.
69. "The Text of President Bush's Address Tuesday Night, After Terrorist Attacks on New York and Washington," *CNN*, September 11, 2001.
70. "President Bush Addresses the Nation," *Washington Post*, September 20, 2001.
71. "Return of the Taliban," *Frontline*, October 3, 2006.
72. "Deputy Secretary Wolfowitz on the Reasons for Iraq War," *Caltech Peace and Justice News*, May 9, 2003.
73. "Text of Bush's Speech at West Point," *New York Times*, June 1, 2002.
74. "The National Security Strategy of the United States of America" (Washington, DC: Office of the President of the United States of America, 2002), i.
75. "President Bush's Speech on Terrorism," *New York Times*, September 6, 2006.
76. Bill Clinton, "Remarks at a Memorial Service for the Bombing Victims in Oklahoma City," April 23, 1995, PPP. This attack was perpetrated by an American, Timothy Nichols.
77. Bill Clinton, "Address to the Nation on Military Action Against Terrorist Sites in Afghanistan and Sudan," August 20, 1998, PPP.
78. "President Bush's Speech to Congress Declaring War on Terror."
79. Ronald R. Krebs, *Narrative and the Making of US National Security* (Cambridge: Cambridge University Press, 2015), 3.
80. Quoted in Harris, *The Watchers*, 151.
81. Quoted in Harris, *The Watchers*, 152.
82. Krebs and Lobasz, "Fixing the Meaning of 9/11."
83. It should be noted that the succeeding Obama administration made an effort to bring the United States off of a war footing in fighting terrorism, of which the move to drone attacks was a part. Kojm, conversation with author.
84. This reflects the way that the fight against the propagandists was characterized as being against "anarchy" as an idea. Greenwald echoes this sentiment: "The NSA explicitly states that none of the targeted individuals is a member of a terrorist organization or involved in any terror plots. Instead, their crime is the views they express." Glenn Greenwald, *No Place to Hide: Edward Snowden, the NSA, and the U.S. Surveillance State* (New York: Metropolitan Books, 2014), 187.
85. "The National Security Strategy of the United States of America," 2002, i.

4. THE BOUNDARIES OF THE TWENTY-FIRST CENTURY   193

86. Pillar, conversation with author.
87. Rommel C. Banlaoi, "The Abu Sayyaf Group: From Mere Banditry to Genuine Terrorism," *Southeast Asian Affairs* 2006, no. 1 (2006): 247–62; Soliman M. Santos Jr. and Octavio A. Dinampo, "Abu Sayyaf Reloaded: Rebels, Agents, Bandits, Terrorists (Case Study)," in Soliman M. Santos Jr. and Paz Verdades M. Santos, *Primed and Purposeful: Armed Groups and Human Security Efforts in the Philippines* (Geneva: Small Arms Survey, Graduate Institute of International and Development Studies, 2010), 115–38; McKenzie O'Brien, "Fluctuations Between Crime and Terror: The Case of Abu Sayyaf's Kidnapping Activities," *Terrorism and Political Violence* 24, no. 2 (2012): 320–36.
88. Barak Mendelsohn, "Sovereignty Under Attack: The International Society Meets the Al Qaeda Network," *Review of International Studies* 31, no. 1 (2005): 45–68; Oded Lowenheim and Brent J. Steele, "Institutions of Violence, Great Power Authority, and the War on Terror," *International Political Science Review* 31, no. 1 (2010): 23–39.
89. Dana Priest and William M. Arkin, *Top Secret America: The Rise of the New American Security State* (New York: Little, Brown, 2011), xx–xxi.
90. Lee Tien, phone conversation with author, July 22, 2014. Harris mentions that this was one of the biggest effects of the War on Terror. Harris, conversation with author.
91. Levitt, conversation with author.
92. This was specifically mentioned by Zelikow, who sees public distrust as a consequence of "policy judgments on what to collect, or the absence of such judgments, combined with a wider erosion of trust in intelligence agencies caused by abuses elsewhere." Zelikow, conversation with author.
93. Byman, conversation with author; Benjamin, conversation with author; Kojm, conversation with author; Levitt, conversation with author; Marcus, conversation with author; Pillar, conversation with author.
94. The significance of the Patriot Act was a point of difference between the privacy advocates I interviewed. For instance, D.S. (a Washington, DC, attorney and privacy advocate who wished to remain anonymous) and Lee Tien saw the act as vitally important, while David Husband believed that it was epiphenomenal to the rise of technology. D.S., Skype conversation with author, July 31, 2014; Tien, conversation with author; David Husband, personal conversation with author, Washington, DC, August 22, 2014.
95. Alfred W. McCoy, *A Question of Torture: CIA Interrogation, from the Cold War to the War on Terror* (New York: Holt Paperbacks, 2006); Mark Fallon, *Unjustifiable Means: The Inside Story of How the CIA, Pentagon, and US Government Conspired to Torture* (New York: Regan Arts, 2017).
96. Shaw, *Predator Empire*, 122; Fuller, *See It/Shoot It*, 18, 185–90.
97. Byman, conversation with author.
98. "Iraq Coalition Casualty Count," iCasualties.org, February 15, 2021, http://icasualties.org/App/Fatalities.
99. It should be noted that the Afghanistan War also had many critics among my interviewees, especially with regards to its conduct. Wertheimer said that he wished the United States had tried to work with the Taliban: "We will give you aid if you give us

100. bin Laden. . . . I would like to have given that approach a try . . . [not] kill a soul, that would have been huge." Wertheimer, conversation with author.
100. Hayden called the Afghan invasion a major success but warned that this success was not guaranteed to continue if resources were shifted away. Michael Hayden, personal conversation with author, Washington, DC, August 22, 2014.
101. "Iraq Body Count," http://www.iraqbodycount.org/.
102. Pillar, conversation with author.
103. Robert Kagan and William Kristol, *Present Dangers: Crisis and Opportunity in American Foreign and Defense Policy* (San Francisco: Encounter Books, 2000). Terrorism is conspicuously missing from this collection of essays from future Bush administration officials and their allies.
104. "Deputy Secretary Wolfowitz on the Reasons for Iraq War."
105. Zelikow, conversation with author. Micah Zenko and Kathleen Hicks expressed similar sentiments. Zenko, conversation with author; Hicks, conversation with author.
106. Poindexter was the lone defender of the Iraq War among my interviewees. He justified the claims of WMD: "A lot of the intelligence we had was what his people were telling him, which was not true." Poindexter, conversation with author.
107. Benjamin, conversation with author; see also Byman, conversation with author, and Krebs and Lobasz, "Fixing the Meaning of 9/11."
108. Zelikow, conversation with author.
109. "Testimony of U.S. Secretary of Defense Donald Rumsfeld Before the Senate Armed Services Committee Regarding Iraq (Transcript)," September 19, 2002, http://www.defense.gov/speeches/speech.aspx?speechid=287.
110. "Deputy Secretary Wolfowitz on the Reasons for Iraq War."
111. "The 9/11 Commission Report," 336.
112. "The National Security Strategy of the United States of America" (Washington, DC: Office of the President of the United States of America, 2006), i.
113. Alexandre Debs and Nuno P. Monteiro, "Known Unknowns: Power Shifts, Uncertainty, and War," *International Organization* 68, no. 1 (2014): 1–31.
114. Fuller, *See It/Shoot It*, 9–10.
115. Spencer Ackerman, "U.S. Drones Never Left Libya; Will Hunt Benghazi Thugs," *Danger Room*, September 12, 2012. Micah Zenko told me that drone operations have almost nothing to do with counterterrorism and are more focused on counterinsurgency. This was not a common opinion. Zenko, conversation with author.
116. For more on JSOC and drones, see Shaw, *Predator Empire*, 111–54.
117. Benjamin, conversation with author.
118. "The Drone War in Pakistan," accessed September 1, 2021, https://www.newamerica.org/international-security/reports/americas-counterterrorism-wars/the-drone-war-in-pakistan/.
119. It should be mentioned that Michael Hayden told me that the program was ramped up beginning in 2008, even if annual numbers do not reflect this. Hayden, conversation with author.

120. "The War in Yemen," accessed September 1, 2021, https://www.newamerica.org/international-security/reports/americas-counterterrorism-wars/the-war-in-yemen.
121. Attacks tend to occur in bunches. In the two-week period between July 27 and August 8, 2013, thirty-four militants were killed by drone strikes in Yemen, based on intelligence of future al-Qaeda attacks on embassies in Sana'a and on shipping in the Red Sea. "Yemen Drone Strikes: 3 Attacks Kill 12 Suspected Militants," *Huffington Post*, August 8, 2013.
122. Closings and reallocations may be part of a larger strategy to make sure that operations are not interrupted by the attention given to any single base. See Farhan Bokhari, "Officials Confirm CIA Drones In Pakistan," *CBS News*, February 19, 2009.
123. Chris Allbritton, "Pakistan Army Chief Sought More Drone Coverage in '08: Wikileaks," *Reuters*, May 20, 2011.
124. For more, see Fuller, *See It/Shoot It*, 104–21.
125. Benjamin and Simon, *The Age of Sacred Terror*, 321–22, 336–38, 343–46.
126. Quoted in Fuller, *See It/Shoot It*, 120.
127. Quoted in Fuller, *See It/Shoot It*, 117.
128. Quoted in Jane Mayer, "The Predator War," *New Yorker*, October 26, 2009.
129. Quoted in Peter W. Singer, *Wired for War: The Robotics Revolution and Conflict in the 21st Century* (New York: Penguin Books, 2009), 53–54.
130. Obama's attorney general Eric Holder has suggested a similarity between a drone strike and tracking the plane of Japanese general Isoroku Yamamoto during the Second World War. "Attorney General Eric Holder Speaks at Northwestern University School of Law," Evanston, IL, March 5, 2012, http://www.justice.gov/iso/opa/ag/speeches/2012/ag-speech-1203051.html. Fuller argues the United States sought extensive legal cover for drones. Fuller, *See It/Shoot It*, 129–77.
131. Singer, *Wired for War*, 62.
132. Greenwald, *No Place to Hide*, 101–8.
133. As one NSA document boasts, "Prism is a team sport!" Quoted in Greenwald, *No Place to Hide*, 109–18, quote on 116; Glenn Greenwald and Ewen MacAskill, "NSA Prism Program Taps in to User Data of Apple, Google and Others," *Guardian*, June 6, 2013; Chris Huhne, "Prism and Tempora: The Cabinet Was Told Nothing of the Surveillance State's Excesses," *Guardian*, October 6, 2013; James Ball, Julian Borger, and Glenn Greenwald, "Revealed: How US and UK Spy Agencies Defeat Internet Privacy and Security," *Guardian*, September 5, 2013; Barton Gellman and Laura Poitras, "U.S., British Intelligence Mining Data from Nine U.S. Internet Companies in Broad Secret Program," *Washington Post*, June 7, 2013.
134. "U.S. Phone Companies Never Once Challenged NSA Data Requests," *Washington Post*, September 27, 2013; "The NSA Paid Silicon Valley Millions to Spy on Taxpayers," *Washington Post*, August 23, 2013.
135. Glenn Greenwald et al., "Microsoft Handed the NSA Access to Encrypted Messages," *Guardian*, July 11, 2013.
136. James Ball, Luke Harding, and Juliette Garside, "BT and Vodafone Among Telecoms Companies Passing Details to GCHQ," *Guardian*, August 2, 2013.

137. Hayley Tsukayama, "Facebook Report: 74 Countries Sought Data on 38,000 Users," *Washington Post*, August 27, 2013.
138. Greenwald and MacAskill, "NSA Prism Program"; Greenwald, *No Place to Hide*; James Ball, "NSA Stores Metadata of Millions of Web Users for up to a Year, Secret Files Show," *Guardian*, September 30, 2013; Spencer Ackerman and James Ball, "Optic Nerve: Millions of Yahoo Webcam Images Intercepted by GCHQ," *Guardian*, February 27, 2014; Glenn Greenwald and Ewen MacAskill, "Boundless Informant: The NSA's Secret Tool to Track Global Surveillance Data," *Guardian*, June 11, 2013.
139. There are disagreements about the usefulness of these two statutes. Many of the people I talked to agreed that 702 is useful but that 215 is "of dubious legality." Kojm, conversation with author.
140. "Order Granting Governments Motion to Dismiss ACLU Motion," ACLU, https://www.aclu.org/files/assets/order_granting_governments_motion_to_dismiss_and_denying_aclu_motion_for_preliminary_injunction.pdf.
141. Byman, conversation with author; D.S., conversation with author; Tien, conversation with author.
142. There is also some debate and question over how much data the NSA actually collects. It claims that it can collect only 1.6 percent of all internet communication and 0.00004 percent of all internet use. However, Jeff Jarvis claims that, after streaming, HTTP, and person-to-person file sharing are taken into account, the NSA can monitor "practically everything that matters." Jeff Jarvis, "How Much Data the NSA Really Gets," *Guardian*, August 13, 2013.
143. Timothy B. Lee, "The House Just Overwhelmingly Voted to Rein In the NSA," *Vox*, June 20, 2014.
144. Brian Fung, "Everything You Need to Know About Obama's NSA Reforms, in Plain English," *Washington Post*, January 17, 2014.
145. Ball, Borger, and Greenwald, "Revealed."
146. Glenn Greenwald and James Ball, "The Top Secret Rules That Allow NSA to Use US Data Without a Warrant," *Guardian*, June 20, 2013.
147. Nick Hopkins and Luke Harding, "GCHQ Accused of Selling Its Services After Revelations of Funding by NSA," *Guardian*, August 2, 2013; Glenn Greenwald, Laura Poitras, and Ewen MacAskill, "NSA Shares Raw Intelligence Including Americans' Data with Israel," *Guardian*, September 11, 2013; "NSA and Israeli Intelligence: Memorandum of Understanding—Full Document," *Guardian*, September 11, 2013.
148. Nick Hopkins, and Julian Borger, "Exclusive: NSA Pays £100m in Secret Funding for GCHQ," *Guardian*, August 1, 2013; Hopkins and Harding, "GCHQ Accused of Selling Its Services."
149. Nick Hopkins and Spencer Ackerman, "Flexible Laws and Weak Oversight Give GCHQ Room for Manoeuvre," *Guardian*, August 2, 2013.
150. Angelique Chrisafis, "France 'Runs Vast Electronic Spying Operation Using NSA-Style Methods,'" *Guardian*, July 4, 2013.

151. "The National Security Agency: Missions, Authorities, Oversight and Partnerships," National Security Agency, August 9, 2013, 6, http://www.nsa.gov/public_info/_files/speeches_testimonies/2013_08_09_the_nsa_story.pdf.
152. Quoted in Harris, *The Watchers*, 159.
153. H. G. Wells, *World Brain* (London: Methuen, 1938).
154. Kirstie Ball and Frank Webster, "The Intensification of Surveillance," in *The Intensification of Surveillance: Crime, War and Terrorism in the Information Age*, ed. Kirstie Ball and Frank Webster (Sterling, VA: Pluto Press, 2003), 1–15.
155. Harris, *The Watchers*, 15–36.
156. Poindexter, conversation with author.
157. David Lyon, "Surveillance After September 11, 2001," in Ball and Webster, *The Intensification of Surveillance*, 16–25.
158. Michael Hayden told me that data collection "had been going on since the late 1990s." Hayden, conversation with author. Paul Pillar worked in the CIA during this time and related the following story: "Back in 1997 I got involved in the Defense Science Board summer study [a workshop hosted by private-sector workers].... One of the big emphases that these people in private industry talked about was we need to do more in the area of data mining. In other words, using algorithms to sift through bulk collections stuff.... What they [the NSA] are doing is exactly what the community was urged to be doing more of back in the late 1990s." Pillar, conversation with author.
159. D.S., conversation with author.
160. Pillar, conversation with author.
161. Quoted in Peter C. Baker, "'We Can't Go Back to Normal': How Will Coronavirus Change the World?," *Guardian*, March 31, 2020.
162. Wertheimer, conversation with author.
163. Poindexter was Reagan's national security advisor and was convicted of five felonies in the aftermath of Iran-Contra in 1990. However, his sentence was overturned on appeal in 1991.
164. Poindexter, conversation with author.
165. Bush's decision relied on the Supreme Court case *Smith v. Maryland*. Bush believed it was a separation-of-powers issue; national security allowed the executive to claim control of metadata from Congress. Hayden, conversation with author.
166. Glenn Greenwald, Ewen MacAskill, and Laura Poitras, "Edward Snowden: The Whistleblower Behind the NSA Surveillance Revelations," *Guardian*, June 9, 2013.
167. Eric Lichtblau and James Risen, "Bank Data Is Sifted by U.S. in Secret to Block Terror," *New York Times*, June 23, 2006.
168. Harris, *The Watchers*, 201–5.
169. "'Peeling Back the Layers of Tor with EgotisticalGiraffe'—Read the Document," *Guardian*, October 4, 2013.
170. "The National Security Agency," 1.
171. Andrea Peterson, "Government Board Report Refutes 9/11 Argument for NSA Phone Records Program," *Washington Post*, January 23, 2014.

172. Peterson, "Government Board Report."
173. Glenn Greenwald, "XKeyscore: NSA Tool Collects 'Nearly Everything a User Does on the Internet,'" *Guardian*, July 31, 2013.
174. A. G. Sulzberger and William K. Rashbaum, "Najibullah Zazi Pleads Guilty in Plot to Bomb Subway," *New York Times*, February 22, 2010.
175. Nick Hopkins, "MI5 Chief: GCHQ Surveillance Plays Vital Role in Fight Against Terrorism," *Guardian*, October 8, 2013.
176. Ellen Nakashima, "Independent Review Board Says NSA Phone Data Program Is Illegal and Should End," *Washington Post*, January 24, 2014.
177. Poindexter, conversation with author.
178. Wertheimer, conversation with author.
179. Davison, conversation with author; Hamilton, conversation with author; Zelikow, conversation with author.
180. Brannen, conversation with author; Marcus, conversation with author.
181. Brannen and Kojm were skeptical of the strategic successes.
182. Poindexter, conversation with author.
183. Hicks, conversation with author.
184. Davison, conversation with author; Zelikow, conversation with author.
185. Davison, conversation with author. Similar sentiments were expressed by Benjamin, conversation with author; Brannen, conversation with author; Zelikow, conversation with author.
186. Kojm, conversation with author.
187. Felbab-Brown, conversation with author; Hamilton, conversation with author; Zelikow, conversation with author.
188. Graeme Wood, "What ISIS Really Wants," *Atlantic*, March 2015.
189. Abu Bakr al-Baghdadi, "A Message to the Mujahidin and the Muslim Ummah in the Month of Ramadan," *al-Hayyat Media Center*, July 5, 2014.
190. Audrey Kurth Cronin, "ISIS Is Not a Terrorist Group," *Foreign Affairs* 94, no. 2 (2015): 87–98.
191. Nadia Al-Dayel and Aaron Anfinson, "'In the Words of the Enemy': The Islamic State's Reflexive Projection of Statehood," *Critical Studies on Terrorism* 11, no. 1 (2018): 45–64; Aaron Anfinson, "The Treachery of Images: Visualizing 'Statehood' as a Tactic for the Legitimization of Non-State Actors," *Terrorism and Political Violence* (April 2019): 1–23.
192. Donald Holbrook, *Al-Qaeda 2.0: A Critical Reader* (London: Hurst, 2017).
193. Levitt, conversation with author.
194. The topic of IS will be taken up again in the Conclusion.
195. Jeff Gruenewald, "Do Targeted Killings Increase or Decrease Terrorism?" *Criminology and Public Policy* 16, no. 1 (2017): 187–90; Daniel P. Hepworth, "Terrorist Retaliation? An Analysis of Terrorist Attacks Following the Targeted Killing of Top-Tier al Qaeda Leadership," *Journal of Policing, Intelligence and Counter Terrorism* 9, no. 1 (2014): 1–18; Javier Jordan, "The Effectiveness of the Drone Campaign Against Al Qaeda Central: A Case Study," *Journal of Strategic Studies* 37, no. 1 (2014): 4–29; Alex S.

Wilner, "Targeted Killings in Afghanistan: Measuring Coercion and Deterrence in Counterterrorism and Counterinsurgency," *Studies in Conflict and Terrorism* 33, no. 4 (2010): 307–29; Steven R. David, *Fatal Choices: Israel's Policy of Targeted Killing* (Tel Aviv: Bar-Ilan University, 2002); Mohammed M. Hafez and Joseph M. Hatfield, "Do Targeted Assassinations Work? A Multivariate Analysis of Israel's Controversial Tactic During Al-Aqsa Uprising," *Studies in Conflict and Terrorism* 29, no. 4 (2006): 359–82; Leila Hudson, Colin S. Owens, and Matt Flannes, "Drone Warfare: Blowback from the New American Way of War," *Middle East Policy* 18, no. 3 (2011): 122–32; Jenna Jordan, "When Heads Roll: Assessing the Effectiveness of Leadership Decapitation," *Security Studies* 18, no. 4 (2009): 719–55; Charli Carpenter, "Crunching Drone Death Numbers," *Duck of Minerva*, August 17, 2011; Jennifer Varriale Carson, "Assessing the Effectiveness of High-Profile Targeted Killings in the 'War on Terror,'" *Criminology and Public Policy* 16, no. 1 (2017): 191–220; Brian Forst, "Targeted Killings," *Criminology and Public Policy* 16, no. 1 (2017): 221–24.

196. Benjamin, conversation with author. This dynamic was also mentioned in Byman, conversation with author; Brannen, conversation with author; Felbab-Brown, conversation with author; Hayden, conversation with author; Kojm, conversation with author; Pillar, conversation with author; Zelikow, conversation with author.

197. Brannen, conversation with author.

198. The New American Foundation estimates that drones have killed between 375 and 475 civilians through June 2017, while the Bureau of Investigative Journalism claimed 881 civilian deaths through 2012. See Jo Becker and Scott Shane, "Secret 'Kill List' Tests Obama's Principles," *New York Times*, May 29, 2012; "The Drone War in Pakistan"; "Living Under Drones: Death, Injury, and Trauma to Civilians from U.S. Drone Practices in Pakistan," International Human Rights and Conflict Resolution Clinic at Stanford Law School and Global Justice Clinic at New York University School of Law, 2012, vi.; Erik Voeten, "The Problems with Studying Civilian Casualties from Drone Usage in Pakistan: What We Can't Know," *Monkey Cage*, August 17, 2011.

199. "Living Under Drones," vii; Shaw, *Predator Empire*, 234.

200. Ackerman, "U.S. Drones Never Left Libya."

201. The United States has recently declassified information stating that drone attacks have "close to the same number of civilian casualties per incident as manned aircraft, and were an order of magnitude more likely to result in civilian casualties per engagement." "Drone Strikes: Civilian Casualty Considerations," Joint and Coalition Operational Command, June 18, 2013, 1. https://www.cna.org/sites/default/files/research/Drone_Strikes.pdf.

202. "The War in Yemen."

203. Robert F. Mazzetti, Mark Worth, and Scott Shane, "With Brennan Pick, a Light on Drone Strikes' Hazards," *New York Times*, February 5, 2013.

204. Lauren Wilcox, "Embodying Algorithmic War: Gender, Race, and the Posthuman in Drone Warfare," *Security Dialogue* 48, no. 1 (2017): 11–28.

205. Pillar, conversation with author.

206. Wertheimer, conversation with author.

207. Christian Davenport, "How the Pentagon Is Preparing for the Coming Drone Wars," *Washington Post*, November 24, 2017.
208. Jason Burke, "Bin Laden Letters Reveal Al-Qaida's Fears of Drone Strikes and Infiltration," *Guardian*, March 1, 2016.
209. Daniel J. Rosenthal and Loren DeJonge Schulman, "Trump's Secret War on Terror," *Atlantic*, August 10, 2018.
210. Kojm, conversation with author.
211. Andrea Peterson, "Obama Can't Point to a Single Time the NSA Call Records Program Prevented a Terrorist Attack," *Washington Post*, December 23, 2013.
212. Zelikow, conversation with author. Poindexter echoed these concerns; Poindexter, conversation with author.
213. Husband, conversation with author.
214. Wertheimer, conversation with author.
215. Jeremy Scahill and Glenn Greenwald, "The NSA's Secret Role in the U.S. Assassination Program," *Intercept*, February 10, 2014.
216. Fuller, *See It/Shoot It*, 95.
217. Tien, conversation with author.
218. Wertheimer, conversation with author.
219. Peter Baker, "In Terror Shift, Obama Took a Long Path," *New York Times*, May 27, 2013; Siobhan Gorman and Carol E. Lee, "Obama Readies Revamp of NSA," *Wall Street Journal*, January 10, 2014; Fung, "Everything You Need to Know"; Andrea Peterson, "The Senate Has Another Go at NSA Surveillance Reform," *Washington Post*, July 29, 2014.
220. Steven Bernstein et al., "Social Science as Case-Based Diagnostics," in *Theory and Evidence in Comparative Politics and International Relations*, ed. Richard Ned Lebow and Mark I. Lichbach (New York: Palgrave Macmillan, 2007), 229–60.
221. Blair Wilkinson and Randy Lippert, "Moving Images Through an Assemblage: Police, Visual Information, and Resistance," *Critical Criminology* 20, no. 3 (2012): 312; Kevin D. Haggarty and Richard V. Erickson, "The Surveillant Assemblage," *British Journal of Sociology* 51, no. 4 (2000): 605–22.
222. Lyon, "Surveillance After September 11," 21.
223. Google and other companies are attempting to encrypt data to keep it proprietary. Craig Timberg and Jia Lynn Yang, "Google Is Encrypting Search Globally. That's Bad for the NSA and China's Censors," *Washington Post*, March 12, 2014, http://www.washingtonpost.com/blogs/the-switch/wp/2014/03/12/google-is-encrypting-search-worldwide-thats-bad-for-the-nsa-and-china/. However, Wertheimer argues that Google's encryption would actually help keep attacks anonymous and is about protecting from lawsuits and keeping data proprietary. Wertheimer, conversation with author.
224. Gilles Deleuze, "Postscript on the Societies of Control," *October* 59 (Winter 1992): 3–7. Of course many of the exclusionary aspects of borders, like passports, have not gone away but they are becoming less important as collection points become more important.
225. Ed Romein and Marc Schuilenburg, "Are You On the Fast Track? The Rise of Surveillant Assemblages in a Post Industrial Age," *Architectural Theory Review* 13, no. 3

(2008): 337–48; Alexandra Hall and Jonathan Mendel, "Threatprints, Threads and Triggers," *Journal of Cultural Economy* 5, no. 1 (2012): 9–27.
226. Tamara Vukov and Mimi Sheller, "Border Work: Surveillant Assemblages, Virtual Fences, and Tactical Counter-Media," *Social Semiotics* 23, no. 2 (2013), 227.
227. Shaw, *Predator Empire*, 159.
228. Louise Amoore and Rita Raley, "Securing with Algorithms: Knowledge, Decision, Sovereignty," *Security Dialogue* 48, no. 1 (2017): 3–10.
229. "The 2014 Quadrennial Homeland Security Review" (Washington, DC: Department of Homeland Security, 2014), 16.
230. Adam Segal, "Huawei, 5G, and Weaponized Interdependence," in *Uses and Abuses of Weaponized Interdependence*, ed. Dan Drezner, Henry Farrell, and Abraham L. Newman (Washington, DC: Brookings Institution Press, 2021), 149–67.
231. "China Has the World's Most Centralised Internet System," *Economist*, June 28, 2018; "China Moves Towards Nationalization with Probe Into Alibaba," *Radio Free Asia*, December 25, 2020; Anna Mitchell and Larry Diamond, "China's Surveillance State Should Scare Everyone," *Atlantic*, February 2, 2018.
232. Ewen MacAskill, "New NSA Leaks Show How US Is Bugging Its European Allies," *Guardian*, June 30, 2013; Jason Burke, "NSA Spied on Indian Embassy and UN Mission, Edward Snowden Files Reveal," *Guardian*, September 25, 2013.
233. Robert H. Jackson, *Quasi-States: Sovereignty, International Relations, and the Third World* (Cambridge: Cambridge University Press, 1990); Robert I. Rotberg, *When States Fail: Causes and Consequences* (Princeton, NJ: Princeton University Press, 2003); for more on various institutional attempts to rank or warn about such states, see Javier Fabra Mata and Sebastian Ziaja, "User's Guide on Measuring Fragility" (Bonn: Deutsches Institut für Entwicklungspolitik and United Nations Development Program, 2009), https://gsdrc.org/document-library/users-guide-on-measuring-fragility/; for critiques of the concept, see Naeem Inayatullah, "Beyond the Sovereignty Dilemma: Quasi-States as Social Construct," in *State Sovereignty as Social Construct*, ed. Thomas J. Biersteker and Cynthia Weber (Cambridge: Cambridge University Press, 1996), 50–77; Jonathan Hill, "Beyond the Other? A Postcolonial Critique of the Failed State Thesis," *African Identities* 3, no. 2 (2005): 139–54; Branwen Gruffyd Jones, "The Global Political Economy of Social Crisis: Towards a Critique of the 'Failed State' Ideology," *Review of International Political Economy* 15, no. 2 (2008): 180–205.
234. Michael Hardt and Antonio Negri, *Empire* (Cambridge, MA: Harvard University Press, 2000). Frontiers in this conception are not too dissimilar form the idea of "buffer zones" discussed in chapter 2. They are not hard separations between political entities, which necessitate locality, but instead, in the words of Frederick Jackson Turner, "the meeting point between savagery and civilization." Frederick Jackson Turner, *The Significance of the Frontier in American History* (London: Penguin, 2008), 3.
235. Shaw, *Predator Empire*, 119.
236. Michael Hardt and Antonio Negri, *Multitude: War and Democracy in the Age of Empire* (New York: Penguin, 2004), 21.
237. Wilcox, "Embodying Algorithmic War," 13.

238. Shaw, *Predator Empire*, 128.
239. Alfred W. McCoy, *Policing America's Empire: The United States, the Philippines, and the Rise of America's Surveillance State* (Madison: University of Wisconsin Press, 2009), 19.
240. Stuart Elden, *Terror and Territoriality: The Spatial Extent of Sovereignty* (Minneapolis: University of Minnesota Press, 2009).
241. Katharine Hall Kindervater, "Drone Strikes, Ephemeral Sovereignty, and Changing Conceptions of Territory," *Territory, Politics, Governance* 5, no. 2 (2017): 207–21.
242. Wilcox, "Embodying Algorithmic War."
243. Katharine Hall Kindervater, "The Emergence of Lethal Surveillance: Watching and Killing in the History of Drone Technology," *Security Dialogue* 47, no. 3 (2016): 223–38; "Lawfulness of a Lethal Operation Directed Against a US Citizen," Department of Justice White Paper, November 8, 2011, https://fas.org/irp/eprint/doj-lethal.pdf.
244. Jason Burke, "Pressure Builds on Sri Lankan Officials as Isis Claims Easter Attacks," *Guardian*, April 24, 2019.
245. Craig Whitlock, "Remote U.S. Base at Core of Secret Operations," *Washington Post*, December 1, 2012; Craig Whitlock, "U.S. Expands Secret Intelligence Operations in Africa," *Washington Post*, June 14, 2012.
246. Craig Whitlock, "U.S. Drone Base in Ethiopia Is Operational," *Washington Post*, November 16, 2011.
247. Most of the policy makers I interviewed were adamant that sovereignty has rarely, if ever, been breached in drone attacks since permission has been asked and granted. Benjamin, conversation with author; Byman, conversation with author; Brannen, conversation with author; Davison, conversation with author; Felbab-Brown, conversation with author; Pillar, conversation with author; Zelikow, conversation with author. One dissenter was Chris Kojm, who said that drone attacks "definitely violate Pakistani sovereignty." Kojm, conversation with author.
248. Hamilton, conversation with author.
249. David Lyon, *Surveillance as Social Sorting: Privacy, Risk, and Digital Discrimination* (London: Routledge, 2003).
250. Louie Amoore and Marieke de Goede, "Introduction: Data and the War by Other Means," *Journal of Cultural Economy* 5, no. 1 (2012): 5.
251. Roger Clarke, "Information Technology and Dataveillance," *Communications of the ACM* 31, no. 5 (1988): 498–512; David Murakami Wood, "What Is Global Surveillance? Towards a Relational Political Economy of the Global Surveillant Assemblage," *Geoforum* 49 (2013): 317–26.
252. Hall and Mendel, "Threatprints, Threads and Triggers," 11.
253. Tyler Wall and Torin Monahan, "Surveillance and Violence from Afar: The Politics of Drones and Liminal Security-Scapes," *Theoretical Criminology* 15, no. 3 (2011): 239.
254. Wall and Monahan, "Surveillance and Violence from Afar," 239; see also Kelly Gates, "The Cultural Labor of Surveillance: Video Forensics, Computational Objectivity, and the Production of Visual Evidence," *Social Semiotics* 23, no. 2 (2013): 242–60.

255. This is a common critique of neoliberal and algorithmic methods of governance. If drones and data surveillance are a part of this larger story, that story would unfold differently than without them. As regards the state, drones and data surveillance are connected to the use of violence in ways that Facebook and employee assessment, for example, are not.
256. Rosemary E. Shinko, "Ethics After Liberalism: Why (Autonomous) Bodies Matter," *Millennium—Journal of International Studies* 38, no. 3 (2010): 723–45; Christine Sylvester, "War Experiences/War Practices/War Theory," *Millennium—Journal of International Studies* 40, no. 3 (2012): 483–503; Linda Ahall, "The Dance of Militarisation: A Feminist Security Studies Take on the Political," *Critical Studies on Security* 4, no. 2 (2016): 154–68; Kandida Purnell, "Grieving, Valuing, and Viewing Differently: The Global War on Terror's American Toll," *International Political Sociology* 12, no. 2 (2018): 156–71; Lauren B. Wilcox, *Bodies of Violence: Theorizing Embodied Subjects in International Politics* (Oxford: Oxford University Press, 2015).
257. Haggarty and Erickson, "The Surveillant Assemblage."
258. Hall and Mendel, "Threatprints, Threads and Triggers."
259. Hasan Elahi, personal conversation with author, University of Maryland, August 26, 2014. Elahi reminded me that while we met for the first time during the interview, our data doubles had been interacting for some time through email conversation, my visit to his website, etc. Despite never talking to each other and not being sure what the other looked like, we were already connected.
260. Shaw, *Predator Empire*, 210–18, 234–40.

CONCLUSION

1. John Robert McNeill, *Mosquito Empires: Ecology and War in the Greater Caribbean, 1620–1914* (Cambridge: Cambridge University Press, 2010).
2. John Dewey, *Reconstruction in Philosophy* (New York: Cosimo, 2008), 167, 169.
3. John Dewey, "Creative Democracy: The Task Before Us," in *The Philosopher of the Common Man: Essays in Honor of John Dewey to Celebrate His Eightieth Birthday* (New York: Greenwood Press, 1968), 220–28.
4. Disagreements over whose access to data is more dangerous—the government's or corporations'—depends on whether one focuses on restrictions to access or potential actions taken. Paul Pillar told me, "General [Keith] Alexander [former director of the NSA] has assured us, and I know that he is speaking the truth, that there are only twenty-two people in the whole NSA that are able to log into this kind of database. Verizon has all of my metadata, they know everybody I have called and when, and so on. How many people at Verizon have access to that database? I haven't the faintest idea." Paul Pillar, phone conversation with author, July 3, 2014. Zelikow echoed: "In general, our government is somewhat more careful and more regulated." Philip Zelikow, personal conversation with author, July 22, 2014. Meanwhile, privacy

advocate D.S. told me that "the state can bring all its forces to bear on an individual whether that be the criminal justice system or things of that ilk." D.S., Skype conversation with author, July 31, 2014.
5. Laura K. Donohue, "Bulk Metadata Collection: Statutory and Constitutional Considerations," *Harvard Journal of Law and Public Policy* 37 (2014): 757–900.
6. D.S., conversation with author.
7. Lee Tien, phone conversation with author, July 22, 2014.
8. David Husband, personal conversation with author, Washington, DC, August 22, 2014. Husband mentioned that rolling back policy is more popular with older privacy advocates, while younger ones are willing to live with data collection.
9. D.S., conversation with author.
10. Shane Harris, personal conversation with author, Washington, DC, July 24, 2014.
11. Tien, conversation with author.
12. Jeffrey Rosen, "Total Information Awareness," *New York Times*, December 15, 2002; Shane Harris, *The Watchers: The Rise of America's Surveillance State* (New York: Penguin, 2011).
13. The Defense Department Spending Bill pledged that "none of the funds appropriated or otherwise made available in this or any other act may be obligated for the Terrorism Information Awareness Program." However, there was a caveat: "provided: this limitation shall not apply to the program hereby authorized for processing, analysis, and collaboration tools for counterterrorism foreign intelligence, as described in the classified annex." Harris, *The Watchers*, 247.
14. Harris, *The Watchers*, 244–45.
15. As Harris told me, "Activists have done themselves no favors when they allow themselves to be portrayed, sometimes unjustifiably, sometimes justifiably, as their real aim being to stop the government from doing surveillance." Harris, conversation with author.
16. Renée Marlin-Bennett, *Knowledge Power: Intellectual Property, Information, and Privacy* (Boulder, CO: Lynne Rienner Publishers, 2004), 169.
17. Elahi's project website is http://trackingtransience.net/. Elahi told me that his project is now largely obsolete as everyone on social media is basically doing this anyway. Hasan Elahi, personal conversation with author, University of Maryland, August 26, 2014.
18. Quoted in Ed Romein and Marc Schuilenburg, "Are You on the Fast Track? The Rise of Surveillant Assemblages in a Post Industrial Age," *Architectural Theory Review* 13, no. 3 (2008): 344.
19. Elahi, conversation with author.
20. Elahi, conversation with author.
21. Elahi, conversation with author; Michael Hayden, personal conversation with author, Washington, DC, August 22, 2014; Pillar, conversation with author.
22. Hayden, conversation with author.
23. Daniel Byman, personal conversation with author, Washington, DC, June 27, 2014.
24. Ethan Zuckerman, "The Internet's Original Sin," *Atlantic*, August 14, 2014.

25. D.S., conversation with author.
26. Silvia D'Amato, "Terrorists Going Transnational: Rethinking the Role of States in the Case of AQIM and Boko Haram," *Critical Studies on Terrorism* 11, no. 1 (2018): 151–72.
27. Eric Schmitt, "U.S. Drone Strikes Stymie ISIS in Southern Libya," *New York Times*, November 18, 2019; "Top ISIS Commanders Among 6 Killed in U.S. Drone Strikes in East of Afghanistan," *Khaama Press News Agency*, March 2, 2020.
28. Zach Beauchamp, "The Surprising Reason Why ISIS May Be Lashing Out: Because It's Losing," *Vox*, November 16, 2015.
29. Daniel Byman, "ISIS' Big Mistake," *Foreign Affairs*, November 15, 2015.
30. Eliott Abrams, et al. "What Comes After ISIS?," *Foreign Policy*, July 10, 2017; Daniel Byman, "What Comes After ISIS?," *Foreign Policy*, February 22, 2019.
31. Tore Refslund Hamming, "The Al Qaeda–Islamic State Rivalry: Competition Yes, but No Competitive Escalation," *Terrorism and Political Violence* 32, no. 1 (2020): 20–37.
32. Jason Burke, "'A More Dangerous Long-Term Threat': Al-Qaida Grows as Isis Retreats," *Guardian*, December 29, 2016.
33. Vera Mironova and Ekaterina Sergatskova, "Cracks in the Islamic State," *Foreign Affairs*, February 15, 2017.
34. Léa Eveline Jeanne Stéphanie Massé, "Losing Mood(s): Examining Jihadi Supporters' Responses to ISIS' Territorial Decline," *Terrorism and Political Violence* (March 2020): 1–21.
35. Brian Katz and Michael Carpenter, "ISIS Is Already Rising from the Ashes," *Foreign Affairs*, October 18, 2019; Aki Peritz, "The Coming ISIS Jailbreak," *Foreign Affairs*, October 25, 2019.
36. Daniel Byman, "You Can't Defeat Tomorrow's Terrorists by Fighting Yesterday's Enemy," *Foreign Policy*, May 16, 2019.
37. Sarah Marusek, "Inventing Terrorists: The Nexus of Intelligence and Islamophobia," *Critical Studies on Terrorism* 11, no. 1 (2018): 65–87.
38. Kurt M. Campbell and Rush Doshi, "The Coronavirus Could Reshape Global Order," *Foreign Affairs*, March 20, 2020; Henry Farrell and Abraham L. Newman, "Will the Coronavirus End Globalization as We Know It?," *Foreign Affairs*, March 16, 2020; Daniel W. Drezner, "The Song Remains the Same: International Relations After COVID-19," *International Organization*, Special Online Issue (2020), 1–18; Thomas J. Wright, "Stretching the International Order to Its Breaking Point," *Atlantic*, April 4, 2020.
39. Jennifer Rankin, "Coronavirus Could Be Final Straw for EU, European Experts Warn," *Guardian*, April 1, 2020; Colin Kahl and Ariana Berengaut, "Aftershocks: The Coronavirus Pandemic and the New World Disorder," *War on the Rocks*, April 10, 2020; See also the *International Organization* COVID-19 Online Supplemental Issue: https://www.cambridge.org/core/journals/international-organization/information/io-covid-19-online-supplemental-issue.
40. Daniel H. Nexon, *The Struggle for Power in Early Modern Europe: Religious Conflict, Dynastic Empires, and International Change* (Princeton, NJ: Princeton University Press, 2009).

41. Matthew Levitt, personal conversation with author, Washington, DC, July 23, 2014..
42. Lee Hamilton, phone conversation with author, July 24, 2014.
43. Jean-François Lyotard, *The Postmodern Condition: A Report on Knowledge* (Minneapolis: University of Minnesota Press, 1984); David Harvey, *The Condition of Postmodernity: An Enquiry Into the Origins of Cultural Change* (Oxford: Wiley-Blackwell, 1991); Jean Baudrillard, *Simulacra and Simulation*, trans. Sheila Faria Glaser (Ann Arbor: University of Michigan Press, 1995).

BIBLIOGRAPHY

Abbott, Andrew. *Processual Sociology*. Chicago: University of Chicago Press, 2016.
Abrams, Eliott, Robert Malley, Cole Bunzel, Noah Bonsey, Amr al-Azm, and Renad Mansour. "What Comes After ISIS?" *Foreign Policy*, July 10, 2017.
Abrams, Philip. "Notes on the Difficulty of Studying the State." *Journal of Historical Sociology* 1, no. 1 (March 1988): 58–89.
Acharya, Amitav. *Constructing Global Order: Agency and Change in World Politics*. Cambridge: Cambridge University Press, 2018.
———. *The End of American World Order*. Cambridge: Polity, 2018.
Ackerman, Spencer. "U.S. Drones Never Left Libya; Will Hunt Benghazi Thugs." *Danger Room*, September 12, 2012.
Ackerman, Spencer, and James Ball. "Optic Nerve: Millions of Yahoo Webcam Images Intercepted by GCHQ." *Guardian*, February 27, 2014.
Adelman, Jeremy. *Sovereignty and Revolution in the Iberian Atlantic*. Princeton, NJ: Princeton University Press, 2009.
Adler, Emanuel, and Vincent Pouliot. "International Practices." *International Theory* 3, no. 1 (2011): 1–36.
Adler-Nissen, Rebecca. "Towards a Practice Turn in EU Studies: The Everyday of European Integration." *Journal of Common Market Studies* 54, no. 1 (2016): 87–103.
Agnew, John. *Globalization and Sovereignty: Beyond the Territorial Trap*. London: Rowman and Littlefield, 2017.
Agnew, John, and Luca Muscarà. *Making Political Geography*. London: Rowman and Littlefield, 2012.
Ahall, Linda. "The Dance of Militarisation: A Feminist Security Studies Take on the Political." *Critical Studies on Security* 4, no. 2 (2016): 154–68.

al-Baghdadi, Abu Bakr. "A Message to the Mujahidin and the Muslim Ummah in the Month of Ramadan." *Al-Hayyat Media Center*, July 5, 2014.

Al-Dayel, Nadia, and Aaron Anfinson. "'In the Words of the Enemy': The Islamic State's Reflexive Projection of Statehood." *Critical Studies on Terrorism* 11, no. 1 (2018): 45–64.

Allbritton, Chris. "Pakistan Army Chief Sought More Drone Coverage in '08: Wikileaks." *Reuters*, May 20, 2011.

Allison, Graham T. "Conceptual Models and the Cuban Missile Crisis." *American Political Science Review* 63, no. 3 (1969): 689–718.

"Al-Qaida Timeline: Plots and Attacks." *MSNBC*, April 23, 2004. http://www.nbcnews.com/id/4677978/ns/world_news-hunt_for_al_qaida/t/al-qaida-timeline-plots-attacks/.

Amirell, Stefan Eklof. *Pirates of Empire: Colonisation and Maritime Violence in Southeast Asia*. Cambridge: Cambridge University Press, 2019.

Amoore, Louise, and Marieke de Goede. "Introduction: Data and the War by Other Means." *Journal of Cultural Economy* 5, no. 1 (2012): 3–8.

Amoore, Louise, and Rita Raley. "Securing with Algorithms: Knowledge, Decision, Sovereignty." *Security Dialogue* 48, no. 1 (2017): 3–10.

Anarchism and Outrage. London: C. M. Wilson, 1893.

Anderson, Benedict R. *Under Three Flags: Anarchism and the Anti-Colonial Imagination*. London: Verso, 2005.

Anderson, M. S. *Europe in the Eighteenth Century, 1713–1783*. London: Longman, 1987.

Anderson, Perry. *Lineages of the Absolutist State*. London: Verso, 1979.

Anfinson, Aaron. "The Treachery of Images: Visualizing 'Statehood' as a Tactic for the Legitimization of Non-State Actors." *Terrorism and Political Violence* (April 2019): 1–23.

Antony, Robert J. *Like Froth Floating on the Sea: The World of Pirates and Seafarers in Late Imperial South China*. Berkeley, CA: Institute of East Asian Studies, 2003.

Australian Capital Territory Government. "ACT Legislation Register—Offences at Sea Act 1536 28 Hen 8 c 15." http://www.legislation.act.gov.au/a/db_1803//.

Avrich, Paul. *The Haymarket Tragedy*. Princeton, NJ: Princeton University Press, 1984.

———. *Sacco and Vanzetti: The Anarchist Background*. Princeton, NJ: Princeton University Press, 1991.

Axelrod, Robert M. *The Evolution of Cooperation*. New York: Basic Books, 1984.

Ayers, Cynthia E. *Rethinking Sovereignty in the Concept of Cyberspace*. Cyber Sovereignty Workshop Series. Carlisle, PA: U.S. Army War College, 2016.

Baer, Joel H. "Bold Captain Avery in the Privy Council: Early Variants of a Broadside Ballad from the Pepys Collection." *Folk Music Journal* 7, no. 1 (1995): 4–26.

Bailyn, Bernard. "Idea of Atlantic History." *Itinerario* 20 (1996): 19–44.

Baker, Peter. "In Terror Shift, Obama Took a Long Path." *New York Times*, May 27, 2013.

Baker, Peter C. "'We Can't Go Back to Normal': How Will Coronavirus Change the World?" *Guardian*, March 31, 2020.

Ball, James. "NSA Stores Metadata of Millions of Web Users for Up to a Year, Secret Files Show." *Guardian*, September 30, 2013.

Ball, James, Julian Borger, and Glenn Greenwald. "Revealed: How US and UK Spy Agencies Defeat Internet Privacy and Security." *Guardian*, September 5, 2013.

Ball, James, Luke Harding, and Juliette Garside. "BT and Vodafone Among Telecoms Companies Passing Details to GCHQ." *Guardian*, August 2, 2013.
Ball, Kirstie, and Frank Webster. "The Intensification of Surveillance." In *The Intensification of Surveillance: Crime, War and Terrorism in the Information Age*, ed. Kirstie Ball and Frank Webster, 1–15. Sterling, VA: Pluto Press, 2003.
Ball, Kirstie, and David Murakami Wood. "Political Economies of Surveillance." *Surveillance and Society* 11, no. 1/2 (2013): 1–3.
Balzacq, Thierry. *Understanding Securitisation Theory: How Security Problems Emerge and Dissolve*. London: Routledge, 2010.
Banlaoi, Rommell C. "The Abu Sayyaf Group: From Mere Banditry to Genuine Terrorism." *Southeast Asian Affairs* 2006, no. 1 (2006): 247–62.
——. "The Abu Sayyaf Group: Threat of Maritime Piracy and Terrorism." In *Violence at Sea: Piracy in the Age of Global Terrorism*, ed. Peter Lehr, 121–23. New York: Routledge, 2007.
Bantman, Constance. *The French Anarchists in London, 1880–1914: Exile and Transnationalism in the First Globalisation*. Liverpool: Liverpool University Press, 2013.
——. "Internationalism Without an International? Cross-Channel Anarchist Networks, 1880–1914." *Revue Belge de Philologie et d'histoire* 84, no. 4 (2006): 961–81.
Barkawi, Tarak. "Democratic States and Societies at War: The Global Context." *Comparative Social Research* 20 (2002): 361–76.
Barkawi, Tarak, and Mark Laffey. "Retrieving the Imperial: Empire and International Relations." *Millennium—Journal of International Studies* 31, no. 1 (2002): 109–27.
Barkin, J. Samuel, and Bruce Cronin. "The State and the Nation: Changing Norms and the Rules of Sovereignty in International Relations." *International Organization* 48, no. 1 (1994): 107–30.
Barlow, John Perry. "A Declaration of the Independence of Cyberspace." Electronic Frontier Foundation, January 20, 2016, https://www.eff.org/cyberspace-independence.
Bartelson, Jens. *A Genealogy of Sovereignty*. Cambridge: Cambridge University Press, 1995.
Baudrillard, Jean. *Simulacra and Simulation*. Trans. Sheila Faria Glaser. Ann Arbor: University of Michigan Press, 1995.
——. *The Spirit of Terrorism and Other Essays*. Ed. Chris Turner. New York: Verso, 2012.
Bauer, Harry, and Elisabetta Brighi, eds. *Pragmatism in International Relations*. London: Routledge, 2011.
Baugh, Daniel A. "Maritime Strength and Atlantic Commerce: The Uses of a Grand Marine Empire." In *An Imperial State at War: Britain from 1689 to 1815*, ed. Lawrence Stone, 185–223. London: Routledge, 1994.
Bayer, Osvaldo. *Anarchism and Violence: Severino Di Giovanni in Argentina, 1923–1931*. London: Elephant Editions, 1985.
Bayly, C. A., Sven Beckert, Matthew Connelly, Isabel Hofmeyr, Wendy Kozol, and Patricia Seed. "AHR Conversation: On Transnational History." *American Historical Review* 111, no. 5 (2006): 1441–64.
Bayly, Martin J. *Taming the Imperial Imagination: Colonial Knowledge, International Relations, and the Anglo-Afghan Encounter, 1808–1878*. Cambridge: Cambridge University Press, 2016.

Bean, Richard. "War and the Birth of the Nation State." *Journal of Economic History* 33, no. 1 (1973): 203–21.

Beauchamp, Zach. "The Surprising Reason Why ISIS May Be Lashing Out: Because It's Losing." *Vox*, November 16, 2015.

Becker, Jo, and Scott Shane. "Secret 'Kill List' Tests Obama's Principles." *New York Times*, May 29, 2012.

Becker, Peter. "The Standardized Gaze: The Standardization of the Search Warrant in Nineteenth Century Germany." In *Documenting Individual Identity: The Development of State Practices in the Modern World*, ed. Jane Caplan and John Torpey, 139–63. Princeton, NJ: Princeton University Press, 2001.

Bell, Duncan. "Founding the World State: H. G. Wells on Empire and the English-Speaking Peoples." *International Studies Quarterly* 62, no. 4 (2018): 867–79.

———, ed. *Victorian Visions of Global Order: Empire and International Relations in Nineteenth-Century Political Thought*. Cambridge: Cambridge University Press, 2007.

Benjamin, Daniel, and Steve Simon. *The Age of Sacred Terror*. New York: Random House, 2002.

Bentley, Jerry H. "Sea and Ocean Basins as Frameworks of Historical Analysis." *Geographical Review* 89 (1999): 215–24.

Benton, Lauren. *A Search for Sovereignty: Law and Geography in European Empires 1400–1900*. Cambridge: Cambridge University Press, 2010.

Bernstein, Steven, Richard Ned Lebow, Janice Gross Stein, and Stephen Weber. "Social Science as Case-Based Diagnostics." In *Theory and Evidence in Comparative Politics and International Relations*, ed. Richard Ned Lebow and Mark I. Lichbach, 229–60. New York: Palgrave Macmillan, 2007.

Bialuschewski, Arne. "Between Newfoundland and the Malacca Strait: A Survey of the Golden Age of Piracy, 1695–1725." *Mariner's Mirror* 90, no. 2 (2004): 167–86.

———. "Pirates, Markets and Imperial Authority: Economic Aspects of Maritime Depredations in the Atlantic World, 1716–1726." *Global Crime* 9, no. 1/2 (2008): 52–65.

bin Laden, Osama. *Messages to the World: The Statements of Osama bin Laden*. Ed. Bruce Lawrence. Trans. James Howarth. New York: Verso, 2005.

Birn, Raymond. *Crisis, Absolutism, Revolution: Europe and the World, 1648–1789*. Ontario: Broadview Press, 2005.

Black, Jeremy. *Eighteenth-Century Europe*. New York: St. Martin's Press, 1999.

Blom, Philipp. *The Vertigo Years: Europe, 1900–1914*. New York: Basic Books, 2008.

Bobbitt, Philip. *The Shield of Achilles: War, Peace, and the Course of History*. New York: Knopf, 2002.

———. *Terror and Consent: The Wars for the Twenty-First Century*. New York: Knopf, 2008.

Boersma, Kees, Rosamunde Van Brakel, Chiara Fonio, and Pieter Wagenaar, eds. *History of State Surveillance in Europe and Beyond*. London: Routledge, 2014.

Bokhari, Farhan. "Officials Confirm CIA Drones in Pakistan." *CBS News*, February 19, 2009.

Bonner, Philip, Jonathan Hyslop, and Lucien van der Walt. "Worker's Movements." In *The Palgrave Dictionary of Transnational History*, ed. Akira Iriye and Pierre-Yves Saunier, 1121–28. London: Palgrave, 2009.

Borriello, Arthur, and Nathalie Brack. "'I Want My Sovereignty Back!' A Comparative Analysis of the Populist Discourses of Podemos, the 5 Star Movement, the FN and UKIP During the Economic and Migration Crises." *Journal of European Integration* 41, no. 7 (2019): 833–53.

Bookchin, Murray. *The Spanish Anarchists: The Heroic Years 1868–1936*. Chico, CA: AK Press, 2001.

Bourdieu, Pierre. "The Field of Cultural Production, or the Economic World Reversed." *Poetics* 12 (1983): 311–56.

———. *The Logic of Practice*. Stanford, CA: Stanford University Press, 1990.

———. *On the State: Lectures at the College de France, 1989–1992*. London: Polity, 2015.

———. *Outline of a Theory of Practice*. Cambridge: Cambridge University Press, 1977.

———. "Some Properties of Fields." In *Sociology in Question*, ed. Pierre Bourdieu, 72–77. London: Sage, 1993.

Branch, Jordan. *The Cartographic State: Maps, Territory, and the Origins of Sovereignty*. Cambridge: Cambridge University Press, 2014.

———. "'Colonial Reflection' and Territoriality: The Peripheral Origins of Sovereign Statehood." *European Journal of International Relations* 18, no. 2 (2012): 277–97.

Brenner, Robert. "Agrarian Class Structure and Economic Development in Pre-Industrial Europe." *Past and Present* 70, no. 1 (1976): 30–75.

Brenner, William J. *Confounding Powers: Anarchy and International Society from the Assassins to Al Qaeda*. Cambridge: Cambridge: University Press, 2016.

Brewer, John. *The Sinews of Power: War, Money, and the English State*. New York: Knopf, 1989.

Brown, Rupert. "Social Identity Theory: Past Achievements, Current Problems and Future Challenges." *European Journal of Social Psychology* 30, no. 6 (2000): 745–78.

Bueger, Christian. "Practice, Pirates and Coast Guards: The Grand Narrative of Somali Piracy." *Third World Quarterly* 34, no. 10 (2013): 1811–27.

Bueger, Christian, and Frank Gadinger. "The Play of International Practice." *International Studies Quarterly* 59, no. 3 (2015): 449–60.

Bukovansky, Mlada. *Legitimacy and Power Politics: The American and French Revolutions in International Political Culture*. Princeton, NJ: Princeton University Press, 2002.

Bull, Hedley. *The Anarchical Society: A Study of Order in World Politics*. New York: Columbia University Press, 2002.

Burbank, Jane, and Frederick Cooper. *Empires in World History: Power and the Politics of Difference*. Princeton, NJ: Princeton University Press, 2011.

Burdin Asumi, Judith. "Understanding the Armed Groups of the Niger Delta." Working paper, Council on Foreign Relations, 2009.

Burg, B. R. *Sodomy and the Pirate Tradition: English Sea Rovers in the Seventeenth-Century Caribbean*. New York: New York University Press, 1995.

Burgess, Douglas R., Jr. "Piracy in the Public Sphere: The Henry Every Trials and the Battle for Meaning in Seventeenth-Century Print Culture." *Journal of British Studies* 48, no. 4 (2009): 887–913.

Burke, Jason. "Bin Laden Letters Reveal Al-Qaida's Fears of Drone Strikes and Infiltration." *Guardian*, March 1, 2016.

———. "'A More Dangerous Long-Term Threat': Al-Qaida Grows as Isis Retreats." *Guardian*, December 29, 2016.

———. "NSA Spied on Indian Embassy and UN Mission, Edward Snowden Files Reveal." *Guardian*, September 25, 2013.

———. "Pressure Builds on Sri Lankan Officials as Isis Claims Easter Attacks." *Guardian*, April 24, 2019.

Butel, Paul. *The Atlantic*. Trans. Iain Hamilton Grant. London: Routledge, 1999.

Butterworth, Alex. *The World That Never Was: A True Story of Dreamers, Schemers, Anarchists, and Secret Agents*. New York: Pantheon Books, 2010.

Buzan, Barry, and George Lawson. *The Global Transformation: History, Modernity and the Making of International Relations*. Cambridge: Cambridge University Press, 2015.

Buzan, Barry, and Richard Little. *The Logic of Anarchy: Neorealism to Structural Realism*. New York: Columbia University Press, 1993.

Byman, Daniel. "ISIS' Big Mistake." *Foreign Affairs*, November 15, 2015.

———. "What Comes After ISIS?" *Foreign Policy*, February 22, 2019.

———. "You Can't Defeat Tomorrow's Terrorists by Fighting Yesterday's Enemy." *Foreign Policy*, May 16, 2019.

Cafiero, Carlo. "Action." In *Anarchism: A Documentary History of Libertarian Ideas*, ed. Robert Graham, 152–53. Tonawanda, NY: Black Rose Books, 2005.

Cahm, Caroline. *Kropotkin and the Rise of Revolutionary Anarchism, 1872–1886*. Cambridge: Cambridge University Press, 1989.

Campbell, Kurt M., and Rush Doshi. "The Coronavirus Could Reshape Global Order." *Foreign Affairs*, March 20, 2020.

Caplan, Jane. "Illegibility: Reading and Insecurity in History, Law and Government." *History Workshop Journal* 68, no. 1 (2009): 99–121.

Caplan, Jane, and John Torpey, eds. *Documenting Individual Identity: The Development of State Practices in the Modern World*. Princeton, NJ: Princeton University Press, 2001.

Capouya, Emile, and Keitha Tompkins, eds. *The Essential Kropotkin*. New York: Liveright, 1975.

Carlson, Andrew R. *Anarchism in Germany*. Metuchen: Scarecrow Press, 1972.

Carpenter, Charli. "Crunching Drone Death Numbers." *Duck of Minerva*, August 17, 2011. https://www.duckofminerva.com/2011/08/crunching-drone-death-numbers.html.

Carson, Jennifer Varriale. "Assessing the Effectiveness of High-Profile Targeted Killings in the 'War on Terror.'" *Criminology and Public Policy* 16, no. 1 (2017): 191–220.

Carvalho, Benjamin de, Halvard Leira, and John M. Hobson. "The Big Bangs of IR: The Myths That Your Teachers Still Tell You About 1648 and 1919." *Millennium—Journal of International Studies* 39, no. 3 (2011): 735–58.

Cederlof, Gunnar. *Founding an Empire on India's North-Eastern Frontiers, 1790–1840: Climate, Commerce, Polity*. Oxford: Oxford University Press, 2014.

Cerny, Philip G. "Globalization and the Erosion of Democracy." *European Journal of Political Research* 36, no. 1 (1999): 1–26.

Chaliand, Gerard, and Arnaud Blin. "The 'Golden Age' of Terrorism." In *The History of Terrorism: From Antiquity to Al Qaeda*, ed. Gérard Chaliand and Arnaud Blin, 175–96. Berkeley: University of California Press, 2007.

"China Has the World's Most Centralised Internet System." *Economist*, June 28, 2018.

"China Moves Towards Nationalization with Probe Into Alibaba." *Radio Free Asia*, December 25, 2020.

Chrisafis, Angelique. "France 'Runs Vast Electronic Spying Operation Using NSA-Style Methods.'" *Guardian*, July 4, 2013.

Clark, Gordon L., and Michael Dear. *State Apparatus: Structures and Language of Legitimacy*. Boston: Allen and Unwin, 1984.

Clarke, Richard A. "Presidential Policy Initiative/Review—The Al-Qida Network." NSC Memorandum, January 25, 2001. http://www2.gwu.edu/~nsarchiv/NSAEBB/NSAEBB147/clarke%20memo.pdf.

Clarke, Roger. "Information Technology and Dataveillance." *Communications of the ACM* 31, no. 5 (1988): 498–512.

Coben, Stanley. *A. Mitchell Palmer: Politician*. New York: Columbia University Press, 1963.

Cochran, Molly. "Pragmatism and International Relations. A Story of Closure and Opening." *European Journal of Pragmatism and American Philosophy* 4, no. 1 (2012): 1–22.

Coclanis, Peter A, ed. *The Atlantic Economy During the Seventeenth and Eighteenth Centuries: Organization, Operation, Practice, and Personnel*. Columbia: University of South Carolina Press, 2005.

———. "Drang Nach Osten: Bernard Bailyn, the World-Island, and the Idea of Atlantic History." *Journal of World History* 13, no. 1 (2002): 169–82.

Colas, Alejandro, and Bryan Mabee. "The Flow and Ebb of Private Seaborne Violence in Global Politics." In *Mercenaries, Pirates, Bandits, and Empires: Private Violence in Historical Context*, ed. Alejandro Colas and Bryan Mabee, 83–106. New York: Columbia University Press, 2011.

Cole, Simon A. "The 'Opinionization' of Fingerprint Evidence." *BioSocieties* 3, no. 1 (2008): 105–13.

Conrad, Joseph. *The Secret Agent*. Champaign, IL: Project Gutenberg, 1999.

Cooley, Alexander, and Daniel Nexon. *Exit from Hegemony: The Unraveling of American Global Order*. Oxford: Oxford University Press, 2020.

Cooley, Alexander, Daniel Nexon, and Stephen Ward. "Revising Order or Changing the Balance of Military Power? An Alternative Typology of Revisionist and Status Quo States." *Review of International Studies* 45, no. 4 (2019): 689–708.

Corrigan, Philip. *Capitalism, State Formation, and Marxist Theory: Historical Investigations*. London: Quartet Books, 1980.

Crawford, Emily, and Rosemary Rayfuse. "Climate Change, Sovereignty, and Statehood." In *International Law in the Era of Climate Change*, ed. Rosemary Rayfuse and Shirley Scott, 243–53. Cheltenham, UK: Edward Elgar, 2012.

Cronin, Audrey Kurth. "How Al Qaeda Ends: The Decline and Demise of Terrorist Groups." *International Security* 31, no. 1 (2006): 7–48.

———. "ISIS Is Not a Terrorist Group." *Foreign Affairs* 94, no. 2 (2015): 87–98.

Cutler, A. Claire, Virginia Haufler, and Tony Porter, eds. *Private Authority and International Affairs*. Albany: State University of New York Press, 1999.

D'Amato, Silvia. "Terrorists Going Transnational: Rethinking the Role of States in the Case of AQIM and Boko Haram." *Critical Studies on Terrorism* 11, no. 1 (2018): 151–72.

Darwin, John. *The End of the British Empire: The Historical Debate.* Oxford: Wiley-Blackwell, 2006.
Dasgupta, Rana. "The Demise of the Nation-State." *Guardian*, April 5, 2018.
Davenport, Christian. "How the Pentagon Is Preparing for the Coming Drone Wars." *Washington Post*, November 24, 2017.
Davenport, Frances Gardiner. *European Treaties Bearing on the History of the United States and Its Dependencies.* Clark, NJ: Lawbook Exchange, 2012.
David, Steven R. *Fatal Choices: Israel's Policy of Targeted Killing.* Tel Aviv: Bar-Ilan University, 2002.
Davis, Ralph. *The Rise of the English Shipping Industry in the Seventeenth and Eighteenth Centuries.* London: Macmillan, 1962.
Debs, Alexandre, and Nuno P. Monteiro. "Known Unknowns: Power Shifts, Uncertainty, and War." *International Organization* 68, no. 1 (2014): 1–31.
DeFlem, Mathieu. "Wild Beasts Without Nationality: The Uncertain Origins of Interpol, 1898–1910." In *Handbook of Transnational Crime and Justice*, ed. Philip Reichel, 275–85. Thousand Oaks, CA: Sage Publications, 2005.
DeFoe, Daniel. *A General History of the Robberies and Murders of the Most Notorious Pyrates.* Ed. Manuel Schonhorn. Mineola, NY: Dover Publications, 1999.
Delbrück, Jost. "Global Migration—Immigration—Multiethnicity: Challenges to the Concept of the Nation-State." *Indiana Journal of Global Legal Studies* 2, no. 1 (1994): 45–64.
Deleuze, Gilles. "Postscript on the Societies of Control." *October* 59 (Winter 1992): 3–7.
Delis, Apostolos. "A Hub of Piracy in the Aegean: Syros During the Greek War of Independence." In *Corsairs and Pirates in the Eastern Mediterranean, Fifteenth–Nineteenth Centuries*, ed. Gelina Harlaftis, Dimitris Dimitropolous, and David J. Starkey, 41–54. Athens: Sylvia Ioannou Foundation, 2016.
"Deputy Secretary Wolfowitz on the Reasons for Iraq War." *Caltech Peace and Justice News*, May 9, 2003.
Descartes, René. *Discourse on Method and Meditations on First Philosophy.* Trans. Donald A. Cress. Indianapolis, IN: Hackett, 1980.
Devji, Faisal. *Landscapes of the Jihad: Militancy, Morality, Modernity.* Ithaca, NY: Cornell University Press, 2005.
Dewey, John. "Creative Democracy: The Task Before Us." In *The Philosopher of the Common Man: Essays in Honor of John Dewey to Celebrate His Eightieth Birthday*, 220–28. New York: Greenwood Press, 1968.
———. *Democracy and Education.* New York: Free Press, 1997.
———. *Experience and Nature.* McCutchen Press, 2013.
———. *The Public and Its Problems.* Athens: Ohio University Press, 1954.
———. *Reconstruction in Philosophy.* New York: Cosimo, 2008.
Dewey, John, and Arthur Fisher Bentley. *Knowing and the Known.* Boston: Beacon Press, 1949.
Dickinson, E. D. "Is the Crime of Piracy Obsolete." *Harvard Law Review* 38, no. 3 (1925): 334–60.
Di Paola, Pietro. "The Spies Who Came in from the Heat: The International Surveillance of the Anarchists in London." *European History Quarterly* 37, no. 2 (2007): 189–215.

Documents Related to the Colonial History of New York: Procured in England, Holland, and France. Vol. 4. Trans. and ed. E. B. O'Callaghan. Albany, NY: Weed Parsons, 1854.

Donohue, Laura K. "Bulk Metadata Collection: Statutory and Constitutional Considerations." *Harvard Journal of Law and Public Policy* 37 (2014): 757–900.

Downing, Brian M. *The Military Revolution and Political Change: Origins of Democracy and Autocracy in Early Modern Europe.* Princeton, NJ: Princeton University Press, 1992.

Doyle, Arthur Conan. *Sherlock Holmes: The Complete Novels and Stories.* New York: Bantam Books, 1986.

Doyle, William. *The Old European Order: 1660–1800.* Short Oxford History of the Modern World. Oxford: Oxford University Press, 1978.

Drezner, Daniel W. "The Song Remains the Same: International Relations After COVID-19." *International Organization*, Special Online Issue (2020), 1–18.

Drolet, Jean-François, and Michael C. Williams. "Radical Conservatism and Global Order: International Theory and the New Right." *International Theory* 10, no. 3 (2018): 285–313.

"Drone Strikes: Civilian Casualty Considerations." Joint and Coalition Operational Command, June 18, 2013. https://www.cna.org/sites/default/files/research/Drone_Strikes.pdf.

"The Drone War in Pakistan." Accessed September 1, 2021. https://www.newamerica.org/international-security/reports/americas-counterterrorism-wars/the-drone-war-in-pakistan/.

Dryzek, John S., Richard B. Norgaard, and David Schlosberg. "Climate Change and Society: Approaches and Responses." In *The Oxford Handbook of Climate Change and Society*, ed. Dryzek, Norgaard, and Schlosberg, 3–17. Oxford: Oxford University Press, 2011.

DuPlessis, Robert S. "Cloth and the Emergence of the Atlantic Economy." In *The Atlantic Economy During the Seventeenth and Eighteenth Centuries: Organization, Operation, Practice, and Personnel*, ed. Peter A. Coclanis, 72–94. Columbia: University of South Carolina Press, 2005.

Earle, Peter. *The Pirate Wars.* New York: St. Martin's Press, 2003.

Elden, Stuart. *Terror and Territoriality: The Spatial Extent of Sovereignty.* Minneapolis: University of Minnesota Press, 2009.

Emirbayer, Mustafa. "Manifesto for a Relational Sociology." *American Journal of Sociology* 103, no. 2 (1997): 281–317.

Engel, Pamela. "Watertown Resident Describes Finding Boston Bombing Suspect Dzhokhar Tsarnaev in His Boat." *Business Insider*, October 16, 2013.

Evans, Peter B, Dietrich Rueschemeyer, and Theda Skocpol, eds. *Bringing the State Back In.* Cambridge: Cambridge University Press, 1985.

Exquemelin, Alexander O. *The Buccaneers of America.* Trans. Alexis Brown. Mineola, NY: Dover Publications, 1969.

Fallon, Mark. *Unjustifiable Means: The Inside Story of How the CIA, Pentagon, and US Government Conspired to Torture.* New York: Regan Arts, 2017.

Farley, Robert, and Yoav Gortzak. "Fighting Piracy: Experiences in Southeast Asia and Off the Horn of Africa." *Journal of Strategic Security* 2, no. 1 (2009): 1–24.

Farrell, Henry, and Abraham L. Newman. "Weaponized Interdependence: How Global Economic Networks Shape State Coercion." *International Security* 44, no. 1 (2019): 42–79.

———. "Will the Coronavirus End Globalization as We Know It?" *Foreign Affairs*, March 16, 2020.

Fazal, Tanisha Z. "Health Diplomacy in Pandemical Times." *International Organization* 74, no. S1 (2020): E78–E97.

Feldman, Jay. *Manufacturing Hysteria: A History of Scapegoating, Surveillance, and Secrecy in Modern America*. New York: Pantheon, 2011.

Ferguson, Kathy E. "Anarchist Printers and Presses: Material Circuits of Politics." *Political Theory* 42, no. 4 (2014): 391–414.

Ferguson, Yale H., and Richard W. Mansbach. "Polities Past and Present." *Millennium* 37, no. 2 (2008): 365–79.

Fernandez-Armesto, Felipe. "Origins of the European Atlantic." *Itinerario* 24 (2000): 111–23.

Festenstein, Matthew. "Pragmatism's Boundaries." *Millennium—Journal of International Studies* 31, no. 3 (2002): 549–71.

Finnemore, Martha. *The Purpose of Intervention: Changing Beliefs About the Use of Force*. Ithaca, NY: Cornell University Press, 2003.

Fleming, Marie. "Propaganda by the Deed: Terrorism and Anarchist Theory in Late Nineteenth Century Europe." In *Terrorism in Europe*, ed. Yonah Alexander and Kenneth A. Myers, 8–28. New York: St. Martin's Press, 1982.

Ford, Franklin L. "Reflections on Political Murder: Europe in the Nineteenth and Twentieth Centuries." In *Social Protest, Violence, and Terror in Nineteenth and Twentieth Century Europe*, ed. Wolfgang J. Mommsen and Gerhard Hirschfeld, 1–12. New York: St. Martin's Press, 1982.

Forman, Michael. *Nationalism and the International Labor Movement: The Idea of the Nation in Socialist and Anarchist Theory*. State College: Pennsylvania State University Press, 1998.

Forst, Brian. "Targeted Killings." *Criminology and Public Policy* 16, no. 1 (2017): 221–24.

Foucault, Michel. *The Birth of Biopolitics*. Trans. Graham Burchell. New York: Palgrave Macmillan, 2008.

———. *Security, Territory, Population: Lectures at the College de France*. Ed. Michael Senellart. Trans. Graham Burchell. New York: Picador, 2009.

Fox, E. T. "Jacobitism and the 'Golden Age' of Piracy, 1715–1725." *International Journal of Maritime History* 22, no. 2 (2010): 277–303.

Friedman, Thomas L. *Longitudes and Attitudes: Exploring the World After September 11*. New York: Farrar, Strauss and Giroux, 2002.

Friedrichs, Jorg, and Friedrich Kratochwil. "On Acting and Knowing: How Pragmatism Can Advance International Relations Research and Methodology." *International Organization* 63, no. 4 (2009): 701–31.

Frykman, Niklas. "Pirates and Smugglers: Political Economy in the Red Atlantic." In *Mercantilism Reimagined: Political Economy in Early Modern Britain and Its Empire*, ed. Philip J. Stern and Carl Wennerlind, 218–38. Oxford: Oxford University Press, 2014.

Fuller, Christopher J. *See It/Shoot It: The Secret History of the CIA's Lethal Drone Program*. New Haven, CT: Yale University Press, 2017.

Fung, Brian. "Everything You Need to Know About Obama's NSA Reforms, in Plain English." *Washington Post*, January 17, 2014.

Galtung, Johan. "A Structural Theory of Imperialism." *Journal of Peace Research* 8, no. 2 (1971): 81–117.

Games, Alison. "Introduction, Definitions, and Historiography: What Is Atlantic History?" *OAH Magazine of History* 18 (2004): 3–7.

Gates, Kelly. "The Cultural Labor of Surveillance: Video Forensics, Computational Objectivity, and the Production of Visual Evidence." *Social Semiotics* 23, no. 2 (2013): 242–60.

Gates, Robert. M. *Duty: Memoirs of a Secretary at War.* New York: Knopf, 2014.

Gellman, Barton, and Laura Poitras. "U.S., British Intelligence Mining Data from Nine U.S. Internet Companies in Broad Secret Program." *Washington Post*, June 7, 2013.

Gerges, Fawaz A. *The Far Enemy: Why Jihad Went Global.* Cambridge: Cambridge University Press, 2009.

Gilpin, Robert. "The Politics of Transnational Economic Relations." In *Transnational Relations and World Politics*, ed. Robert O. Keohane and Joseph S. Nye, 48–69. Cambridge, MA: Harvard University Press, 1972.

Glanville, Luke. "The Myth of 'Traditional' Sovereignty." *International Studies Quarterly* 57, no. 1 (March 2013): 79–90.

Glete, Jan. *War and the State in Early Modern Europe: Spain, the Dutch Republic, and Sweden as Fiscal-Military States, 1500–1600.* London: Routledge, 2002.

———. *Warfare at Sea, 1500–1650: Maritime Conflicts and the Transformation of Europe.* New York: Routledge, 2000.

Go, Julian. *Patterns of Empire: The British and American Empires, 1688 to the Present.* Cambridge: Cambridge University Press, 2011.

Go, Julian, and George Lawson, eds. *Global Historical Sociology.* Cambridge: Cambridge University Press, 2017.

Goddard, Stacie E. "Embedded Revisionism: Networks, Institutions, and Challenges to World Order." *International Organization* 72, no. 4 (2018): 763–97.

———. *When Might Makes Right: Rising Powers and World Order.* Ithaca, NY: Cornell University Press, 2018.

Goddard, Stacie E., and Ronald R. Krebs. "Rhetoric, Legitimation, and Grand Strategy." *Security Studies* 24, no. 1 (2015): 5–36.

Goddard, Stacie E., Paul K. MacDonald, and Daniel H. Nexon. "Repertoires of Statecraft: Instruments and Logics of Power Politics." *International Relations* 33, no. 2 (2019): 304–21.

Goddard, Stacie E., and Daniel H. Nexon. "The Dynamics of Global Power Politics: A Framework for Analysis." *Journal of Global Security Studies* 1, no. 1 (2016): 4–18.

Goettlich, Kerry. "The Rise of Linear Borders in World Politics." *European Journal of International Relations* 25, no. 1 (2019): 203–28.

Goldstein, Robert J. "The Anarchist Scare of 1908: A Sign of Tensions in the Progressive Era." *American Studies* 15, no. 2 (1974): 55–78.

Goodwin, Joshua Michael. "Universal Jurisdiction and the Pirate: Time for an Old Couple to Part." *Vanderbilt Journal of Transnational Law* 39, no. 3 (2006): 973–1011.

Gorman, Siobhan, and Carol E. Lee. "Obama Readies Revamp of NSA." *Wall Street Journal*, January 10, 2014.

Gorski, Philip S. *The Disciplinary Revolution: Calvinism and the Rise of the State in Early Modern Europe*. Chicago: University of Chicago Press, 2003.
Gould, Eliga H. "Zones of Law, Zones of Violence: The Legal Geography of the British Atlantic, Circa 1772." *William and Mary Quarterly* 60, no. 3 (2003): 471–510.
Gould, Harry. "Cicero's Ghost: Rethinking the Social Construction of Piracy." In *Maritime Piracy and the Construction of Global Governance*, ed. Jon D. Carlson, Mark T. Nance, and Michael J. Struett, 23–46. London: Routledge, 2012.
Gray, John. *Al Qaeda and What It Means to Be Modern*. New York: The New Press, 2003.
Green, Daniel M, ed. *Bifurcated Century: The Two Worlds of Nineteenth Century International Relations*. London: Routledge, 2018.
Greenwald, Glenn. *No Place to Hide: Edward Snowden, the NSA, and the U.S. Surveillance State*. New York: Metropolitan Books, 2014.
———. "XKeyscore: NSA Tool Collects 'Nearly Everything a User Does on the Internet.'" *Guardian*, July 31, 2013.
Greenwald, Glenn, and James Ball. "The Top Secret Rules That Allow NSA to Use US Data Without a Warrant." *Guardian*, June 20, 2013.
Greenwald, Glenn, and Ewen MacAskill. "Boundless Informant: The NSA's Secret Tool to Track Global Surveillance Data." *Guardian*, June 11, 2013.
———. "NSA Prism Program Taps in to User Data of Apple, Google and Others." *Guardian*, June 6, 2013.
Greenwald, Glenn, Ewen MacAskill, and Laura Poitras. "Edward Snowden: The Whistleblower Behind the NSA Surveillance Revelations." *Guardian*, June 9, 2013.
Greenwald, Glenn, Ewen MacAskill, Laura Poitras, Spencer Ackerman, and Dominic Rushe. "Microsoft Handed the NSA Access to Encrypted Messages." *Guardian*, July 11, 2013.
Greenwald, Glenn, Laura Poitras, and Ewen MacAskill. "NSA Shares Raw Intelligence Including Americans' Data with Israel." *Guardian*, September 11, 2013.
Grotius, Hugo. *The Law of War and Peace. De Jure Belli Ac Pacis, Libri Tres*. Indianapolis, IN: Bobbs-Merrill, 1962.
Gruenewald, Jeff. "Do Targeted Killings Increase or Decrease Terrorism?" *Criminology and Public Policy* 16, no. 1 (2017): 187–90.
Hafez, Mohammed M., and Joseph M. Hatfield. "Do Targeted Assassinations Work? A Multivariate Analysis of Israel's Controversial Tactic During Al-Aqsa Uprising." *Studies in Conflict and Terrorism* 29, no. 4 (2006): 359–82.
Haggarty, Kevin D., and Richard V. Erickson. "The Surveillant Assemblage." *British Journal of Sociology* 51, no. 4 (2000): 605–22.
Hall, Alexandra, and Jonathan Mendel. "Threatprints, Threads and Triggers." *Journal of Cultural Economy* 5, no. 1 (2012): 9–27.
Hall, Rodney Bruce. *National Collective Identity: Social Constructs and International Systems*. New York: Columbia University Press, 1999.
Hall, Rodney Bruce, and Thomas J. Biersteker, eds. *The Emergence of Private Authority in Global Governance*. Cambridge: Cambridge University Press, 2002.
Hameiri, Shahar, and Lee Jones. *Governing Borderless Threats: Non-Traditional Security and the Politics of State Transformation*. Cambridge: Cambridge University Press, 2015.

Hamming, Tore Refslund. "The Al Qaeda–Islamic State Rivalry: Competition Yes, but No Competitive Escalation." *Terrorism and Political Violence* 32, no. 1 (2020): 20–37.

Hanna, Mark G. *Pirate Nests and the Rise of the British Empire, 1570–1740*. Chapel Hill: University of North Carolina Press, 2015.

Hardt, Michael, and Antonio Negri. *Empire*. Cambridge, MA: Harvard University Press, 2000.

———. *Multitude: War and Democracy in the Age of Empire*. New York: Penguin Press, 2004.

Harris, Shane. *The Watchers: The Rise of America's Surveillance State*. New York: Penguin Press, 2011.

Hart, B. H. Liddell. *A History of the Second World War*. London: Pan, 2014.

Harvey, David. *The Condition of Postmodernity: An Enquiry Into the Origins of Cultural Change*. Oxford: Wiley-Blackwell, 1991.

Head, David. "New Nations, New Connections: Spanish American Privateering from the United States and the Development of Atlantic Relations." *Early American Studies* 11, no. 1 (2013): 161–75.

Hechter, Michael, and William Brustein. "Regional Modes of Production and Patterns of State Formation in Western Europe." *American Journal of Sociology* 85, no. 5 (1980): 1061–94.

Hellmich, Christina. "'Here Come the Salafis': The Framing of Al Qaeda's Ideology Within Terrorism Research." In *Knowing Al Qaeda: The Epistemology of Terrorism*, ed. Andreas Behnke and Christina Hellmich, 12–27. Abingdon, UK: Ashgate Publishing, 2012.

Hepworth, Daniel P. "Terrorist Retaliation? An Analysis of Terrorist Attacks Following the Targeted Killing of Top-Tier al Qaeda Leadership." *Journal of Policing, Intelligence and Counter Terrorism* 9, no. 1 (2014): 1–18.

Higginbotham, Don. "War and State Formation in the Revolutionary Atlantic." In *Empire and Nation: The American Revolution in the Atlantic World*, ed. Peter S. Onuf and Eliga H. Gould, 54–71. Baltimore, MD: Johns Hopkins University Press, 2005.

Higgs, Edward. *The Information State in England: The Central Collection of Information on Citizens Since 1500*. London: Palgrave Macmillan, 2004.

Hill, Jonathan. "Beyond the Other? A Postcolonial Critique of the Failed State Thesis." *African Identities* 3, no. 2 (2005): 139–54.

Hirsch, Steven, and Lucien van der Walt, eds. *Anarchism and Syndicalism in the Colonial and Postcolonial World, 1870–1940: The Praxis of National Liberation, Internationalism, and Social Revolution*. Boston: Brill, 2010.

Hobson, John M. "Provincializing Westphalia: The Eastern Origins of Sovereignty." *International Politics* 46, no. 6 (2009): 671–90.

Hogg, Michael A. "Social Identity Theory." In *Contemporary Social Psychological Theories*, ed. Peter J. Burke. Stanford, CA: Stanford Social Sciences, 2006.

Holbrook, Donald. *Al-Qaeda 2.0: A Critical Reader*. London: Hurst, 2017.

Holder, Eric. "Attorney General Eric Holder Speaks at Northwestern University School of Law." Evanston, IL, March 5, 2012. http://www.justice.gov/iso/opa/ag/speeches/2012/ag-speech-1203051.html.

Holsti, K. J. *Taming the Sovereigns: Institutional Change in International Politics*. Cambridge: Cambridge University Press, 2004.

Hopf, Ted. "The Logic of Habit in International Relations." *European Journal of International Relations* 16, no. 4 (2010): 539–61.
Hopkins, Nick. "MI5 Chief: GCHQ Surveillance Plays Vital Role in Fight Against Terrorism." *Guardian*, October 8, 2013.
Hopkins, Nick, and Spencer Ackerman. "Flexible Laws and Weak Oversight Give GCHQ Room for Manoeuvre." *Guardian*, August 2, 2013.
Hopkins, Nick, and Julian Borger. "Exclusive: NSA Pays £100m in Secret Funding for GCHQ." *Guardian*, August 1, 2013.
Hopkins, Nick, and Luke Harding. "GCHQ Accused of Selling Its Services After Revelations of Funding by NSA." *Guardian*, August 2, 2013.
"The House Just Overwhelmingly Voted to Rein In the NSA." *Vox*, June 20, 2014. http://www.vox.com/2014/6/20/5826482/the-house-just-overwhelmingly-voted-to-rein-in-the-nsa.
Hudson, Leila, Colin S. Owens, and Matt Flannes. "Drone Warfare: Blowback from the New American Way of War." *Middle East Policy* 18, no. 3 (2011): 122–32.
Huhne, Chris. "Prism and Tempora: The Cabinet Was Told Nothing of the Surveillance State's Excesses." *Guardian*, October 6, 2013.
Hume, David. *Treatise of Human Nature*. Amherst, NY: Prometheus Books, 1992.
Hurrell, Andrew. *On Global Order: Power, Values, and the Constitution of International Society*. Oxford: Oxford University Press, 2007.
Huysmans, Jef. "Security! What Do You Mean? From Concept to Thick Signifier." *European Journal of International Relations* 4, no. 2 (1998): 226–55.
Ikenberry, G. John. *Liberal Leviathan: The Origins, Crisis, and Transformation of the American World Order*. Princeton, NJ: Princeton University Press, 2012.
Ikenberry, G. John, and Daniel H. Nexon. "Hegemony Studies 3.0: The Dynamics of Hegemonic Orders." *Security Studies* 28, no. 3 (2019): 395–421.
Inayatullah, Naeem. "Beyond the Sovereignty Dilemma: Quasi-States as Social Construct." In *State Sovereignty as Social Construct*, ed. Thomas J. Biersteker and Cynthia Weber, 50–77. Cambridge: Cambridge University Press, 1996.
"Interview: Richard A. Clarke." *Frontline*, March 20, 2002.
"Investigation Into Alleged Misconduct by Senior DoD Officials Concerning the Able Danger Program and Lt. Col. Anthony A. Shaffer, U.S. Army Reserve (Case Number H05L97905217)." Memorandum for Undersecretary of Defense. Arlington, VA: Department of Defense, Inspector General, September 18, 2006. http://fas.org/irp/agency/dod/ig-abledanger.pdf.
"Iraq Body Count." http://www.iraqbodycount.org/.
Iriye, Akira. *Global and Transnational History: The Past, Present, and Future*. New York: Springer, 2012.
Jablonski, Ryan S., and Steven Oliver. "The Political Economy of Plunder: Economic Opportunity and Modern Piracy." *Journal of Conflict Resolution* 57, no. 4 (2013): 682–70.
Jackson, Patrick Thaddeus. *Civilizing the Enemy: German Reconstruction and the Invention of the West*. Ann Arbor: University of Michigan Press, 2006.
———. *The Conduct of Inquiry in International Relations: Philosophy of Science and Its Implications for the Study of World Politics*. London: Routledge, 2010.

Jackson, Patrick Thaddeus, and Daniel H. Nexon. "Globalization, the Comparative Method, and Comparing Constructions." In *Constructivism and Comparative Politics*, ed. Daniel M. Green, 88–120. Armonk, NY: M. E. Sharpe, 2002.

———. "Relations Before States: Substance, Process, and the Study of World Politics." *European Journal of International Relations* 5, no. 3 (1999): 291–332.

Jackson, Robert H. *Quasi-States: Sovereignty, International Relations, and the Third World*. Cambridge: Cambridge University Press, 1990.

James, Daniel. *Resistance and Integration: Peronism and the Argentine Working Class, 1946–1976*. Cambridge: Cambridge University Press, 1988.

James, William. *Pragmatism and Other Writings*. New York: Penguin Books, 2000.

Jameson, J. Franklin, ed. *Privateering and Piracy in the Colonial Period, Illustrative Documents*. Kindle Edition, 2012.

Jarvis, Jeff. "How Much Data the NSA Really Gets." *Guardian*, August 13, 2013.

Jarvis, Michael J. *In the Eye of All Trade: Bermuda, Bermudians, and the Maritime Atlantic World, 1680–1783*. Chapel Hill: University of North Carolina Press, 2012.

Jensen, Richard Bach. "Anarchist Terrorism and Global Diasporas, 1878–1914." *Terrorism and Political Violence* 27, no. 3 (2015): 441–53.

———. *The Battle Against Anarchist Terrorism: An International History, 1878–1934*. Cambridge: Cambridge University Press, 2014.

———. "Criminal Anthropology and Anarchist Terrorism in Spain and Italy." *Mediterranean Historical Review* 16, no. 2 (2001): 31–44.

———. "Daggers, Rifles and Dynamite: Anarchist Terrorism in 19th Century Europe." *Terrorism and Political Violence* 16, no. 1 (2004): 116–53.

———. "The Evolution of Anarchist Terrorism in Europe and the United States from the Nineteenth Century to World War I." In *Terror: From Tyrannicide to Terrorism*, ed. Brett Bowden and Michael T. Davis, 134–60. Queensland: University of Queensland Press, 2008.

———. "The International Anti-Anarchist Conference of 1898 and the Origins of Interpol." *Journal of Contemporary History* 16, no. 2 (1981): 323–47.

———. "The International Campaign Against Anarchist Terrorism, 1880–1930s." *Terrorism and Political Violence* 21, no. 1 (2009): 89–109.

———. "Police Reform and Social Reform: Italy from the Crisis of the 1890s to the Giolittian Era." *Criminal Justice History: An International Annual* 10 (1989): 179–200.

———. "The United States, International Policing and the War Against Anarchist Terrorism, 1900–1914." *Terrorism and Political Violence* 13, no. 1 (2001): 15–46.

Jervis, Robert, Francis J. Gavin, Joshua Rovner, and Diane N. Labrosse, eds. *Chaos in the Liberal Order: The Trump Presidency and International Politics in the Twenty-First Century*. New York: Columbia University Press, 2018.

Jessop, Bob. *State Power: A Strategic-Relational Approach*. Malden, MA: Polity, 2007.

———. *State Theory: Putting the Capitalist State in Its Place*. State College: Pennsylvania State University Press, 1990.

Joas, Hans. *The Creativity of Action*. Chicago: University of Chicago Press, 1996.

———. *Pragmatism and Social Theory*. Chicago: University of Chicago Press, 1993.

Joll, James. *The Anarchists*. Cambridge, MA: Harvard University Press, 1980.
Jones, Branwen Gruffydd. "The Global Political Economy of Social Crisis: Towards a Critique of the 'Failed State' Ideology." *Review of International Political Economy* 15, no. 2 (2008): 180–205.
Jordan, Javier. "The Effectiveness of the Drone Campaign Against Al Qaeda Central: A Case Study." *Journal of Strategic Studies* 37, no. 1 (2014): 4–29.
Jordan, Jenna. "When Heads Roll: Assessing the Effectiveness of Leadership Decapitation." *Security Studies* 18, no. 4 (2009): 719–55.
Joughin, Louis, and Edmund M. Morgan. *The Legacy of Sacco and Vanzetti*. Princeton, NJ: Princeton University Press, 1976.
Juergensmeyer, Mark. *Global Rebellion: Religious Challenges to the Secular State, from Christian Militias to al Qaeda*. Berkeley: University of California Press, 2009.
Kagan, Robert, and William Kristol. *Present Dangers: Crisis and Opportunity in American Foreign and Defense Policy*. San Francisco: Encounter Books, 2000.
Kahl, Colin, and Ariana Berengaut. "Aftershocks: The Coronavirus Pandemic and the New World Disorder." *War on the Rocks*, April 10, 2020.
Kaluszynski, Martine. "Republican Identity: Bertillonage as Government Technique." In *Documenting Individual Identity: The Development of State Practices in the Modern World*, ed. Jane Caplan and John Torpey, 124–38. Princeton, NJ: Princeton University Press, 2001.
Kaplan, Temma. *Anarchists of Andalusia, 1868–1903*. Princeton, NJ: Princeton University Press, 1977.
Kassel, Whitney. "Terrorism and the International Anarchist Movement of the Late Nineteenth and Early Twentieth Centuries." *Studies in Conflict and Terrorism* 32, no. 3 (2009): 237–52.
Katz, Brian, and Michael Carpenter. "ISIS Is Already Rising from the Ashes." *Foreign Affairs*, October 18, 2019.
Kayaoglu, Turan. "The Extension of Westphalian Sovereignty: State Building and the Abolition of Extra-Territoriality." *International Studies Quarterly* 51, no. 3 (2007): 649–75.
Keck, Margaret E., and Kathryn Sikkink. *Activists Beyond Borders: Advocacy Networks in International Politics*. Ithaca, NY: Cornell University Press, 1998.
Kempe, Michael. "'Even in the Remotest Corners of the World': Globalized Piracy and International Law, 1500–1900." *Journal of Global History* 5, no. 3 (2010): 353–72.
Kenwick, Michael R., and Beth A. Simmons. "Pandemic Response as Border Politics." *International Organization* 74, no. S1 (December 2020): 36–58.
Keohane, Robert O, and Helen V. Milner. *Internationalization and Domestic Politics*. Cambridge: Cambridge University Press, 1996.
Kestnbaum, Meyer. "Mars Revealed: The Entry of Ordinary People Into War Among States." In *Remaking Modernity: Politics, History, and Sociology*, ed. Julia Adams, Elisabeth S. Clemens, and Ann Shola Orloff, 249–85. Durham, NC: Duke University Press, 2005.
Kindervater, Katharine Hall. "Drone Strikes, Ephemeral Sovereignty, and Changing Conceptions of Territory." *Territory, Politics, Governance* 5, no. 2 (2017): 207–21.
———. "The Emergence of Lethal Surveillance: Watching and Killing in the History of Drone Technology." *Security Dialogue* 47, no. 3 (2016): 223–38.

Kinna, Ruth, ed. *Early Writings on Terrorism*. 4 vols. London: Routledge, 2006.
Kiser, Edgar, and April Linton. "Determinants of the Growth of the State: War and Taxation in Early Modern Europe." *Social Forces* 80, no. 2 (2001): 411–48.
Klabbers, Jan. "Setting the Scene." In *The Constitutionalization of International Law*, ed. Jan Klabbers, Anne Peters, and Geir Ulfstein, 1–44. Oxford: Oxford University Press, 2009.
Knepper, Paul. *The Invention of International Crime: A Global Issue in the Making, 1881–1914*. New York: Palgrave, 2010.
Kobrin, Stephen J. "Back to the Future: Neomedievalism and the Postmodern Digital World Economy." *Journal of International Affairs* 51, no. 2 (1998): 361–86.
Koskenniemi, Martti. "What Use for Sovereignty Today?" *Asian Journal of International Law* 1, no. 1 (2011): 61–70.
Krasner, Stephen D. "Abiding Sovereignty." *International Political Science Review* 22, no. 3 (2001): 229–51.
Kratochwil, Friedrich V. *Rules, Norms, and Decisions: On the Conditions of Practical and Legal Reasoning in International Relations and Domestic Affairs*. Cambridge: Cambridge University Press, 1991.
———. "Sovereignty, Property, and Propriety." In *The Puzzles of Politics: Inquiries Into the Genesis and Transformation of International Relations*, 64–80. London: Routledge, 2011.
Krebs, Ronald R. *Narrative and the Making of US National Security*. Cambridge: Cambridge University Press, 2015.
Krebs, Ronald R., and Patrick Thaddeus Jackson. "Twisting Tongues and Twisting Arms: The Power of Political Rhetoric." *European Journal of International Relations* 13, no. 1 (2007): 35–66.
Krebs, Ronald R., and Jennifer K. Lobasz. "Fixing the Meaning of 9/11: Hegemony, Coercion and the Road to War in Iraq." *Security Studies* 16, no. 3 (2007): 409–51.
Kroenig, Matthew, and Jay Stowsky. "War Makes the State, but Not as It Pleases: Homeland Security and American Anti-Statism." *Security Studies* 15, no. 2 (2006): 225–70.
Kuhn, Gabriel. *Life Under the Jolly Roger: Reflections on Golden Age Piracy*. Oakland, CA: PM Press, 2010.
Labaree, Leonard Woods, ed. *Royal Instructions to British Colonial Governors*. New York: Octagon Books, 1967.
Lake, David A. *Hierarchy in International Relations*. Ithaca, NY: Cornell University Press, 2009.
Lamont, Michele, and Virag Molnar. "The Study of Boundaries in the Social Sciences." *Annual Review of Sociology* 28 (2002): 167–95.
Land, Chris. "Flying the Black Flag: Revolt, Revolution and the Social Organization of Piracy in the 'Golden Age.'" *Management and Organizational History* 2, no. 2 (2007): 169–92.
Land, Isaac, ed. *Enemies of Humanity: The Nineteenth-Century War on Terrorism*. New York: Palgrave Macmillan, 2008.
———. "Men with the Faces of Brutes: Physiognomy, Urban Anxieties, and Politics States." In *Enemies of Humanity: The Nineteenth Century War on Terrorism*, ed. Isaac Land, 117–35. London: Palgrave Macmillan, 2008.
Lascurettes, Kyle M. *Orders of Exclusion: Great Powers and the Strategic Sources of Foundational Rules in International Relations*. Oxford: Oxford University Press, 2020.

"Lawfulness of a Lethal Operation Directed Against a US Citizen." Department of Justice White Paper, November 8, 2011. https://fas.org/irp/eprint/doj-lethal.pdf.

Lee, Timothy B. "The House Just Overwhelmingly Voted to Rein In the NSA." *Vox*, June 24, 2014.

Legro, Jeffrey. *Rethinking the World: Great Power Strategies and International Order*. Ithaca, NY: Cornell University Press, 2005.

Lemnitzer, Jan Martin. "'That Moral League of Nations Against the United States': The Origins of the 1856 Declaration of Paris." *International History Review* 35, no. 5 (2013): 1068–88.

Les Lois Scélérates de 1893–1894. Paris: Revue Blanche, 1899.

Levine, Daniel. *Recovering International Relations: The Promise of Sustainable Critique*. Oxford: Oxford University Press, 2012.

Levy, Carl. "Anarchism, Internationalism, and Nationalism in Europe, 1860–1939." *Australian Journal of Politics and History* 50, no. 3 (2004): 330–42.

Lewis, Bernard. *The Crisis of Islam: Holy War and Unholy Terror (Modern Library Chronicles)*. New York: Modern Library, 2003.

Lewis, Flora. "The End of Sovereignty." *New York Times*, May 23, 1992.

Lichtblau, Eric, and James Risen. "Bank Data Is Sifted by U.S. in Secret to Block Terror." *New York Times*, June 23, 2006.

Linden, Marcel van der, and Wayne Thorpe. *Revolutionary Syndicalism: An International Perspective*. Brookfield, VT: Scolar Press, 1990.

Linebaugh, Peter, and Marcus Rediker. *The Many-Headed Hydra: Sailors, Slaves, Commoners, and the Hidden History of the Revolutionary Atlantic*. Boston: Beacon Press, 2000.

Ling, L. H. M. "Worlds Beyond Westphalia: Daoist Dialectics and the 'China Threat.'" *Review of International Studies* 39, no. 3 (2013): 549–68.

"Living Under Drones: Death, Injury, and Trauma to Civilians from U.S. Drone Practices in Pakistan." International Human Rights and Conflict Resolution Clinic at Stanford Law School and Global Justice Clinic at New York University School of Law, 2012.

Lloyd, Martin. *The Passport: The History of Man's Most Travelled Document*. Gloucestershire: Sutton Publishing, 2003.

Lombroso, Cesare. *Criminal Man*. Trans. Mary Gibson and Nicole Hahn Rafter. Durham, NC: Duke University Press, 2006.

Long, David, and Brian C. Schmidt, eds. *Imperialism and Internationalism in the Discipline of International Relations*. Albany: State University of New York Press, 2005.

Lowenheim, Oded, and Brent J. Steele. "Institutions of Violence, Great Power Authority, and the War on Terror." *International Political Science Review* 31, no. 1 (2010): 23–39.

Lydon, James G. *Pirates, Privateers, and Profits*. Upper Saddle River, NJ: Gregg Press, 1970.

Lynch, Michael. "Ehtnomethodology and the Logic of Practice." In *The Practice Turn in Contemporary Theory*, ed. Theodore R. Schatzki, Karin Knorr Cetina, and Eike von Savigny. London: Routledge, 2001.

Lyon, David. *The Electronic Eye: The Rise of Surveillance Society*. Minneapolis: University of Minnesota Press, 1994.

———. "Surveillance After September 11, 2001." In *The Intensification of Surveillance: Crime, Terrorism, and Warfare in the Information Age*, ed. Kirstie Ball and Frank Webster, 16–25. Sterling, VA: Pluto Press, 2003.

———. *Surveillance as Social Sorting: Privacy, Risk, and Digital Discrimination.* London: Routledge, 2003.

Lyotard, Jean-Francois. *The Postmodern Condition: A Report on Knowledge.* Minneapolis: University of Minnesota Press, 1984.

Mabee, Bryan. "Pirates, Privateers, and the Political Economy of Private Violence." *Global Change, Peace, and Security* 21, no. 2 (2009): 139–52.

MacAskill, Ewen. "New NSA Leaks Show How US Is Bugging Its European Allies." *Guardian*, June 30, 2013.

MacDonald, Arthur. "Assassins of Rulers." *Journal of the American Institute of Criminal Law and Criminology* 2, no. 4 (1911): 505–20.

Machiavelli, Niccolo. *The Prince and the Discourses.* Ed. Max Lerner. New York: McGraw Hill, 1950.

MacKay, Joseph. "Pirate Nations: Maritime Pirates as Escape Societies in Late Imperial China." *Social Science History* 37, no. 4 (2013): 551–73.

Malato, Charles. "Some Anarchist Portraits." *Fortnightly Review* 62 (1894): 315–33.

Mann, Jim. *The Great Rift: Dick Cheney, Colin Powell, and the Broken Friendship That Defined an Era.* New York: Henry Holt, 2020.

Mansfield, Laura. *His Own Words: Translation and Analysis of the Writings of Dr. Ayman al Zawahiri.* Old Tappan, NJ: TLG Publications, 2006.

Manwaring, Max G. "A Contemporary Challenge to State Sovereignty: Gangs and Other Illicit Criminal Organizations in Central America, El Salvador, Mexico, Jamaica, and Brazil." Carlisle, PA: Strategic Studies Institute, 2007.

Marlin-Bennett, Renee. *Knowledge Power: Intellectual Property, Information, and Privacy.* Boulder, CO: Lynne Rienner Publishers, 2004.

Marshall, Peter. *Demanding the Impossible: A History of Anarchism.* London: HarperCollins, 1992.

Marusek, Sarah. "Inventing Terrorists: The Nexus of Intelligence and Islamophobia." *Critical Studies on Terrorism* 11, no. 1 (2018): 65–87.

Marx, Karl, and Friedrich Engels. *The Marx-Engels Reader.* Ed. Richard Tucker. New York: Norton, 1978.

Massé, Léa Eveline Jeanne Stéphanie. "Losing Mood(s): Examining Jihadi Supporters' Responses to ISIS' Territorial Decline." *Terrorism and Political Violence* (March 2020): 1–21.

Mata, Javier Fabra, and Sebastian Ziaja. "User's Guide on Measuring Fragility." Bonn: Deutsches Institut fur Entwicklngspolitik and United Nations Development Program, 2009. http://www.gaportal.org/sites/default/files/usersguide_measure_fragility_ogc09_0.pdf.

Mattingly, Garrett. "No Peace Beyond What Line?" *Transactions of the Royal Historical Society* 5, no. 13 (1963): 145–62.

Mayall, James. *Nationalism and International Society.* Cambridge: Cambridge University Press, 1990.

Mayer, Jane. "The Predator War." *New Yorker*, October 26, 2009.

Mayrl, Damon, and Sarah Quinn. "Defining the State from Within: Boundaries, Schemas, and Associational Policymaking." *Sociological Theory* 34, no. 1 (2016): 1–26.

Mazzetti, Robert F., Mark Worth, and Scott Shane. "With Brennan Pick, a Light on Drone Strikes' Hazards." *New York Times*, February 5, 2013.

McCarthy, Matthew. "'A Delicate Question of a Political Nature': The Corso Insurgente and British Commercial Policy During the Spanish-American War of Independence, 1810–1824." *International Journal of Maritime History* 23, no. 1 (2011): 277–92.

McCourt, David M. "Practice Theory and Relationalism as the New Constructivism." *International Studies Quarterly* 60, no. 3 (2016): 475–85.

McCoy, Alfred W. *Policing America's Empire: The United States, the Philippines, and the Rise of America's Surveillance State*. Madison: University of Wisconsin Press, 2009.

———. *A Question of Torture: CIA Interrogation, from the Cold War to the War on Terror*. Holt Paperbacks, 2006.

McDonald, Kevin P. "'A Man of Courage and Activity': Thomas Tew and Pirate Settlements of the Indo-Atlantic Trade World, 1645–1730." Working paper, University of California–Berkeley, 2005. http://escholarship.org/uc/item/7tm078mp.

McNeill, John Robert. *Mosquito Empires: Ecology and War in the Greater Caribbean, 1620–1914*. Cambridge: Cambridge University Press, 2010.

Mendelsohn, Barak. *Combating Jihadism: American Hegemony and Interstate Cooperation in the War on Terrorism*. Chicago: University of Chicago Press, 2009.

———. "Sovereignty Under Attack: The International Society Meets the Al Qaeda Network." *Review of International Studies* 31, no. 1 (2005): 45–68.

Merriman, John. *The Dynamite Club: How a Bombing in Fin-de-Siècle Paris Ignited the Age of Terror*. New York: Houghton Mifflin Harcourt, 2009.

Mieville, China. *The City and the City*. London: Del Rey, 2010.

Miller, Scott. *The President and the Assassin: McKinley, Terror, and Empire at the Dawn of the American Century*. New York: Random House, 2011.

Milner, Helen V. "International Theories of Cooperation Among Nations." *World Politics* 44, no. 3 (1992): 466–96.

Mironova, Vera, and Ekaterina Sergatskova. "Cracks in the Islamic State." *Foreign Affairs*, February 15, 2017.

Mitchell, Anna, and Larry Diamond. "China's Surveillance State Should Scare Everyone." *Atlantic*, February 2, 2018.

Mitchell, Timothy. *Colonising Egypt*. Cambridge: Cambridge University Press, 1988.

———. "The Limits of the State: Beyond Statist Approaches and Their Critics." *American Political Science Review* 85, no. 1 (1991): 77–96.

Mitzen, Jennifer. "Ontological Security in World Politics: State Identity and the Security Dilemma." *European Journal of International Relations* 12, no. 3 (2006): 341–70.

———. *Power in Concert*. Chicago: University of Chicago Press, 2013.

Monatte, Pierre, and Errico Malatesta. "Syndicalism—For and Against." In *Anarchism: A Documentary History of Libertarian Ideas*, ed. Robert Graham, 206–11. London: Black Rose Books, 2005.

Moore, Barrington. *Social Origins of Dictatorship and Democracy: Lord and Peasant in the Making of the Modern World*. Boston: Beacon Press, 2003.

Moravscik, Andrew. "Taking Preferences Seriously: A Liberal Theory of International Politics." *International Organization* 51, no. 4 (1997): 513–53.
Morgan, Kimberly J., and Ann Shola Orloff, eds. *The Many Hands of the State: Theorizing Political Authority and Social Control.* Cambridge: Cambridge University Press, 2017.
Morris, Brian. *Bakunin: The Philosophy of Freedom.* New York: Black Rose Books, 1993.
Motyl, Alexander. *Imperial Ends: The Decay, Collapse, and Revival of Empires.* New York: Columbia University Press, 2001.
———. *Revolutions, Nations, Empires: Conceptual Limits and Theoretical Possibilities.* New York: Columbia University Press, 1999.
Mulich, Jeppe. "Microregionalism and Intercolonial Relations: The Case of the Danish West Indies, 1730–1830." *Journal of Global History* 8, no. 1 (2013): 72–94.
———. "Republican Privateering: Local Networks and Political Order in the Western Atlantic." In *The Two World of Nineteenth Century International Relations: The Bifurcated Century*, ed. Daniel M. Green, 43–59. London: Routledge, 2018.
Murakami Wood, David. "What Is Global Surveillance? Towards a Relational Political Economy of the Global Surveillant Assemblage." *Geoforum* 49 (2013): 317–26.
Murray, Dian. "Living and Working Conditions in Chinese Pirates Communities 1750–1850." In *Pirates and Privateers: New Perspectives on the War on Trade in the Eighteenth and Nineteenth Centuries*, ed. David J. Starkey, E. S. Van Eych van Heslinga, and J. A. de Moor, 47–68. Exeter, UK: University of Exeter Press, 1997.
Musgrave, Paul. "Bringing the State Police In: The Diffusion of U.S. Statewide Policing Agencies, 1905–1941." *Studies in American Political Development* 34, no. 1 (2020): 3–23.
Mylonakis, Leonidas. *Piracy in the Eastern Mediterranean.* London: Bloomsbury, 2021.
Nacos, Brigitte Lebens. *Mass-Mediated Terrorism: The Central Role of the Media in Terrorism and Counterterrorism.* Basingstoke: Rowman and Littlefield, 2007.
Naimark, Norman M. "Terrorism and the Fall of Imperial Russia*." *Terrorism and Political Violence* 2, no. 2 (1990): 171–92.
Nakashima, Ellen. "Independent Review Board Says NSA Phone Data Program Is Illegal and Should End." *Washington Post*, January 24, 2014.
"The National Security Agency: Missions, Authorities, Oversight and Partnerships." National Security Agency, August 9, 2013. http://www.nsa.gov/public_info/_files/speeches_testimonies/2013_08_09_the_nsa_story.pdf.
"The National Security Strategy of the United States of America." Washington, DC: Office of the President of the United States of America, 2002.
"The National Security Strategy of the United States of America." Washington, DC: Office of the President of the United States of America, 2006.
Nexon, Daniel H. *The Struggle for Power in Early Modern Europe: Religious Conflict, Dynastic Empires, and International Change.* Princeton, NJ: Princeton University Press, 2009.
———. "Zeitgeist? The New Idealism in the Study of International Change." *Review of International Political Economy* 12, no. 4 (2005): 700–719.
Nexon, Daniel H., and Iver B. Neumann. "Hegemonic-Order Theory: A Field-Theoretic Account." *European Journal of International Relations* 24, no. 3 (2018): 662–86.

Nexon, Daniel H., and Thomas Wright. "What's at Stake in the American Empire Debate." *American Political Science Review* 101, no. 2 (2007): 253–71.

Nietzsche, Friedrich. *On the Genealogy of Morality*. Ed. Keith Ansell-Pearson. Trans. Carol Diethe. Cambridge: Cambridge University Press, 2007.

"The 9/11 Commission Report: Final Report of the National Commission on Terrorist Attacks Upon the United States." Washington, DC: 2004. http://www.9-11commission.gov/report/911Report.pdf.

North, Douglass C. *Institutions, Institutional Change and Economic Performance*. 2nd ed. Cambridge: Cambridge University Press, 1990.

Norton, Matthew. "Classification and Coercion: The Destruction of Piracy in the English Maritime System." *American Journal of Sociology* 119, no. 6 (2014): 1537–75.

———. "Real Mythic Histories: Circulatory Networks and State-Centrism." In *Global Historical Sociology*, ed. Julian Go and George Lawson, 37–57. Cambridge: Cambridge University Press, 2017.

"NSA and Israeli Intelligence: Memorandum of Understanding—Full Document." *Guardian*, September 11, 2013.

"The NSA Paid Silicon Valley Millions to Spy on Taxpayers." *Washington Post*, August 23, 2013.

Nwalozie, Chijioke J. "Exploring Contemporary Sea Piracy in Nigeria, the Niger Delta and the Gulf of Guinea." *Journal of Transportation Security* 13, no. 3 (2020): 159–78.

Nye, Joseph S., and Robert O. Keohane. "Transnational Relations and World Politics: An Introduction." *International Organization* 25, no. 3 (1971): 329–49.

O'Brien, McKenzie. "Fluctuations Between Crime and Terror: The Case of Abu Sayyaf's Kidnapping Activities." *Terrorism and Political Violence* 24, no. 2 (2012): 320–36.

O'Driscoll, Cian. "From Versailles to 9/11: Non-State Actors and Just War in the Twentieth Century." In *Ethics, Authority, and War: Non-State Actors and the Just War Tradition*, ed. Eric Heinze and Brent J. Steele, 21–46. New York: Palgrave, 2009.

Officer, Lawrence H., and Samuel H. Williamson. "Five Ways to Compute the Relative Value of the UK Pound Amount, 1270 to Present." Measuring Worth, 2015. https://www.measuringworth.com/ukcompare/result.php.

Ogbonnaya, Maurice. "From Nationalist Movements to Organised Crime Groups." *ENACT Research Papers*, no. 22 (2020): 1–22.

Oliver, Hermia. *The International Anarchist Movement in Late Victorian London*. New York: St. Martin's Press, 1983.

Onuf, Nicholas Greenwood. *World of Our Making: Rules and Rule in Social Theory and International Relations*. Columbia: University of South Carolina Press, 1989.

Osiander, Andreas. "Sovereignty, International Relations, and the Westphalian Myth." *International Organization* 55, no. 2 (2001): 251–87.

Oye, Kenneth A. "Explaining Cooperation Under Anarchy: Hypotheses and Strategies." *World Politics* 38, no. 1 (1985): 1–24.

Pachuki, Mark A., Sabrina Pendergrass, and Michele Lamont. "Boundary Processes: Recent Developments and New Theoretical Contributions." *Poetics* 35, no. 6 (2007): 331–51.

Partington, John S. "H. G. Wells and the World State: A Liberal Cosmopolitan in a Totalitarian Age." *International Relations* 17, no. 2 (2003): 233–46.

"'Peeling Back the Layers of Tor with EgotisticalGiraffe'—Read the Document." *Guardian*, October 4, 2013.

Peritz, Aki. "The Coming ISIS Jailbreak." *Foreign Affairs*, October 25, 2019.

Peterson, Andrea. "Government Board Report Refutes 9/11 Argument for NSA Phone Records Program." *Washington Post*, January 23, 2014.

———. "Obama Can't Point to a Single Time the NSA Call Records Program Prevented a Terrorist Attack." *Washington Post*, December 23, 2013.

———. "The Senate Has Another Go at NSA Surveillance Reform." *Washington Post*, July 29, 2014.

Phillips, Andrew. "Contesting the Confucian Peace: Civilization, Barbarism and International Hierarchy in East Asia." *European Journal of International Relations* 24, no. 2 (2018): 740–64.

———. *War, Religion and Empire: The Transformation of International Orders*. Cambridge: Cambridge University Press, 2011.

Phillips, Andrew, and J. C. Sharman. *International Order in Diversity: War, Trade and Rule in the Indian Ocean*. Cambridge: Cambridge University Press, 2015.

Phillips, Hugh. "The War Against Terrorism in Late Imperial and Early Soviet Russia." In *Enemies of Humanity*, ed. Isaac Land, 203–22. New York: Palgrave Macmillan, 2008.

Philpott, Daniel. *Revolutions in Sovereignty: How Ideas Shaped Modern International Relations*. Princeton, NJ: Princeton University Press, 2001.

"Pirate Utopias: Under the Banner of King Death." *Dum De Dum De Dum* (blog). http://dumdedumdedum.wordpress.com/pirate-utopias/.

Poggi, Gianfranco. *The Development of the Modern State: A Sociological Introduction*. Stanford, CA: Stanford University Press, 1978.

Poulantzas, Nicos. *State, Power, Socialism*. London: Verso, 2014.

Pratt, Simon Frankel. "Pragmatism as Ontology, Not (Just) Epistemology: Exploring the Full Horizon of Pragmatism as an Approach to IR Theory." *International Studies Review* 18, no. 3 (2016): 508–27.

Pratt, Simon Frankel, and Sebastian Schmidt. "Pragmatism in IR: The Prospects for Substantive Theorizing." *International Studies Review* (May 2021). https://doi.org/10.1093/isr/viab019.

"President Bush's Speech on Terrorism." *New York Times*, September 6, 2006.

"President Bush Addresses the Nation." *Washington Post*, September 20, 2001.

Preston, William, Jr. *Aliens and Dissenters: Federal Suppression of Radicals, 1903–1933*. Cambridge, MA: Harvard University Press, 1963.

Priest, Dana, and William M. Arkin. *Top Secret America: The Rise of the New American Security State*. New York: Little, Brown, 2011.

Pritchard, James S. *In Search of Empire: The French in the Americas, 1670–1730*. Cambridge: Cambridge University Press, 2004.

Purnell, Kandida. "Grieving, Valuing, and Viewing Differently: The Global War on Terror's American Toll." *International Political Sociology* 12, no. 2 (2018): 156–71.

Putnam, Robert D. "Diplomacy and Domestic Politics: The Logic of Two-Level Games." *International Organization* 42, no. 3 (1988): 428–60.

Qutb, Sayyid. *Milestones*. Islamic Book Service, 2006.

Rankin, Hugh F. *The Golden Age of Piracy*. Williamsburg, VA: Holt, Rinehart and Winston, 1969.

Rankin, Jennifer. "Coronavirus Could Be Final Straw for EU, European Experts Warn." *Guardian*, April 1, 2020.

Rediker, Marcus. "Hydrarchy and Libertalia: The Utopian Dimensions of Atlantic Piracy in the Early Eighteenth Century." In *Pirates and Privateers: New Perspectives on the War on Trade in the Eighteenth and Nineteenth Centuries*, ed. David J. Starkey, E. S. Van Eych van Heslinga, and J. A. de Moor, 29–46. Exeter, UK: University of Exeter Press, 1997.

——. "Liberty Beneath the Jolly Roger: The Lives of Anne Bonny and Mary Read, Pirates." In *Bandits at Sea: A Pirates Reader*, ed. C. R. Pennell, 299–320. New York: New York University Press, 2001.

——. *Villains of All Nations: Atlantic Pirates in the Golden Age*. Boston: Beacon Press, 2004.

"Return of the Taliban." *Frontline*, October 3, 2006.

Reus-Smit, Christian. *The Moral Purpose of the State: Culture, Social Identity, and Institutional Rationality in International Relations*. Princeton, NJ: Princeton University Press, 1999.

Rewald, John. "Extracts of an Unedited Journal by Paul Signac." *Gazzette Des Beaux-Arts* 6, no. 36 (1949): 97–128.

Ringmar, Erik. "On the Ontological Status of the State." *European Journal of International Relations* 2, no. 4 (1996): 439–66.

——. "Performing International Systems: Two East-Asian Alternatives to the Westphalian Order." *International Organization* 66, no. 1 (2012): 1–25.

Ritchie, Robert C. *Captain Kidd and the War Against the Pirates*. Cambridge, MA: Harvard University Press, 1986.

Roberts, Molly. "Facebook Has Declared Sovereignty." *Washington Post*, January 31, 2019.

Robertson, Craig. *The Passport in America: The History of a Document*. Oxford: Oxford University Press, 2010.

Robertson, Robbie. *The Three Waves of Globalization: A History of a Developing Global Consciousness*. New York: Zed Books, 2002.

Robertson, Roland. *Globalization: Social Theory and Global Culture*. London: Sage, 1992.

Roest, Friso, Johan Van Someren, Miek Wijnberg, Kees Boersma, and Pieter Wagenaar. "Policy Windows for Surveillance: The Phased Introduction of the Identification Card in the Netherlands Since the Early Twentieth Century." In *History of State Surveillance in Europe and Beyond*, ed. Kees Boersma, Rosamunde Van Brakel, Chiara Fonio, and Pieter Wagenaar, 150–69. London: Routledge, 2014.

Romein, Ed, and Marc Schuilenburg. "Are You on the Fast Track? The Rise of Surveillant Assemblages in a Post Industrial Age." *Architectural Theory Review* 13, no. 3 (2008): 337–48.

Rosecrance, Richard N. *Action and Reaction in World Politics; International Systems in Perspective*. Boston: Little, Brown, 1963.

Rosen, Jeffrey. "Total Information Awareness." *New York Times*, December 15, 2002.

Rosenau, James N. *Turbulence in World Politics: A Theory of Change and Continuity*. Princeton, NJ: Princeton University Press, 1990.

Rosenthal, Daniel J., and Loren DeJonge Schulman. "Trump's Secret War on Terror." *Atlantic*, August 10, 2018.

Rotberg, Robert I. *When States Fail: Causes and Consequences*. Princeton, NJ: Princeton University Press, 2003.

Roy, Olivier. *Globalized Islam: The Search for a New Ummah*. New York: Columbia University Press, 2006.

Rubin, Alfred P. *The Law of Piracy*. Newport, RI: Naval War College Press, 1988.

Ruggie, John Gerard. "Continuity and Transformation in the World Polity: Toward a Neorealist Synthesis." *World Politics* 35, no. 2 (1983): 261–85.

Salter, Mark. *Rights of Passage: The Passport in International Relations*. Boulder, CO: Lynne Rienner Publishers, 2003.

Santos, Soliman M., Jr., and Octavio A. Dinampo. "Abu Sayyaf Reloaded: Rebels, Agents, Bandits, Terrorists (Case Study)." In Soliman M. Santos Jr. and Paz Verdades M. Santos, *Primed and Purposeful: Armed Groups and Human Security Efforts in the Philippines*, 115–38. Geneva: Small Arms Survey, Graduate Institute of International and Development Studies, 2010.

Sassen, Saskia. *Losing Control? Sovereignty in the Age of Globalization*. New York: Columbia University Press, 1996.

———. *Territory, Authority, Rights: From Medieval to Global Assemblages*. Princeton, NJ: Princeton University Press, 2006.

Savelle, Max. *Empires to Nations: Expansion in America, 1713–1824*. Minneapolis: University of Minnesota Press, 1974.

Scahill, Jeremy, and Glenn Greenwald. "The NSA's Secret Role in the U.S. Assassination Program." *The Intercept*, February 10, 2014.

Scarlett, George Chandler. *The Treaty of Utrecht: Considered from the Viewpoints of the Past and Present State of Spain, the Slave Trade Monopoly That Set It Up, Christian Colonization, and the International Struggle*. New York: Cosmos Greek-American Printing, 1939.

Schinkel, Willem. "Dignitas Non-Moritur? The State of the State in an Age of Social Hypochondria." In *Globalization and the State: Sociological Perspectives on the State of the State*, ed. Willem Schinkel, 1–22. New York: Palgrave Macmillan, 2009.

Schmidt, Vivien A. "Putting the Political Back into Political Economy by Bringing the State Back in Yet Again." *World Politics* 61, no. 3 (2009): 516–46.

Schmitt, Eric. "U.S. Drone Strikes Stymie ISIS in Southern Libya." *New York Times*, November 18, 2019.

Scott, James C. *The Art of Not Being Governed: An Anarchist History of Upland Southeast Asia*. New Haven, CT: Yale University Press, 2009.

———. *Seeing Like a State: How Certain Schemes to Improve the Human Condition Have Failed*. New Haven, CT: Yale University Press, 1998.

Segal, Adam. "Huawei, 5G, and Weaponized Interdependence." In *Uses and Abuses of Weaponized Interdependence*, ed. Dan Drezner, Henry Farrell, and Abraham L. Newman, 149–67. Washington, DC: Brookings Institution Press, 2021.

Sekula, Allan. "The Body and the Archive." *October* 39 (1986): 3–64.

Shaffer, Kirwin Ray. *Anarchism and Countercultural Politics in Early Twentieth Century Cuba*. Gainesville: University of Florida Press, 2005.

Sharma, Aradhana, and Akhil Gupta, eds. *The Anthropology of the State: A Reader*. Oxford: Blackwell, 2006.

Shaw, George Bernard. *The Impossibilities of Anarchism*. Kypros Press, 2016.

Shaw, Ian G. R. *Predator Empire: Drone Warfare and Full Spectrum Dominance*. Minneapolis: University of Minnesota Press, 2016.

Shinko, Rosemary E. "Ethics After Liberalism: Why (Autonomous) Bodies Matter." *Millennium—Journal of International Studies* 38, no. 3 (2010): 723–45.

Shirk, Mark. "Boundaries in the Sea." In *International Relations and the Sea*, ed. Halvard Leira and Benjamin de Carvalho. Manchester: Manchester University Press, forthcoming.

———. "'Bringing the State Back In' to the Empire Turn: Piracy and the Layered Sovereignty of the Eighteenth Century Atlantic." *International Studies Review* 19, no. 2 (2017): 143–65.

———. "Busting Blackbeard's Ghost: Somali Piracy in Historical Context." *Global Change, Peace, and Security* 28, no. 1 (2016): 17–34.

———. "An Evil of Ancient Date: Piracy and the Two Pax Britannicas in Nineteenth-Century Southeast Asia." In *The Two Worlds of Nineteenth Century International Relations: The Bifurcated Century*, ed. Dan Green, 177–95. London: Routledge, 2019.

———. "How Does Violence Threaten the State? Four Narratives on Piracy." *Terrorism and Political Violence* 29, no. 4 (2017): 656–73.

———. "The Universal Eye: Anarchist 'Propaganda of the Deed' and Development of the Modern Surveillance State." *International Studies Quarterly* 63, no. 2 (2019): 334–45.

"Shoe Bomber: Tale of Another Failed Terrorist Attack." *CNN*, December 25, 2009.

Singer, Peter W. *Wired for War: The Robotics Revolution and Conflict in the 21st Century*. New York: Penguin Books, 2009.

Skumsrud Andersen, Morten. "Semi-Cores in Imperial Relations: The Cases of Scotland and Norway." *Review of International Studies* 42, no. 1 (2016): 1–26.

Sonn, Richard D. *Anarchism and Cultural Politics in Fin de Siècle France*. Lincoln: University of Nebraska Press, 1989.

Sorel, Georges. *Sorel: Reflections on Violence*. Ed. Jeremy Jennings. Cambridge: Cambridge University Press, 1999.

Spruyt, Hendrik. *The Sovereign State and Its Competitors: An Analysis of Systems Change*. Princeton, NJ: Princeton University Press, 1994.

Staley, Eugene. *World Economy in Transition: Technology vs. Politics, Laissez Faire vs. Planning, Power vs. Welfare*. New York: Council on Foreign Relations, 1939.

Starkey, David J. "Pirates and Markets." In *Bandits at Sea: A Pirates Reader*, ed. C. R Pennell, 69–81. New York: New York University Press, 2001.

Starr, Paul. "Social Categories and Claims in the Liberal State." *Social Research* 59, no. 2 (1992): 263.

Steele, Brent J. *Ontological Security in International Relations: Self-Identity and the IR State*. London: Routledge, 2008.

Steele, Ian Kenneth. *The English Atlantic, 1675–1740: An Exploration of Communication and Community*. Oxford: Oxford University Press, 1986.

Steinberg, Philip E. *The Social Construction of the Ocean*. Cambridge: Cambridge University Press, 2001.

Steinmetz, George, ed. *State/Culture: State-Formation After the Cultural Turn*. Ithaca, NY: Cornell University Press, 1999.

Stern, Philip J. "British Asia and British Atlantic: Comparisons and Connections." *William and Mary Quarterly* 63, no. 4 (2006): 693–712.

———. "Companies: Monopoly, Sovereignty, and the East Indies." In *Mercantilism Reimagined: Political Economy in Early Modern Britain and Its Empire*, ed. Philip J. Stern and Carl Wennerlind, 177–95. Oxford: Oxford University Press, 2014.

———. *The Company-State: Corporate Sovereignty and the Early Modern Foundations of the British Empire in India*. Oxford: Oxford University Press, 2012.

Strange, Susan. *The Retreat of the State: The Diffusion of Power in the World Economy*. Cambridge: Cambridge University Press, 1996.

Strayer, Joseph R. *On the Medieval Origins of the Modern State*. Princeton, NJ: Princeton University Press, 1970.

Sulzberger, A. G., and William K. Rashbaum. "Najibullah Zazi Pleads Guilty in Plot to Bomb Subway." *New York Times*, February 22, 2010.

Sylvester, Christine. "War Experiences/War Practices/War Theory." *Millennium—Journal of International Studies* 40, no. 3 (2012): 483–503.

Taylor, John. *Jamaica in 1687: The Taylor Manuscripts at the National Library of Jamaica*. Ed. David Buisseret. Kingston: University of the West Indies Press, 2008.

Teschke, Benno. *The Myth of 1648: Class, Geopolitics, and the Making of Modern International Relations*. London: Verso, 2003.

"Testimony of U.S. Secretary of Defense Donald Rumsfeld Before the Senate Armed Services Committee Regarding Iraq (Transcript)." September 19, 2002. http://www.defense.gov/speeches/speech.aspx?speechid=287.

"Text of Bush's Speech at West Point." *New York Times*, June 1, 2002.

"The Text of President Bush's Address Tuesday Night, After Terrorist Attacks on New York and Washington." *CNN*, September 11, 2001.

Thomson, Janice E. *Mercenaries, Pirates, and Sovereigns: State-Building and Extraterritorial Violence in Early Modern Europe*. Princeton, NJ: Princeton University Press, 1994.

———. "State Sovereignty in International Relations." *International Studies Quarterly* 39, no. 2 (1995): 213–33.

Thongchai, Winichakul. *Siam Mapped: A History of the Geo-Body of a Nation*. Honolulu: University of Hawai'i Press, 1994.

Thorleifsson, Cathrine. "In Pursuit of Purity: Populist Nationalism and the Racialization of Difference." *Identities* 28, no. 2 (2021): 186–202.

Tilly, Charles. *Coercion, Capital, and European States, AD 990–1990*. Oxford: Blackwell, 1990.

———. "Mechanisms in Political Processes." *Annual Review of Political Science* 4 (2001): 21–41.

———. "Reflections on the History of European State-Making." In *The Formation of National States in Western Europe*, ed. Charles Tilly, 3–84. Princeton, NJ: Princeton University Press, 1975.

———. "Social Boundary Mechanisms." *Philosophy of the Social Sciences* 34, no. 2 (2004): 211–36.

———. "States, State Transformation, and War." In *Oxford Handbook of World History*, ed. Jerry H. Bentley, 176–92. Oxford: Oxford University Press, 2011.

———. "War Making and State Making as Organized Crime." In *Bringing the State Back In*, ed. Peter B. Evans, Dietrich Rueschemeyer, and Theda Skocpol, 169–91. Cambridge: Cambridge University Press, 1985.

Timberg, Craig, and JIa Lynn Yang. "Google Is Encrypting Search Globally. That's Bad for the NSA and China's Censors." *Washington Post*, March 12, 2014. http://www.washingtonpost.com/blogs/the-switch/wp/2014/03/12/google-is-encrypting-search-worldwide-thats-bad-for-the-nsa-and-china/.

"Timeline: Al Qaeda's Global Context." *Frontline*, 2004.

Tinniswood, Adrian. *Pirates of Barbary: Corsairs, Conquests, and Captivity in the Seventeenth-Century Mediterranean*. New York: Riverhead Books, 2010.

Toft, Monica Duffy, Daniel Philpott, and Timothy Samuel Shah. *God's Century: Resurgent Religion and Global Politics*. New York: Norton, 2011.

"Top ISIS Commanders Among 6 Killed in U.S. Drone Strikes in East of Afghanistan." *Khaama Press News Agency*, March 2, 2020.

Torpey, John. "The Great War and the Birth of the Modern Passport System." In *Documenting Individual Identity: The Development of State Practices in the Modern World*, ed. Jane Caplan and John Torpey, 256–70. Princeton, NJ: Princeton University Press, 2001.

Tsukayama, Hayley. "Facebook Report: 74 Countries Sought Data on 38,000 Users." *Washington Post*, August 27, 2013.

Tuchman, Barbara Wertheim. *The Guns of August and the Proud Tower*. New York: Library of America, 2012.

Turack, Daniel C. "Freedom of Movement and the International Regime of Passports." *Osgoode Hall Law Journal* 6, no. 2 (1968): 230–51.

Turner, Frederick Jackson. *The Significance of the Frontier in American History*. London: Penguin, 2008.

"The 2014 Quadrennial Homeland Security Review." Washington, DC: Department of Homeland Security, 2014.

Ulam, Adam Bruno. *In the Name of the People: Prophets and Conspirators in Prerevolutionary Russia*. New York: Viking Press, 1977.

United States Department of Commerce. *Historical Statistics of the United States, 1789–1945*. Washington, DC: U.S. Government Printing Office, 1949.

United States Department of Labor. *Annual Report of the Secretary of Labor*. Washington, DC: U.S. Government Printing Office, 1920.

"US 'Foils Underwear Bomb' Plot." *BBC*, May 8, 2012.

"U.S. Phone Companies Never Once Challenged NSA Data Requests." *Washington Post*, September 27, 2013.

Vagg, Jon. "Rough Seas? Contemporary Piracy in South East Asia." *British Journal of Criminology* 35, no. 1 (1995): 63–80.

Van Brakel, Rosamunde, and Xavier Van Kerckhoven. "The Emergence of the Identity Card in Belgium and Its Colonies." In *History of State Surveillance in Europe and Beyond*, ed. Kees Boersma, Rosamunde Van Brakel, Chiara Fonio, and Pieter Wagenaar, 170–85. London: Routledge, 2014.

Varias, Alexander. *Paris and the Anarchists: Aesthetes and Subversives During the Fin de Siècle*. New York: St. Martin's Press, 1996.

Vincent, David. *Privacy: A Short History*. Cambridge: Polity, 2016.

Vitalis, Robert. *White World Order, Black Power Politics: The Birth of American International Relations*. Ithaca, NY: Cornell University Press, 2015.

Voeten, Erik. "The Problems with Studying Civilian Casualties from Drone Usage in Pakistan: What We Can't Know." *Monkey Cage*, August 17, 2011.

Vukov, Tamara, and Mimi Sheller. "Border Work: Surveillant Assemblages, Virtual Fences, and Tactical Counter-Media." *Social Semiotics* 23, no. 2 (2013): 225–41.

Waever, Ole. "Securitization and Desecuritization." In *On Security*, ed. Ronnie D. Lipschutz, 46–86. New York: Columbia University Press, 1995.

Wafer, Lionel. *A New Voyage and Description of the Isthmus of America*. Ed. Lillian Elwyn Elliot Joyce. London: Hakluyt Society, 1934.

Walker, R. B. J. "Genealogy, Geopolitics and Political Community: Richard K. Ashley and the Critical Social Theory of International Politics." *Alternatives* 13 (1988): 77–102.

Wall, Tyler, and Torin Monahan. "Surveillance and Violence from Afar: The Politics of Drones and Liminal Security-Scapes." *Theoretical Criminology* 15, no. 3 (2011): 239–54.

"The War in Yemen." Accessed September 1, 2021. https://www.newamerica.org/international-security/reports/americas-counterterrorism-wars/the-war-in-yemen.

Watson, Scott D. "'Framing' the Copenhagen School: Integrating the Literature on Threat Construction." *Millennium—Journal of International Studies* 40, no. 2 (2012): 279–301.

Weber, Max. *Max Weber on the Methodology of the Social Sciences*. Trans. Edward Shils. Glencoe, IL: Free Press, 1949.

——. "Prefatory Remarks to Collected Essays in the Sociology of Religion." In *Protestant Ethic and the Spirit of Capitalism*, trans. Stephen Kalberg, 149–64. London: Roxbury, 2002.

——. *The Vocation Lectures*. Trans. Rodney Livingstone. Indianapolis, IN: Hackett, 2004.

Weller, Toni, ed. *Information History in the Modern World: Histories of the Information Age*. Basingstoke: Palgrave, 2010.

Wells, H. G. *Anticipations of the Reactions of Mechanical and Scientific Progress Upon Human Life and Thought*. Mineola, NY: Dover Publications, 1999.

——. *World Brain*. London: Methuen, 1938.

Wendt, Alexander. *Social Theory of International Politics*. Cambridge: Cambridge University Press, 1999.

Whitlock, Craig. "Remote U.S. Base at Core of Secret Operations." *Washington Post*, December 1, 2012.

———. "U.S. Drone Base in Ethiopia Is Operational." *Washington Post*, November 16, 2011.

———. "U.S. Expands Secret Intelligence Operations in Africa." *Washington Post*, June 14, 2012.

Wiktorowicz, Quintan. "Anatomy of the Salafi Movement." *Studies in Conflict and Terrorism* 29, no. 3 (2006): 207–39.

Wilcox, Lauren. *Bodies of Violence: Theorizing Embodied Subjects in International Politics* (Oxford: Oxford University Press, 2015).

———. "Embodying Algorithmic War: Gender, Race, and the Posthuman in Drone Warfare." *Security Dialogue* 48, no. 1 (2017): 11–28.

Wilkinson, Blair, and Randy Lippert. "Moving Images Through an Assemblage: Police, Visual Information, and Resistance." *Critical Criminology* 20, no. 3 (2012): 311–25.

Wilner, Alex S. "Targeted Killings in Afghanistan: Measuring Coercion and Deterrence in Counterterrorism and Counterinsurgency." *Studies in Conflict and Terrorism* 33, no. 4 (2010): 307–29.

Woloch, Isser. *Eighteenth-Century Europe, Tradition and Progress, 1715–1789.* New York: Norton, 1982.

Wood, Graeme. "What ISIS Really Wants." *Atlantic*, March 2015.

Woodcock, George. *Anarchism: A History of Libertarian Ideas and Movements.* New York: New American Library, 1962.

Woodward, Colin. *The Republic of Pirates: Being the True and Surprising Story of the Caribbean Pirates and the Man Who Brought Them Down.* New York: Harcourt, 2007.

Wright, Thomas J. "Stretching the International Order to Its Breaking Point." *Atlantic*, April 4, 2020.

Wright, Thomas J. *All Measures Short of War: The Contest for the Twenty-First Century and the Future of American Power.* New Haven, CT: Yale University Press, 2018.

"Yemen Drone Strikes: 3 Attacks Kill 12 Suspected Militants." *Huffington Post*, August 8, 2013.

Zarakol, Ayşe, ed. *Hierarchies in World Politics.* Cambridge: Cambridge University Press, 2017.

———. "What Makes Terrorism Modern? Terrorism, Legitimacy, and the International System." *Review of International Studies* 37, no. 5 (2011): 2311–36.

Zuckerman, Ethan. "The Internet's Original Sin." *Atlantic*, August 14, 2014.

INDEX

Able Danger project, 109, 121
Afghanistan, 107, 111, 118; Soviet invasion of, 103, 105; U.S. invasion of, 104, 116, 193n99
agents provocateurs, 88, 89, 97
al-Awlaki, Abdulrahman, 125
al-Baghdadi, Abu Bakr, 143
Alexander, Keith, 202n247
Alexander II (Russian tsar), 69, 74
Alexander VI (pope), 22
Algeria, 80
Aliens Act (UK, 1905), 97
Ali Jaber, Salem Ahmed, 125, 131
al-Libi, Abu Yahya, 125
al-Mihdhar, Khalid, 123
al-Qaeda, 4–9, 20, 54, 102–32; attacks by, 111, 134, 143; boundaries of, 105–11, 115, 127–29; data surveillance of, 103–4, 119–23; drone attacks on, 6, 102–3, 118–19; Earth Liberation Front and, 27–28; globalization and, 103, 105–7; goals of, 105; illegibility of, 5, 105, 110, 112–13, 134; Islamic State and, 124; politics of, 104–7; reinscribing of, 117–26; September 11th attacks by, 4–5; shattering of, 109, 111–17. *See also* War on Terror
al-Shabaab, 118
al-Zawahiri, Ayman, 103, 116, 124
American Revolution, 8, 36, 66
anarchists, 6–7, 69–101; agents provocateurs and, 88, 89, 97; boundaries of, 70–71, 76–79; communism and, 99; conspiracy theories about, 80–82, 88; definitions of, 77, 183n120; as "enemies of humanity," 76, 83, 92, 112–13; fingerprinting and, 32; globalization and, 81–82; illegibility of, 80, 82–84, 113, 134; industrialization and, 70–73, 75–79, 134; Marxism and, 71–72, 74, 75; origins of, 73–75; pirates as, 9, 49–51, 112–13; reinscribing of, 89–99; of Russian Revolution, 72, 84; shattering of, 79–80. *See also* propaganda of the deed
anarcho-syndicalism, 72, 92–93. *See also* labor movements
Angiolillo, Michele, 86, 88
anti-Semitic conspiracy theories, 81–82
Apple Corporation, 120
Arcos, Duke of, 79, 86
Argentina, 98
Armitage, Richard, 113
artificial intelligence, 149

Aurangzeb (Mughal emperor), 43
Austrian Succession, War of, 65
Ayers, Cynthia, 1–2

Bahamas, 44–45, 52, 56, 59–60
Bakunin, Michel, 74, 180n44
Balkan wars, 80, 119
Barbary Corsairs, 48, 169n79.
  See also pirates
Barlow, John, 1
Bartelson, Jens, 159n22
Bellamy, Sam, 49–50, 52, 60, 170n91
Bellomont, Earl of, 43
Benghazi attack (2012), 125
Benjamin, Daniel, 108, 116–17, 124
Benton, Lauren, 41
Berkman, Alexander, 69
Bermuda, 44
Bertillon, Alphonse, 95, 96
Bhutto, Benazir, 111
bin Laden, Osama, 103, 106, 116; Devji on, 105; on drones, 125; intelligence on, 126
biometric databases, 70, 96, 98–99.
  See also data surveillance
Black Bart. *See* Roberts, Bartholomew
Blackbeard. *See* Teach, Edward
Black Lives Matter movement, 141
Blin, Arnaud, 79
Bonnet, Stede, 46, 55, 60, 63
Boston Marathon bombing (2013), 28–29, 111
boundaries, 20–23, 34, 149; al-Qaeda and, 105–11, 115, 127–29; anarchism and, 70–71, 76–79; cyberspace, 127–29; Deleuze on, 127; pandemics and, 146–47; piracy and, 37–45
Boundless Informant program, 128
Bourdieu, Pierre, 26–27
Bourdin, Martial, 91, 185n163
Brousse, Paul, 75
buccaneers, 40, 166n27. *See also* pirates
Buerger, Christian, 17

Bush, George W., 108–9, 142; on data surveillance, 122; drone attacks by, 118; on War on Terror, 112–13
Butterworth, Alex, 72, 81

Cafiero, Carlo, 75
Canovas, Antonio, 69, 88
Cantwell, Thomas, 81
capitalism, 39, 82; free trade, 49, 71, 76, 144–46; mercantilism and, 5, 45, 49.
  See also globalization
Carnot, Sardi, 69, 78, 86, 90
Cartesianism, 20–21, 159n22
Caserio, Sante, 85
Cateau-Cambresis, Treaty of (1559), 38
Central Intelligence Agency (CIA), 89, 109, 110, 114; drone attacks by, 118; torture by, 115–16
Cerny, Philip, 2
Chaliand, Gerard, 79
Chechnya, 106, 111
Cheney, Dick, 4
China, 137, 146
Cicero, 172n139
citizenship, 127, 130–31; aliens and, 102
Clarke, Richard, 108, 109, 119
climate change, 1, 2
Clinton, Bill, 108–9, 113, 119
Club Autonomie (London), 91
Cohen, William, 109
Cold War, 31, 129
collusion, 12, 16, 24–25, 57, 114, 135–37
colonialism, 7, 71; core-periphery relationships and, 21, 25, 37–39, 49, 66; religious freedom and, 165n20.
  See also imperialism
communism, 99, 107. *See also* Marxism
conspiracy theories, 80–82, 88
cotton plantations, 42
counterterrorism, 4, 103, 114, 204n13; Clinton on, 108; counterinsurgency and, 194n115; Fuller on, 103; Levitt on, 148;

"successes" of, 123–26; Wolfowitz on, 117, 126
COVID-19 pandemic, 2, 146–47
Crawford, Emily, 2
crimes against humanity, 112.
    See also "enemies of humanity"
Cromwell, Oliver, 38
cybersecurity, 2, 126
cyberspace boundaries, 127–29

Dalziel, Alexander, 63
Dampier, William, 40
Dasgupta, Rana, 1
data surveillance, 103–4, 119–23, 137, 141–45; fingerprints and, 24, 31–32, 95–96, 130; Kojm on, 125; "success" with, 123–32.
    See also biometric databases
"dataveillance," 130
Davis, Thomas, 52
decolonization, 8, 128
Defense Advanced Research Projects Agency (DARPA), 114, 140
Delbrück, Jost, 2
Deleuze, Gilles, 127
democracy, 8
democratization, 8
Descartes, René, 20–21, 159n22
Devji, Faisal, 105–6
Dewey, John, 31, 139, 146
Di Giovanni, Severino, 98
DNA evidence, 130
Doyle, Arthur Conan, 96
Drake, Francis, 40
drones, 6, 102–3, 118–19, 137, 145, 199n198; African bases for, 129; legal justification for, 128–29, 139; "success" with, 123–32
dynamiteurs (bomb makers), 71, 75, 77–78, 82–83

Earth Liberation Front, 27–28
East India Company (EIC), 19, 43
Ebola, 147
Egypt, 105

Elahi, Hasan, 140–41, 204n17
Elisabeth (Austrian empress), 69, 75, 87
encomienda system, 39
"enemies of humanity," 5; al-Qaeda as, 112; anarchists as, 76, 83, 92, 112–13; pirates as, 53, 57, 62, 112
eugenics, 32, 83, 96
European Union, nationalism in, 2
Every, Henry, 40, 43, 45
extradition policies, 70, 77, 79, 89

Facebook, 2, 139, 203n255
Farrell, Henry, 2
Feldman, Jay, 72
Fénéon, Félix, 75
Fenianism, 80
filibusters, 19. See also pirates
fingerprints, 24, 31–32, 95–96, 130.
    See also data surveillance
Finkelstein, Rob, 119
Fletcher, Benjamin, 59
Fly, William, 50, 52, 56
Foreign Intelligence Surveillance Act (FISA), 120–21, 139–40
Fornara, Giuseppe, 71, 81, 82, 185n162
Franco, Francisco, 100
François, Jean-Pierre, 91
Franklin, Benjamin, 61
Franz Ferdinand (Austrian archduke), 80
Frederick II (Prussian king), 65
freebooters, 44, 45. See also pirates
free trade, 49, 71, 76, 144–46.
    See also globalization
French Revolution, 8; nationalism of, 77
Frick, Henry Clay, 69
Fuller, Christopher, 103

Gadinger, Frank, 17
Gallo, Charles, 75
Galton, Francis, 96
George I (English king), 55
Gibraltar, 65
Giolitti, Giovanni, 91

globalism, 144
globalization, 11–15, 134, 144–46; al-Qaeda and, 103, 105–7; anarchism and, 71, 81–82; future of states and, 146–49; imperialism and, 64–65, 71; industrialization and, 76–79; second wave of, 6, 71; state transformation and, 25; technology and, 107; transboundary processes and, 148–49. *See also* capitalism
gold, 39, 45
Google, 127, 139
governmentality, 16
Gow, John, 52
Grotius, Hugo, 39–40

Haiti, 36, 108
Hall, Alexandra, 130
Hall, Rodney Bruce, 8–9, 36
Hamas, 103, 105, 108; drone attacks on, 119
Hamilton, Archibald, 42, 174n179
Hamilton, Lee, 130, 148
Hamilton, Walter, 56
Hanna, Mark, 61
Hardt, Michael, 129, 201n234
Harris, Shane, 140, 204n15
Hayden, Michael, 121, 122, 194n100
Haymarket Affair (1886), 74
Henneberry, David, 28
Henry, Émile, 74, 78, 85, 90, 182n107
Henry VIII (English king), 53
Hezbollah, 108, 112, 121
hijrah (Muslim pilgrimage), 124
Hoar, George Frisbee, 84
Holder, Eric, 195n130
homosexuality, 50–51
Hornigold, Benjamin, 44, 45, 50, 56, 60
hostes humani generis. See "enemies of humanity"
Hume, David, 17
Husband, David, 125–26, 193n94
Hussein, Saddam, 116–17
Hussin, Iza, 18

Ibn Taymiyyah, 104
illegibility, 12–13, 34, 134; of al-Qaeda, 5, 105, 110, 112–13; of anarchists, 80, 82–84, 113; illegitimacy and, 82–84; of pirates, 5, 48–54, 60–61; of transnational violence, 28. *See also* legibility
immigration policies, 24, 137; anarchists and, 72, 97–98; Argentinian, 98; standardization of, 94; surveillance state and, 90; universal, 6, 72, 96–98; U.S., 86, 96–98
imperialism: core-periphery relationships in, 21, 25, 37–39, 49, 66; globalization and, 64–65, 71. *See also* colonialism
India, 22, 43
industrialization, 70–73, 75–79, 134
Indyk, Martin, 119
Information Defense Agency (IDA), 109
Iran, 108, 109, 112, 197n163
Iraq, 104, 109, 111, 119, 143; War on Terror and, 116–17; weapons of mass destruction and, 117, 194n106
Ireland, 80, 108
Islamic State (IS), 124, 129, 134; fall of, 143; "success" of, 142–44
Italy, 21, 69, 82

Jackson, Patrick Thaddeus, 20
Jacobite pirates, 51, 63
Jamaica, 41, 45
Jenkins, Leoline, 64
Jenkins' Ear, War of. *See* War of Jenkins' Ear
Jennings, Henry, 44, 45, 60
Jensen, Richard Bach, 76, 94; on anarchist repression, 90; on Italian labor unions, 92
jihadism. *See* al-Qaeda
Joas, Hans, 27, 31
Johnson, Robert, 55
Johnson, Samuel, 51

Kashmir, 22
Kayani, Ashfaq, 119
Kenya, 106, 108

KGB (Komitet Gosudarstvennoy
    Bezopasnosti), 89
Kidd, William, 43, 45, 52, 58–59
Klabbers, Jan, 1
Kleinsmith, Eric, 109, 121
Knepper, Paul, 97
Kobrin, Stephen, 1, 2
Koenigstein, François Claudius.
    See Ravachol
Kojm, Chris, 108, 124, 125, 202n247
Koskenniemi, Martti, 1
Kosovo, 119
Kratochwil, Friedrich, 26
Krebs, Ronald, 107, 112–14
Kropotkin, Piotr, 75, 84, 91, 180n44; on
    bombings, 77–78; on syndicalism, 93
Kuhn, Gabriel, 63

labor movements, 6, 71, 89–93, 134;
    anarcho-syndicalism and, 72, 92–93.
    See also syndicalism
La Buse, Olivier, 56
Lebanon, 108, 121
legibility, 12–13; of Boston Marathon
    bomber, 28–29; Hussin on, 18; Scott on,
    3–4. *See also* illegibility
Leopold II (Belgian king), 88
letters of marque, 40–43, 48; pardons
    and, 55–56, 137
Levitt, Mathew, 114–15, 148
Levy, Carl, 72
Lewis, Flora, 2
"Libertalia," 50
Libya, 108, 118, 119
Lobasz, Jennifer, 107, 112
Lombroso, Cesare, 95
Low, Ned, 57, 61
Lynch, Thomas, 41
Lyon, David, 127

Macarty, Daniel, 51, 61–62
MacDonald, Arthur, 79–80
Machiavelli, Niccolò, 17

Madagascar, 44, 50
Mainwaring, Henry, 40
Malatesta, Errico, 75, 84, 93
Malato, Charles, 90
Malay pirates, 48
Mansfield, Joseph, 49
Manwaring, Max, 1
Martinique, 63
Marxism, 16, 99, 107; anarchists and, 71–72,
    74, 75
Massachusetts, 58–59
Mather, Cotton, 53
McIntyre, Patrick, 87
McKinley, William, 69, 78
McNamara, Robert, 121
Mendel, Jonathan, 130
mercantilism, 5, 45, 49
Meunier, Théodule, 82, 85, 91
Microsoft Corporation, 120
Middle East respiratory syndrome
    (MERS), 147
Mieville, China, 15, 32–33
migration. *See* immigration policies
Mirbeau, Octave, 90
Mitchell, Timothy, 21, 22, 159n22
Monahan, Torin, 130
monopoly, 40
Morgan, Henry, 19, 40–43
Morgan, Kimberly, 19
Morris, Thomas, 52
Morris, William, 93
Most, Johann, 83
Mueller, Robert, 123
Muslim Brotherhood, 105, 112

nationalism, 2, 72, 77, 83
nation-states, 1, 8, 17–20, 149; empires
    versus, 37–38; as structural effect, 21
Negri, Antonio, 129, 201n234
New American Foundation, 118–19
Newman, Abraham, 2
New York, 42–44, 60, 66
Nexon, Daniel H., 20, 148

Nietzsche, Friedrich, 26
Niger, 129, 130
9/11. *See* September 11 attacks
Nine Years' War, 43
Nordau, Max, 95
Norton, Matthew, 20, 22, 57
Nychaev, Sergei, 179n40

Obama, Barack, 115–16; on data surveillance, 123; drone attacks by, 118, 199n198; "War on Terror" and, 115
O'Driscoll, Cian, 105–6
Ogle, Channeler, 63, 137
Okhrana (tsarist secret police), 87–89
Oklahoma City bombing (1995), 113
Olson, Scott, 141
Omar, Muhammad, 116
Organization of American States (OAS), 23
Orloff, Ann, 19
Orwell, George, 127
Ottoman Empire, 76, 169n79

Pakistan, 111; drone attacks in, 118–19, 130; Kashmir and, 22
Palestine, 106, 112
Panama City, Morgan's sack of, 41
pardons, pirate, 54–56, 58, 63, 137
Paris Commune (1871), 74
passports, 18, 30, 70, 76, 137
Patriot Act (U.S., 2001), 115, 120, 126, 193n94
Pavitt, James, 119
Pearl Harbor (1941), 4–5
Pennsylvania, 44, 46, 62
Philippines, 106
Pillar, Paul, 116, 197n158, 202n247
Pinkertons, 19
piracy, 133–34, 137–38; boundaries of, 37–45; economic impact of, 46–48; English legislation against, 53; golden age of, 35–37, 44–56, 67–68; political economy and, 41–45; reinscribing of, 19, 54, 56–67; shattering of, 45–46, 56

pirates, 5–7, 29, 35–68, 165n12; anarchists and, 9, 49–51, 112–13; Barbary Corsairs and, 48, 169n79; buccaneers and, 40, 166n27; egalitarianism of, 49–52; as "enemies of humanity," 53, 57, 62, 112; filibusters and, 19; governing articles of, 51; illegibility of, 5, 48–54, 60–61, 134; Jacobite, 51, 63; Samuel Johnson on, 51; legislation against, 53, 57–58; material consequences of, 46–48; nationality of, 40–41; pardons for, 54–56, 58, 63, 137; privateers and, 36, 39–44, 48, 54, 63; propaganda against, 60–61; as proto-anarchists, 9, 49–51; twenty-first-century, 48–49, 54; women, 50–51
Pisacane, Carlo, 75
Poindexter, John, 108, 114, 116, 121, 123; Iran-Contra scandal and, 197n163; TIA and, 140
police: brutality by, 78–79, 86, 94; militarization of, 10
Popp, Bob, 140
portraits parlés, 95, 96, 98
postmodernism, 149
Pouget, Émile, 93
Powell, Colin, 4
practice theory, 10, 16–20, 23–25, 33, 134–36
pragmatism, 31, 139
Princip, Gavrilo, 80
privacy, 120, 138–42, 193n94, 202n247
privateers, 36, 39–44, 54, 63; commission of, 39, 138; definition of, 42; letters of marque for, 40–43, 48. *See also* pirates
propaganda of the deed, 5, 24, 69–75, 99–101, 133–34; definitions of, 69, 177n9; failed solutions to, 84–89; results of, 82–84, 92. *See also* anarchists
propaganda of the word, 77
Protocols of the Elders of Zion, 81
Proudhon, Pierre Joseph, 74

Quadruple Alliance, War of the. *See* War of the Quadruple Alliance

Quelch, John, 43, 59
Qutb, Sayyid, 104–5

race, 50–51
Rachovsky, Peter, 88
racial theories, 83, 96
Rackham, Calico Jack, 44
rationalism, 31, 32
Ravachol (François Claudius Koenigstein), 81, 85, 90, 182n97, 182n107
Rayfuse, Rosemary, 2
Raytheon Corporation, 109
Reagan, Ronald, 119, 197n163
Reclus, Élisée, 75, 93
Red Army Faction, 80
Rediker, Marcus, 43–44, 46, 50, 51
reinscribing, 5, 25–27, 29–34, 133, 148–49; al-Qaeda and, 117–26; anarchism and 89–99; piracy and, 54, 56–63; reimposition and, 5; transnational violence and, 7–11; War on Terror and, 102, 103, 126–31
responsibility to protect (R2P), 3
revolutionary movement, 71–73, 77, 99
Rheinsdorf, August, 179n41
Rhett, William, 55
Rhode Island, 44
Rice, Condoleezza, 4, 109
Ritchie, Robert, 58
Roberts, Bartholomew ("Black Bart") 44, 46, 50–52, 55, 137
Roberts, Molly, 2
Robertson, Craig, 95–96
Robotic Technology, 119
Rogers, Woodes, 56, 58
Rome Conference (1898), 87, 94–95, 137
Roosevelt, Franklin Delano, 4, 92
Roosevelt, Theodore, 77, 83
Rosenau, James, 2
Rubino, Gennaro, 88
Rumsfeld, Donald, 109, 117, 129
Russia, 74–75, 144; passports for, 76; pogroms in, 81
Russian Revolution (1917), 72, 84

Sacco, Nicola, 97
Salafism, 102–4, 105
Salter, Mark, 72, 97
Salvador, Santiago, 86
Schinkel, Willem, 1
Scotland Yard, 88
Scott, James C., 3–4, 28
secret police, 70, 87–88
September 11 attacks, 4–5, 24, 111; reactions to, 104, 109, 121, 127
Seven Years' War (1756–1763), 65, 138
severe acute respiratory virus, 147
Sharia, 105
shattering, 26–29, 34, 133, 149; al-Qaeda and, 109, 111–17; anarchists and, 79–80; pirates and, 45–46, 56
Shaw, George Bernard, 77
Shaw, Ian, 103, 128, 129
silver, 39, 45
slave trade, 36, 66; increase in, 41–42, 46; pirates and, 51, 55
Smith v. Maryland (1979), 120, 197n165
Snowden, Edward, 104, 115, 121, 122
Somalia, 111, 118, 124
sovereignty, 2, 8–9; cyberspace and, 127; drone attacks and, 202n247; "imperial," 129; knowledge and, 159n22; universal jurisdiction and, 57, 63; Westphalian, 2, 8–9, 25, 39
Spanish Civil War, 84, 100
Spanish Succession, War of. *See* War of Spanish Succession
Spottswood, Alexander, 48, 53, 59
Sri Lanka, 129
Staley, Eugene, 2
state agent, 19
state transformation, 15, 18, 23–26, 33–34, 133; future of, 146–49; Tilly on, 154n39; transnational violence and, 135–38
Steele, Ian Kenneth, 165n15
Steinmetz, George, 24
St. Petersburg Protocol (1904), 87, 94–95, 137
Strange, Susan, 1

sugar plantations, 42
surveillance, 6, 89–90, 93–99, 135; "drone stare" of, 130; FISA legislation on, 120–21, 139–40; passports and, 72, 90. *See also* data surveillance
Sweden, 63
syndicalism, 72, 77, 89–93. *See also* labor movements
Syria, 2, 111; drone attacks in, 119; U.S. withdrawal from, 143

Taliban, 105
Teach, Edward ("Blackbeard"), 46, 50–52, 60–61; Bahamas and, 60; pardon of, 55; ship of, 63
Tenet, George, 109, 114, 119
terrorism, 1, 7, 108, 139; anarchist, 177n9; domestic, 124. *See also* counterterrorism; War on Terror
Terrorist Finance Tracking Program (TFTP), 121, 122
Tether, Tony, 122
Tew, Thomas, 43
Thirty Years' War (1618–1648), 8, 9
Thomson, Janice, 36, 63
Tien, Lee, 114, 126, 193n94
Tilly, Charles, 154n39
tobacco plantations, 42
Tordesillas, Treaty of (1494), 22
Torpey, John, 71
Tortuga, 41
Total Information Awareness (TIA) program, 122
transboundary processes, 10–11, 22–23, 148–49
transformation. *See* state transformation
transnational violence, 27–28, 107–8; illegibility of, 28; state transformation and, 7–11, 135–38
Transportation Security Administration (TSA), 115, 140
triangular trade. *See* slave trade
Tropic of Cancer, 38, 39

Trump, Donald, 125, 143, 144, 146
Tsarnaev, Dzhokhar, 28–29
Tuchman, Barbara, 72
Tunisia, 106, 108
Turner, Frederick Jackson, 201n234

Umberto I (Italian king) 69, 91
Ungern-Sternberg, Ernst, 88
Union of Soviet Socialist Republics (USSR), 21; Afghan War of, 103, 105; Chechnya and, 106, 111; Cold War and, 31, 129; KGB of, 89. *See also* Russia
"United Anarchists Groups, London," 81
United Nations (UN), 23
"universal eye," 89–90, 96
unmanned aerial vehicles (UAVs). *See* drones
USS *Cole*, 108, 111
Utrecht, Treaty of (1714), 44, 45, 48, 62, 65, 137
Uyghurs, 137

Vaillant, Auguste, 85
Vane, Charles, 50, 55
Vanzetti, Bartolomeo, 97
Verizon Corporation, 127, 139
Vincent, Howard, 94–95

Wahhabism, 104
Walker, R. B. J., 20–21
Wall, Tyler, 130
War of Jenkins' Ear, 65, 176n218
War of Spanish Succession, 24, 43–48, 59
War of the Quadruple Alliance, 47
War on Terror, 4, 29, 102–32, 137–39; declaration of, 111–15; drones used for, 118–19, 145; failed strategies in, 115–17; state transformation and, 102, 103, 126–31; "success" in, 123–32, 142–44; torture during, 115–16. *See also* al-Qaeda; terrorism
Warsaw Pact, 21
weapons of mass destruction, 117, 194n106

Weather Underground, 80
Weber, Max, 16
welfare state, 8
Wells, H. G., 2, 121
Wertheimer, Michael, 110, 121–23, 125, 126, 193n99
Westphalian sovereignty, 2, 8–9, 25, 39
Wilcox, Lauren, 129
Wilhelm I (German kaiser), 69, 70, 179n41
William III (English king), 43
Wolfowitz, Paul, 109, 113, 117
World Trade Center bombing (1993), 108, 111. *See also* September 11 attacks
World Trade Organization (WTO), 23
World War I, 8, 18, 24, 137; anarchists and, 72
World War II, 8–10, 18, 31; Pearl Harbor and, 4–5

yellow fever, 42
Yemen, 111, 123, 124; drone attacks in, 118, 125, 130
Yugoslavia, 108, 119

Zarakol, Ayse, 106–7
Zazi, Najibullah, 123, 125
Zelikow, Phillip, 109, 116–17, 193n92, 202n247
Zoccoli, Ettore, 77
Zola, Émile, 73–74, 179n32
Zuboff, Shoshana, 121
Zuckerman, Ethan, 142